THE STARK TRUTH

The Most Overrated and Underrated Players in Baseball History

Jayson Stark

TRIUMPH
BOOKS
CHICAGO

Library of Congress Cataloging-in-Publication Data

Stark, Jayson, 1951–
    The stark truth : the most overrated and underrated players in baseball history / Jayson Stark.
        p. cm.
    Includes bibliographical references.
    ISBN-13: 978-1-57243-959-7
    ISBN-10: 1-57243-959-9
    1. Baseball players—United States. 2. Baseball players—United States—History.   I. Title.

GV8673.S73 2007
796.357'64—dc22

                                                                                    2007005143

This book is available in quantity at special discounts for your group or organization. For further information, contact:

Triumph Books
542 South Dearborn Street
Suite 750
Chicago, Illinois 60605
(312) 939-3330
Fax (312) 663-3557

Printed in U.S.A.
ISBN: 978-1-57243-959-7
Design by Patricia Frey
All photos courtesy of AP/Wide World Photos except where otherwise indicated.

To the real *writing talent in the Stark family, June Herder Stark, who taught me to love the written word, who spent a lifetime demonstrating the value of a smile, and who inspires me every day I sit in front of a keyboard.*

Contents

Acknowledgments

You know what's *never* overrated?

Having people who believe in you. Having people who actually have faith you can write a book, even though you've made it through your entire lifetime without ever having written one. Having a family that loves you and roots for you and turns into your own little public-relations squadron right before your eyes. Having friends you can call, any time of day, any day of any year, and ask the kind of questions that define our reason for existence—questions like: "Who was more underrated, Boog Powell or Ken Singleton?"

I'm a lucky man. I have so many people who fit those descriptions, I had no choice but to keep typing away on this opus, because I knew I couldn't let them down.

So this is where I say thanks.

Thanks to Mike Emmerich and Tom Bast of Triumph Books, who had astonishing trust that a first-time author could fulfill our mutual vision for this project.

Thanks to Ken Shouler, whose awesome research was more invaluable than he'll ever know.

Thanks to my very best friends and coworkers in the heavily underrated baseball-writing business—especially Tim Kurkjian, Jerry Crasnick, Jim Caple, and Peter Gammons—who got so pumped about this topic that they devoted way too much of their own lives to serving as my own personal underrated/overrated sounding boards.

Thanks to Dave Kull, Patrick Stiegman, and all my friends and colleagues at ESPN.com—who afforded me the time and leeway to meet this deadline and fulfill this dream.

Thanks to friends like Retrosheet's Dave Smith and David "The Sultan of Swat Stats" Vincent, who were never too busy to help provide the unique, insightful info they have devoted so much of their lives to unearthing. And thanks to Lee Sinins, whose incredible invention—the *Complete Baseball Encyclopedia*—made it possible for me to look up so many of the (hopefully) enlightening factoids that show up all over this book.

Thanks to all the amazing people all over the baseball industry who told me I was right, wrong, brilliant, crazy, perceptive, misguided and everything in between when our conversations somehow evolved, or devolved, into yet another underrated/overrated debate.

Thanks to my mom and dad, June and Ed Stark, for nurturing their son's never-ending passion for writing and baseball (not always in that order). And thanks to my sister, Karen, who must have seen this coming when she wrote a fourth-grade homework assignment about her nutty brother who "makes books and stories about baseball." Hey, who knew somebody would some day *publish* one?

But thanks, above all, to Lisa, Steven, Jessica, and Hali Stark—my Dream Team of a family. To have a wife like this and kids like this is the best sort of royalties any writer ever collected. They never stopped reminding me how proud they were that this real, live member of *their* family was writing a book (as opposed to, say, taking out the trash). They never stopped informing pretty much the entire population of North America that I was writing that book (as opposed to, say, cleaning the garage). They never stopped fantasizing about how this book was definitely going to lead to a guest appearance on the *Today* show, or possibly *The Daily Show,* or maybe even *Dancing with the Stars.* (Uh, would you settle for *Mike and Mike*?) They never stopped checking Amazon to see if I'd made it into the top quarter-million on the best-seller list (despite the slight technicality that I hadn't even finished *writing* yet). They never stopped providing the daily inspiration that makes books worth writing and life worth living. And that, friends and readers, is the part of life that none of us should ever underrate.

INTRODUCTION

Over Here, Under There

Three of the most opinionated scouts in America are sitting at the back of the press box in a waterlogged ballpark in South Philadelphia. With nothing but rain-delay time to kill, they do what they do best:

Argue.

"Who's the best player in the Phillies lineup?" one of them asks, with that edge in his voice that suggests he knows the answer—and none of these other lunkheads will get it.

"Chase Utley," says Scout No. 2, confidently.

"Chase Utley?" laughs Scout No. 1. "C'monnnnnn. He can't throw the ball from me to you."

"Okay, Bobby Abreu," says the third scout, bracing for the onslaught that's coming any second.

"Nope," says Scout No. 1, shaking his head as if he can't believe he's even hanging out with these knuckleheads. "You're *both* wrong. It's Jimmy Rollins."

"Jimmy Rollins?" gulps Scout No. 2. "No way. Overrated."

"Oh, no, he isn't," says Scout No. 1. "Underrated."

I present this slice of rain-delay life because, if you're reading this book, I'm betting you have been here. I'm betting you have done this. I'm betting you have found yourself sucked into this very debate. By a friend. By a talk-show host. Possibly even by one paragraph in a newspaper. It's a game that's practically as much fun as Game 7 of the World Series, a game just as popular as anything you can play on an Xbox.

It's the old underrated-overrated game. If you haven't played it, you're not breathing.

You don't have to work in baseball to play it. You don't have to be a season-ticket holder to play it. You don't need to be any particular race, creed, gender, mammal, amphibian, or extra-terrestrial to play it. You just need to care enough about baseball to have an opinion. On who can play and who can't. On who's great and who stinks. On who makes way, way, way too much money and who's the biggest bargain since the 99-cent quesadilla.

This, friends, is the essence of sports, the essence of why we love sports, the essence of why we especially love *this* sport. We know it. We get it. We feel it.

We argue about it.

Overrated? Underrated? Toss out a name. Just about any name. From A-Rod to Pete Rose. From Hank Aaron to Todd Zeile. Overrated? Underrated? If you can't find somebody on a bar stool near you with an opinion on this, there's a good chance your stool is located in a bar that closed about three hours ago. If you can't find a radio station that's playing this game every day of every year, you've been listening to way too much hip-hop.

"Overrated-underrated is the foundation of sports-talk radio," says my friend Soren Petro, a sports-talker on WHB radio in Kansas City. "You can't beat it, because there's no right answer. So it gives people a chance to do what they love—talk about sports and argue about it. Are the Braves overrated or underrated? Are they overrated because they've only won one World Series? Or are they underrated because they've finished first so many times and they've accomplished something no one else has? If I can't get through an hour talking about that, there's something wrong."

But overrated-underrated is the foundation of more than just slow-news-day radio-thonning. In its own way, overrated-underrated is also the foundation of the real-life decisions baseball's beleaguered general managers make every day. The only difference between what they do and what we do is that, when a GM is making these kinds of calls, this is no little happy-hour game anymore. This is bigger than bases loaded, with nobody out in the ninth.

"In our market, I can never get caught up in overrated," says Cleveland Indians GM Mark Shapiro, a man working with the sixth-lowest payroll in baseball in 2006. "But I'm looking for underrated a lot. I guess another way to say it is, we're looking for value—minimizing risk and finding value. Maybe we're looking for that guy who's a little more dependable, with far less upside."

But remember, this is a general manager with a $56 million payroll talking. You think the Yankees care how overrated some talk-show host thinks a player is? Heck, Boss Steinbrenner *loves* signing those overrated guys—if only because at least half of them used to play for the Mets or Red Sox. He loves them, at least until they play for him—and make the mistake of not hitting .879 or something.

"In New York, they make baseball-card signings," says one GM who couldn't see a $200 million payroll with the Hubble Telescope. "They can go out and get a guy for one year, and if he doesn't do it the next year, so what? They can afford to get someone else."

So in those executive offices, the folks in charge play a very different, real-life edition of the overrated-underrated game. But meanwhile, down there on the fields below them, the overrated-underrated debate swirls around the men who wear the uniforms—from the moment they become anything more than a "Who's-*that*-guy?" kind of player. That debate thunders on every day of their careers, while the players in the middle of it just try to figure out how the heck they got overrated or underrated in the first place.

"Everyone starts out underrated, because nobody knows you," says Mets closer Billy Wagner. "The longer you play, the easier it is to get overrated. By the time I'm done, I'll be so overrated, you'll wonder why I'm still playing."

Ah, but this just in: a player doesn't *have* to get stuck in that either/or quicksand. It *is* possible to avoid being overrated *or* underrated. If you play your career strategy just right, it might actually be possible to float along in the haze of the elusive Unrated Zone, where the talk-show radar never quite detects your existence.

"I always tried to stay away from even being rated," chuckles Astros broadcaster Jim Deshaies, who pitched 12 as-anonymous-as-possible years in the big leagues (1984–95). "As soon as somebody says, 'That guy's a hell of a pitcher,' you know somebody else is saying, 'Nah, he's overrated.' So I always wanted to be the guy where everybody said, 'He's still *here*?' I'd rather be that than be: 'I can't believe that guy has this kind of stuff and he can't get people out.'"

So Deshaies's sweat glands still pump like an oil well every time he thinks back on how close he once came to being sucked into the dreaded rating game. On September 23, 1986, to the shock of just about everyone (especially himself), he kicked off a start against the Dodgers by striking out the first eight hitters in a row. That was more than merely a modern major league record. It terrified Dodgers manager Tom Lasorda into pinch hitting for his pitcher in the *third* inning.

"After I did that, I was probably flirting there with moving into overrated," Deshaies says, two decades later. "If people saw that, there may have been a level of expectation. Then they'd have started describing me as a strikeout pitcher. And then I'm overrated. But I don't think I ever got there. It happened near the end of the season, and Mike Scott saved me. He threw a no-hitter. We clinched first place. And I never quite made it to overrated."

Phew.

But some players don't get off that easy. Sometimes events can conspire to hurtle a guy into the overrated shooting gallery even when he can't recall doing anything to influence those events whatsoever. Take the case of long-time relief pitcher Larry Andersen. There he was in 1990, innocently slideballing his way through his 13th big-league season, when the Red Sox had to go destroy his life forever by trading for him. All because the prospect they dealt away to get him turned out to be Jeff Bagwell.

"At the time the trade happened, I'm pretty sure I was underrated," Andersen says. "But after Bagwell became the Rookie of the Year and the MVP, I became vastly overrated. Just nobody knew at the time how overrated I was. I'm a victim of revisionist overrating."

So all these years later, Andersen is *still* trying to convince people he should be restored to his proper place in underratedhood.

"I've *got* to believe I'm pretty underrated," he says. "How many other people can say they played 17 years in professional baseball and they couldn't hit, couldn't field, couldn't intentionally walk a hitter, couldn't throw pitchouts and only threw one pitch [a slider]? I know some people would say if I couldn't do any of that, I must be overrated. But I think it proves I was underrated. So, see, there are all kinds of twists and turns."

Now think about this for a second. This is a grown-up human being who hasn't played a baseball game in over a decade. Yet he still gets frothed up over whether he once deserved to be overrated or underrated. So no wonder the world needs a book on this topic. It invokes so much passion, it's amazing no one has ever tried to run for president on the old I-represent-the-vast-underrated-minions platform.

It's clear to all the lab-coated scientists who have studied this subject that *nobody* wants to be overrated—especially the guys who are pretty sure that's what they are. So if this book is going to make any sort of serious impact on mankind, it needs to do more than simply rank a bunch of players. It needs to provide some genuine public service for the millions of concerned American ballplayers who walk the streets every day, wondering: "What can I do to become more underrated?"

"What people really need," says former Cubs and Phillies center fielder Doug Glanville, "is a self-help book—some sort of 10-step program on how to be underrated, or how to go from overrated to underrated. Then you'd need some kind of infomercial, something that says: 'Are you feeling like everyone notices every mistake you make? Do you feel like 40,000 fans are booing your every move? Then act now. Order this book and order these DVDs. And in just 10 easy steps, you can be the most underrated player around.' Then you just need a couple of people to endorse it—Dr. Phil, maybe Mark Loretta—saying: 'This really works.' And you've got a bestseller on your hands."

Whoa. A bestseller, huh? Well, if all we need is a 10-step program, then by gosh, we'll give you a 10-step program. Do *you* want to be underrated? Then just memorize these 10 simple tips.

1. BOOK A CRUISE EVERY OCTOBER.

Winning is beautiful. We won't deny that. But the more you show up in those games in October, the better the odds that you might accidentally do something that will cause people to say, "Boy, how overrated is *that* guy." On the other hand, if you're always a prominent name on those annual lists of "Most

Games, Homers, Wins, Root Canals, or Unpaid Speeding Tickets Without Ever Playing a Postseason Game," the world is much more likely to feel like you've gotten screwed all your career. And that's precisely the feeling we're after here at How to Be Underrated headquarters.

2. BEG FOR A PAY CUT.

Now that he has made it to the exalted rank of "overpaid free agent," Billy Wagner says he has figured out how this overrated-underrated stuff works. "People characterize underrated or overrated by your paycheck," Wagner says. "So I guess I'm overrated, because you're never as good as what your paycheck says you are." But those guys on the All-Bargain Team—nobody ever calls *them* overrated. So our advice is: whatever your team is willing to offer you, ask for less. And don't settle for more, whatever you do.

3. LEARN TO SPELL "INTANGIBLE."

The number one quality we look for in underratedness is the ability to make people say: "Numbers can't measure what this guy's all about." Now it would be ideal if you were hitting .392 at the time people say that. But that's not always possible. So if you're hitting closer to .192, you're going to need to take emergency intangible training. Get your shirt as dirty as possible (www.fakedirt.com). Make every takeout slide as if you're trying to get signed by the Green Bay Packers. And watch every pitch of every game from the top step of the dugout—preferably next to either the manager, the starting pitcher, or the cleanup hitter—in order to rack up those all-important unsung-leadership points. After all, no one is quite sure what an intangible is. So use that to your advantage.

4. CLAIM TO BE 5'7".

The bigger you are, the more likely you are to be able to hit a ball 498 feet. And even if you can't, everyone will expect you to anyway. Little guys, on the other hand, just *look* like overachievers. "I've always been underrated, ever since I turned 13," says 5'8" Phillies shortstop Jimmy Rollins. "Then everyone else kept growing. I stayed the same. After that, I was just That Little Guy." We'd advise you to shrink, but that's way too painful. So the next-best thing would be: lie about your height. Never admit you're taller than 5'7", and you're guaranteed to be underrated all your life. Or until somebody finds a ruler, anyhow.

5. SPEND YOUR CAREER IN THE CENTRAL OR MOUNTAIN TIME ZONES.

Does anybody ever accuse Mike Sweeney or Todd Helton of being overrated? How about Roy Oswalt or Michael Young? Never. Ever. Hey, sounds like a trend to us. Steering your career away from those major media megalopolises to the east and west can be hazardous to your endorsement income. But that's not important now. If you're going to immerse yourself in underratedhood, you need to dodge those high-visibility time zones. Oh, it's not impossible to be underrated if you play in New York. But it's way trickier. So our advice is: set your clocks back, join the CST/MST Underrated-Player Protection Program, and you're all set.

6. LIVE IN THE SHADOWS.

Another great secret to underrated bliss: it's serious ammunition to be able to claim you were overshadowed by all the Hall of Famers on your team. Alongside every Ernie Banks there's a Ron Santo. Alongside every Joe Morgan there's a Dave Concepcion. So feel free to ride those coattails all the way to underratedness. Go ahead. It's a tradition more time-honored than the seventh-inning stretch.

7. TAKE BOREDOM LESSONS.

One thing we've noticed is: it's very difficult to make a case that nobody ever notices you if every time people turn on *SportsCenter*, you're yukking it up in the Budweiser Hot Seat. We would never openly suggest that anybody enroll in the Manny Ramirez School of Media Relations, you understand. But if your quest to get more underrated ever reaches the crisis stage, you're going to need to find *some* way to lower your profile. So work on your boredom skills. Suppress that urge to be witty, incisive, or media-friendly, and you'll be amazed by how fast the press can stampede away from your locker. Next thing you know, *voila*—you're underrated.

8. DEMAND TO BE TRADED TO THE ROYALS.

There has never been an overrated Royal. Look it up. Go ahead. It's true. Dan Quisenberry. Frank White. Jeff Montgomery. Buddy Biancalana. They're a veritable Who's Who of Underratedness. Not that there aren't other teams like this. The Devil Rays would work, for instance. But you want people to say: he was a great player, except nobody ever noticed because he played on all those el-stinko teams (in the central time zone).

9. WHATEVER YOU DO, DON'T GET ELECTED TO THE HALL OF FAME.

It's always tough to claim you're underrated when the logical response is: "Oh, yeah? Then what about that plaque in Cooperstown?" Sure, there *are* some underrated Hall of Famers. There are even some in this book. But it's better to have your best friend sending out emails to 500 sportswriters every November that start: "Joe Fobblegoop is the best player *not* in the Hall of Fame. It's time to right this grievous injustice." Nothing stokes the underrated meter like mass sympathy. Remember that.

10. STAR IN *I LOVE THE 80s*.

Radar guns might be the most dangerous technological innovation in the history of underrated people. Why? Because if you ever make the mistake of throwing a baseball, say, 99 miles per hour, there's a pretty good chance you'll be considered a flop unless you go 28–1 every year. But if you're only throwing 89, those expectations will start dropping faster than the value of your 401(k). Don't forget now, every pitcher's favorite synonym for underrated is "crafty."

So there. See how simple this can be? For many of you out there, there's still plenty of time to perfect your underratedness. Simply follow these 10 easy steps, and you're just about guaranteed to star in the sequel to this book. (Author's note: The phrase, "just about," means no requests for your money back, either for this book or any subsequent sequels, will be granted.)

For some of you, however, it's too late. You are what you are, and it's too late to rewrite history. (Author's note: The phrase, "it's too late," means your name could already have rolled off our printing presses. Thus, no appeals of overratedness will be granted.)

So it's time to plow ahead and reveal exactly who the main characters in this opus really are—the most overrated and underrated players in the history of baseball. I should let you know up front that these ratings are completely arbitrary. No team of computer geniuses was employed to write a program that identified who was what. Yes, numbers were used in this process. But no specific methodology of any kind was involved. My old friend Larry Andersen taught me once about the principle that governs this entire book: make the stats work for you. So I did. For all 60,000 words.

Oh, sure. I *could* have gone by some strict mathematical formulas—but everybody knows those mathematical formulas are overrated.

CHAPTER 1

Right-Handed Starting Pitchers

The Most Overrated Right-Handed Starter of All Time

NOLAN RYAN

There are going to be people who think the opinions in this book are dubious. There are going to be people who think the opinions in this book are ludicrous. There are going to be people who think these opinions are clearly the work of a guy who wouldn't know a baseball from a bowling ball. And then there are going to be chapters like this one—chapters that are going to make some of you conclude that this is a book written by a man who has officially lost his mind.

So let me set the record straight on Nolan Ryan.

I know what you're thinking: "I bet this bozo never had to hit against the guy." All right, I'm guilty. I never had to hit against him. That's probably obvious. *Nobody* who ever had to hit against him thought Nolan Ryan was overrated. And even if they possibly thought that for approximately one-trillionth of a second, they then immediately hit the delete button—because they were sure Nolan could read minds, and if he thought that's what *they* were thinking, the next pitch was definitely going to be bearing down on their left eyebrow.

At 98 miles an hour.

So, no, I never had to hit against him. Thank God.

Okay, next point for the record: I loved watching Nolan Ryan. Loved it. Loved watching him. Loved covering him. Loved spending countless otherwise-useful hours figuring out The Greatest Nolan Ryan Factoids Ever Figured. Even loved doing something no other rational human being would ever have done voluntarily—writing every one of his box-score lines in a notebook for the final 10 years of his career. It takes a special kind of nutcase to get actual joy out of writing "10–3–0–0–0–15" with a 10-cent Bic pen on a page of a 12-cent notebook. But that was me. Nutcase. Just writing down those numbers, I could imagine all the funky swings, the dazed eyeballs, the flames pouring out of Ryan's ears. Those weren't just any old pitching lines.

Nobody's saying Nolan Ryan wasn't one of the most exciting pitchers in the history of the game, but most people tend to rate him higher than they really should.

They sure weren't Jose Lima pitching lines or Jaime Navarro pitching lines. They were *Nolan Ryan pitching lines.* And there was nothing—nothing—like them.

nolan ryan

Played From: 1966–1993
Teams: Mets, Angels, Astros, Rangers
Career Record: 807 G, 324–292
W-L, 3.19 ERA, 5,386 IP, 3,923 H,
2,795 BB, 5,714 K

So of all the players in this book who got stuck with that dreaded label, "overrated," none was typed with more second thoughts than this one. Nolan Ryan—overrated? What was I, some kind of lunatic?

But I want this chapter to serve as an important lesson, possibly for our entire civilization. "Overrated" doesn't have to be a synonym for "insult." It's a relative term, see—not an absolute term. It means we've all gotten really, really, realllyyy carried away when we assess what this man was, to the point where we've been way too willing to overlook what he wasn't. So it sure is a good thing this book came along. Where else can we have stuff like that cleared up if not here?

Here's what Nolan Ryan was: the most unhittable pitcher of all time. The supreme strikeout machine of all time. The most durable pitcher of all time. And a legitimate, no-doubt-about-it, first-ballot Hall of Famer.

Cool. Those don't sound like insults, do they? They don't sound like: "I'd rather have Shawn Boskie pitch for my team than that stinking Nolan Ryan," do they? They don't sound like: "This guy couldn't carry Sidney Ponson's wristbands," do they? This, after all, isn't one of those books that was programmed by some talk-radio consultant, where everyone in it is either "great" or "putrid"—and anybody who lands in between will be forced to tumble to the bottom of the Grand Canyon. No need for that. So I blatantly admit to this jury that Nolan Ryan was great. In his own way.

Just not as great as three-quarters of the planet seems to think he was.

So here's what Nolan Ryan *wasn't:* the greatest pitcher of all time. The greatest pitcher of the 20th century. The greatest pitcher of the live-ball era. The greatest pitcher of the division-play era. Our greatest living pitcher. A pitcher worthy of collecting the second-highest Hall of Fame vote percentage (98.79 percent) of any player ever. (Trivia answer you're undoubtedly wondering about: Tom Seaver got the highest percentage, with 98.84.) Or a pitcher who deserved to be elected to the All-Century Team over Seaver, Steve

Carlton, Jim Palmer, Christy Mathewson, Grover Cleveland Alexander or Lefty Grove—let alone a guy who deserved to be *the leading vote-getter among all pitchers on the ballot.*

To characterize him as any of that—as many folks have—is getting massively carried away. Hence opening the door for the proper authorities to grant us permission to use that word, "overrated," to describe him.

Nobody—*nobody*—should ever try to minimize the staggering talent it takes to throw seven no-hitters, or to strike out 5,714 fellow humans. But unless you want Ryan to adopt you or something, you should not overlook the other side of this story:

Of the 22 pitchers in the 300-Win Club, Ryan ranks dead last in winning percentage (.526). Of all those legends, he also has by far the worst walk rate (4.67 per nine innings). Only Don Sutton (with one) reached 300 wins with fewer 20-win seasons than Ryan did (two). And while his teams weren't powerhouses, they weren't as lousy as they're made out to be, either. Ryan's winning percentage was only .027 points higher than the other pitchers on his teams (.499). Compare that to, say, Walter Johnson (.599 to his teammates' .466). Or even Phil Niekro (.537 to .484). Wins can be overblown more than just about any major stat in baseball. But as dominating as he was, Nolan Ryan should have won more than he did. It's that basic.

And isn't it at least troubling that he never won a Cy Young? Or that he finished in the top three in Cy Young voting just three times in 27 seasons? (Sheez, that's less than Dan Quisenberry.) Or that when The Great Nolan Ryan had a three-run lead with six outs to go in an NLCS game that would have carried the Astros into the 1980 World Series, he faced four more hitters, got none of them out, and watched that World Series trip disappear?

Well, it troubled me, anyway. And I'll say this again: I loved the guy. Loved watching him. Loved dealing with him. Loved watching him sign autographs for anyone willing to line up in the parking lot at 8:00 on a spring-training morning. But that doesn't mean your average American baseball fan doesn't drastically overrate him.

When a former teammate of Ryan's found out I was writing this book, he called me. First player he wanted to talk about was his pal, Nolan. This guy's mission, best I could tell, was to try to convince me that Ryan is both under-rated *and* overrated. Or that he has gotten so overrated, he's now underrated. Or something like that.

"The people who argue he's the greatest of all time—those people are over-rating him," Ryan's buddy said. "But the people who argue he's just some freakish guy who just struck a lot of people out but never won—those people are missing the point."

Know what? He's exactly right. So here's my mission: to make sure you *got* the point. And the point is to be able to distinguish what Nolan Ryan was from what he wasn't. If you had to pick one pitcher in history to watch for a day, you might pick him. But if you had to pick one pitcher in history to pitch a game you absolutely positively had to win, you'd pick about 50 pitchers before you got to him. And that's how he ended up in our overrated bin. It's no more complicated than that.

The Rest of the Top Five

2. DON DRYSDALE

He sure was a handsome devil. But outside of two spectacular years (25–9 in 1962 and 23–12 in 1965), Drysdale's career winning percentage was a pedes-trian .526 (exactly the same as Nolan Ryan's). And he had just two other seasons where he even won as many as four more games than he lost. Remember that Drysdale spent all that time pitching for the Dodgers—the team that had the *best* winning percentage in the National League during his career. So how come his numbers don't look a whole lot different than those of, say, Milt Pappas or Jim Perry?

don drysdale

Played From: 1956–1969
Team: Dodgers
Career Record: 518 G, 209–166 W-L, 2.95 ERA, 3,432 IP, 3,084 H, 855 BB, 2,486 K

3. KERRY WOOD

Maybe Wood never should have thrown that 20-strikeout one-hitter against the Astros in 1998, because after that, people started wondering how come he

kerry wood

Played From: 1998–2006 (active)
Team: Cubs
Career Record: 189 G, 71–56 W-L,
3.68 ERA, 1,128⅔ IP, 875 H, 546 BB,
1,299 K

didn't fire off another one about once a month. That game—and the Texas drawl—stamped the dreaded "Next Roger Clemens" label on Wood's forehead. Turned out he was barely the next Roger Pavlik. Never had a 15-win season. never had an ERA under 3.00. Racked up twice as many trips to the disabled list (10) as shutouts (five). Granted, his career isn't over. But, sheez, this man averaged 6.5 wins a year from ages 26 through 29. So at this point, we'd settle for the next Roger Mason.

4. DIZZY DEAN

It's always great to have a guy named "Dizzy" in the Hall of Fame. But let's face it: we're still talking about a player who had five great years—and essentially did zilch the rest of his career. So what's the difference between Dean and, say,

dizzy dean

Played From: 1930–1941
(Also pitched one game in 1947)
Teams: Cardinals, Cubs, Browns
Career Record: 317 G, 150–83
W-L, 3.02 ERA, 1,967⅓ IP, 1,919 H,
453 BB, 1,163 K

Dale Murphy? Or Dave Stewart? Or Mike Scott? Or Mo Vaughn? Was it that "Ol' Diz" (and you've gotta love just saying "Ol' Diz") had a better personality? Or that he was part of a fun brother act? Or that he was a broadcasting icon who actually climbed out of the booth in 1947 to pitch a game six seasons after his "retirement"? Or that we feel sorry for him because his career crashed after he got hurt in an All-Star Game? Yep, there are many reasons to love the Dizmeister. But also many reasons to overrate him.

5. KEVIN BROWN

In these complicated times we live in, you need to nominate somebody as The

kevin brown

Played From: 1986–2005
Teams: Rangers, Orioles, Marlins,
Padres, Dodgers, Yankees
Career Record: 486 G, 211–144
W-L, 3.28 ERA, 3,256⅓ IP, 3,079 H,
901 BB, 2,397 K

Most Overpaid Pitcher of All Time. So Brown makes this list even though he was often almost as nasty *on* the mound as he was off it. (And that's a feat in itself.) It wasn't necessarily Brown's fault that the Dodgers were dumb enough to make him the first $100 million pitcher ($105 million, to be exact) in history, back in December 1998.

But what did they get for their money? One ERA title. Zero postseason games. And one season of 15-plus wins. Let the record show that during the life of that contract, Brown won fewer games (72) than Esteban Loaiza, Kirk Rueter, Woody Williams, and Jeff Suppan. And he got paid $1,458,333 per win. Overrate *that*.

The Most Underrated Right-Handed Starter of All Time

BOB FELLER

Wait. Hear that clattering noise, off in the distance? No, that's not the sound of your kids instant-messaging all their pals (again) to tell them what goofballs their parents are (again). It's actually all those already steamed Nolan Ryan fans typing their emails to protest this choice, of the nowhere-near-as-beloved Bob Feller as most underrated to Ryan's most overrated. Amazingly, I could hear that typing before one copy of this book had even rolled off the presses. I'm perceptive like that. Well, before you get inspired to run for the keyboard yourself, hold on. Read this paragraph. Heck, read them all if you really pride yourself on your open-mindedness. You probably don't have to tell me what you're dying to tell me. I get the irony. I know you can—and will—make the argument that Bob Feller was the Nolan Ryan of his time. His time just happened to be the more easily underrated '30s and '40s, instead of the more heavily videotaped '70s, '80s, and '90s. Trust me. I've heard that argument myself. I've even made it myself.

I know it's Feller, not Ryan, who holds the modern record for most walks in a season (208 in 1938). I know that, of all 127 pitchers in history who worked 3,000 innings or more, Ryan and Feller have the two highest walk ratios. I know Feller and Ryan made the same number of All-Star teams (eight). I know neither of them ever won a major award from the Baseball Writers' Association (although Feller undoubtedly would have had there merely been such an invention as the Cy Young Award in 1940). I know they both had their share of October frustrations. I know that a lot of the nit-picking Ryan hears about his career is the same stuff Feller once heard.

So see? I know all that. And I still say Bob Feller is the most underrated right-hander who ever lived. But only because he is.

Imagine this kid, at 17 years old, pitching an exhibition game in 1936 against a Cardinals team still rolling out most of the lineup that had won the World Series in 1934—and striking out *eight* of the nine hitters he faced. Imagine this kid, a few weeks later, making the first start of his big-league career, and whiffing 15 St. Louis Browns. Imagine him, three weeks after that, ripping off 17 Ks against the Athletics—the biggest strikeout game in American League history at the time. Now imagine him, just a couple of weeks later, heading back home to Iowa—so he could ride the *school bus* with his sister and finish high school. All true. It all happened. In real life. He was the LeBron James of his era—except with a 12-to-6 curve instead of a learning curve.

How many American teenagers have had the impact on their country that Bob Feller once did? His high school graduation was broadcast live—to the whole U.S.A. (on NBC radio). His face was on the *cover* of *Time* magazine before he'd even started 10 big-league games. So it's pretty clear Bob Feller wasn't underrated back then.

But that was then. This is now, all these decades later. And Feller no longer gets his due. When ESPN asked its in-house stable of baseball "experts" (full disclosure: myself included) to rank baseball's greatest living pitchers in May of 2006, Feller finished sixth. But in an accompanying ESPN SportsNation poll of ESPN.com surfers, Feller didn't even make the top 10. (The only other SportsNation omission from the experts' top 10: Juan Marichal.) Seven years earlier, in the fan voting for the All-Century Team, Feller wasn't even close, finishing 13th (with nearly 740,000 fewer votes than Ryan).

So what's up with that?

We'd better remind you—assuming you ever knew—just how enormous a figure Feller was in his time. Over the first 95 seasons in the existence of Major League Baseball, only one pitcher cranked out four straight seasons of 240 strikeouts or more—Bob Feller. In that same period, he and Walter Johnson were the only pitchers who ever led their league in strikeouts 10 or more seasons apart. Through the first nine seasons of Feller's career, he was the most unhittable pitcher in history (allowing just 7.01 hits per nine innings).

And the real proof was all those games in which nobody—or just about nobody—got a hit. This man threw three no-hitters and *12* one-hitters. Until Nolan Ryan came along, the only pitcher in the 20th century with even half as many combined no-hitters and one-hitters was Walter Johnson (one no-hitter, seven one-hitters). And Feller was the only 20th-century pitcher with three no-hitters until Sandy Koufax showed up.

Feller also just might be (ahem) The Hardest Thrower Who Ever Lived. We'll never know for sure, of course. In his day, there weren't radar guns attached to every scoreboard in America—possibly because radar had only been invented about 20 minutes earlier. But there's one expert who *knows* (totally for sure) that Feller was The Hardest Thrower Who Ever Lived. And that would be the ever-modest Feller himself.

Bob Feller wasn't underrated when he was a national icon in the 1930s and '40s, but all these years later he is repeatedly overlooked in debates about the greatest right-handers of all-time.

I'll never forget, back in the 1997 Indians-Marlins World Series, the radar board in Florida threw a "102 mph" up there after one fateful fastball by Marlins closer Robb Nen. Yep, 102. Never saw one of *those* before. Before the game the next day, the *New York Post*'s Tom Keegan and I spotted Feller on the field. So we decided to ask for ourselves whether he thought he'd ever thrown a pitch that traveled 102 miles per hour. "Hell," he said, "that was my *change-up*."

Feller then proceeded to tell a story about some gizmo, or military invention, called the Electric Cell Device. This was some kind of chamber—no longer available at a Wal-Mart near you—that was used back in 1946 to clock his fastball. Feller claimed he whooshed a pitch through the old ECD that was measured at 107.9 miles per hour. Must have been that .9 that made him so hard to hit.

bob feller

Played From: 1936–1956
Team: Indians
Career Record: 570 G, 266–162
W-L, 3.25 ERA, 3,828 IP, 3,271 H,
1,764 BB, 2,581 K

Virtually from the minute he threw his first pitch, there was so much national fascination with Feller and his heater that folks were constantly looking for ways to figure out whether his 100-mile-per-hour flameball was reality or myth. So in 1940, Feller was lined up for his most legendary pitcher's duel—with a speeding motorcycle. Just as the motorcycle varoomed by him at 86 miles per hour, Feller launched his fastball at a target 60'6" away. The baseball won that race so easily, it was calculated that his Harley-ball was traveling at 104 miles per hour. Oh, by the way, a small hole had been cut out of the target so a camera could record this fabled pitch—and Feller launched his fastball right through the target, wiping out the camera. So don't try to buy that historic photo on eBay anytime soon.

Now no doubt you Nolan Ryan fans out there are still saying: "What's the big whoop?" There are all kinds of stories about Ryan that sound just like these, right? Well, there is one significant difference between Ryan and Feller: Feller consistently found ways to convert his smokeball and all his whiffs into wins.

Feller had seven seasons of at least 15 wins and a .600 winning percentage. Ryan had *one* (and it took him 23 seasons to have it). Put another way, Feller had six seasons in which he won at least 10 more games than he lost. Ryan had *none*. True, Feller's teams were generally better than Ryan's teams. But Feller had a much better winning percentage (.621) than his teammates

(.541)—a margin that's almost three times higher than Ryan's. Feller also had a higher winning percentage than the rest of his staff in nine straight seasons. Ryan's longest streak was six.

Ryan, of course, vastly out-accumulated Feller—324 wins to 266, 5,714 strikeouts to 2,581. But who's to say where Feller would have wound up had World War II not lopped nearly four full seasons off his career? When he headed off to war at age 23, Bob Feller already had 1,233 strikeouts and 107 wins. No pitcher, before or since, has equaled those figures at that age. So had the four years he missed gone anything like the four seasons that preceded them, we might be talking about a man with more than 360 wins and more than 3,500 strikeouts. And the only pitcher—ever—who could say he moved into that neighborhood was Walter Johnson.

Oh, it's true that Feller might have blown out his arm. Or he might have been injured in a collision with a motorcycle that spun out of control in a rematch with his fastball. But let's just assume that hadn't happened. Let's just assume there had never been a World War II. Where do you think Bob Feller would sit *then* on those greatest-living-pitcher lists, or in the All-Century Team voting results? Wherever it would have been, you can bet he'd have been high enough that nobody would have to nominate him as The Most Underrated Right-Hander in History.

The Rest of the Top Five

2. JUAN MARICHAL

It would be worth including Marichal on this list just for having the coolest delivery of the last half-century—part Ray Sadecki, part Ray Guy. But once Marichal finished kicking that left leg toward the sky, incredible things happened. He not only was the winningest pitcher of the 1960s, but he also matched or beat the great Bob Gibson's win total in *every* season in the 1960s. In fact, Marichal and some guy named Sandy

juan marichal

Played From: 1960–1975
Teams: Giants, Red Sox, Dodgers
Career Record: 471 G, 243–142
W-L, 2.89 ERA, 3,506 IP, 3,153 H, 709 BB, 2,303 K

Koufax were the only pitchers in the 1960s who won 25 games or more in three different seasons. Marichal also led his league, at one time or another, in wins, ERA, shutouts, innings, and complete games. He had back-to-back seasons (1965–1966) in which the *on-base percentage* against him was under .240. And in eight All-Star Games, he gave up exactly one earned run in 18 innings—which still gives him the lowest ERA (0.50) in All-Star history. Yet he finished 20th in the All-Century Team voting. Outrageous.

3. BERT BLYLEVEN

Full confession: it took me nine years to convince myself to hand Blyleven a Hall of Fame vote. So, obviously, I'm acutely aware of all his potholes. But look where he stacks up in the division-play era versus some big-time peers: Number one on the whole list in complete games. Second in shutouts (one behind Nolan Ryan). Second in innings pitched (again trailing only Ryan). Fifth in strikeouts. And seventh in wins (behind only Hall of Famers and future Hall of Famers). The pride of Zeist, Netherlands, was no Clemens or Seaver. But considering he still has no plaque in Cooperstown, he's got to be the most underrated 287-game winner of all time.

bert blyleven

Played From: 1970–1992
Teams: Twins, Rangers, Pirates, Indians, Angels
Career Record: 692 G, 287–250 W-L, 3.31 ERA, 4,970 IP, 4,632 H, 1,322 BB, 3,701 K

4. CHARLEY "OLD HOSS" RADBOURN

There's probably only one reason Old Hoss is on this list. Because it gives me a chance to tell the story of good old Charlie Leibrandt, back in 1992, when it became clear that the Braves' rotation was turning into *the Braves' rotation*. So off I headed to Atlanta to write a piece about how this crew—John Smoltz, Tom Glavine, Steve Avery, and Leibrandt—was obviously The Most Stupendous Rotation since Columbus Discovered America. Only Leibrandt put it all in proper perspective, by mentioning that somebody had hung Old Hoss's stats on the clubhouse bulletin board. "And that guy won like 60 games and threw 75 complete games one

charley "old hoss" radbourn

Played From: 1881–1891
Teams: Grays, Beaneaters, Red Stockings, Reds
Career Record: 528 G, 309–195 W-L, 2.67 ERA, 4,535⅓ IP, 4,335 H, 875 BB, 1,830 K

year all by himself," Leibrandt said. "So I don't see how people can say we're that great. The four of us combined aren't even as good as him." All right, so he exaggerated. Old Hoss only won 59 and completed 73 that year (1884). But if 59–12, with a 1.38 ERA and 73 CG—in a year when he also pitched *27 freaking games in a row* down the stretch—isn't the greatest season by any pitcher ever, then what the heck is?

5. JOHN SMOLTZ

Speaking of Smoltz, isn't it about time we all recognized he's the most underrated active pitcher of our time? We've never had a member of the 200-Win, 150-Save Club. But Smoltz is about to found that club in 2007 unless his elbow has a Richter scale incident—which should establish him as an automatic Hall of Famer. He's the Dennis Eckersley of his generation, only better. Smoltz's career ERA as a starter is more than a third of a run below Eckersley's. Smoltz's ERA as a reliever

john smoltz

Played From: 1988–2006 (active)
Team: Braves
Career Record: 670 G, 193–137 W-L, 154 SV, 3.27 ERA, 3,161⅓ IP, 2,758 H, 937 BB, 2,778 K

was a half-run lower than the Eck's. And Smoltz gets a slew of extra points for being the best postseason starter of his era (15–4, 2.65 ERA, plus four saves). Even as he approached age 40, he still had That Aura as a pitcher nobody wanted to face. So give this man some hoopla already (not to mention some Rogaine).

CHAPTER 2

Left-Handed Starting Pitchers

The Most Overrated Left-Handed Starter of All Time

SANDY KOUFAX

Hoo boy. Now we're really in trouble. There are certain people in this world you're not supposed to impugn. Ever. The Pope comes to mind. Julia Roberts. Springsteen. Oprah. Homer Simpson. And then there's Sandy.

It's easy to understand how The Great and Mighty Koufax made it to this exalted, Teflon-ish plateau. He gets to live forever in a fuzzy black-and-white 8-millimeter film clip. Dazzling the Yankees and the Twins in the October shadows. Then walking away at 30 years old—*30*—at a time when there was nobody in this solar system pitching better than he was. And, yeah, you heard that right. That word was *nobody*.

So how does a man who was clearly once the greatest pitcher of his time suddenly turn into the most overrated left-hander of *all* time four decades later? No, not because the author of this volume is trying to convince you he's the king of the blockheads. It's because those four decades of memories have rubbed a giant eraser over That Other Half of Koufax's career. As if it never happened. Or as if it wasn't his fault it happened. Or as if what transpired in the glory years made That Other Half irrelevant.

Sorry, that's not how it works. Not in this book, anyway.

Remember way back there, in the *last* chapter, when I tried to explain how Nolan Ryan got to be the right-handed half of this overrated tag team? The same standards apply to his left-handed partner in overratedness. Can I make this clear enough before we plow on? To call a player overrated is not the same thing as calling him, say, useless. It's not the same thing as suggesting he should have been a door-to-door dinnerware salesman. It just means we live in a world where people prefer fairy tales to real life.

And that's okay. Nothing wrong with it. It's just that, in real life, good stuff happens and bad stuff happens. To everybody. And once it's done happening, we start spinning it so it works in our own minds. Every once in a while, the spin cycle gets so out of whack, we concoct versions of the truth that don't match the actual truth as all that truthhood was going down. When that happens in the case of someone like Sandy Koufax, it's the job of us killjoys here at reality-police headquarters to blow the whistle. And out of that whistle, on this very page, comes that dreaded word, "overrated."

Oh, there was nothing overrated about the last six years of Koufax's career. We can all agree on that. At least not unless you were another All-Star pitcher of that era, wondering how come those Cy Young voters never seemed to notice you even existed. Over those last six stupendous seasons, here's the damage Koufax unleashed on the portion of the baseball earth known as Not the Dodgers:

How about a won-lost record of 129–47, an outrageous .733 winning percentage, with a 2.19 ERA and not even six and a half hits allowed for every nine innings he was out there? He ranked number one among starters in the whole darned sport, in every one of those categories, over those six years.

Just for amusement, he also tossed in three Cy Young Awards; a perfect game; three other no-hitters; five straight years leading the league in ERA; four seasons leading the league in strikeouts; one mind-warping, record-setting season of 382 strikeouts; plus a career World Series ERA under (gulp) 1.00. (It was, to be precise, 0.95, if you're calculating October ERAs at home.)

That, friends and readers, is some kind of ridiculous domination. Especially in the final four seasons of his career (97–27, with a 1.86 ERA), when Koufax vs. The Batsmiths wasn't even a fair fight. It was actually *those* four seasons that built the Legend of Sandy. It was *those* four seasons that truly comprise Koufax's indisputable period of "greatness." I'm just throwing in the previous two seasons (18–13, with a strikeout title, in 1961; 14–7, with an ERA title, in 1962) to prove I'm not even attempting to pile on here. I could, you understand, because in those two years, Koufax was merely really good, as opposed to bring-in-the-documentary-crew awesome. But we're all about fairness here at Overrated and Underrated Central. So we're cool with dividing Koufax's career into two distinct halves.

And in that good half—i.e., the only half people appear to think counts— he was Lefty Grove.

As dominant as he was during his prime, people often tend to forget that Sandy Koufax was only slightly better than average (if even that, actually) during the other half of his career.

(*The astute portion of our reading audience's exact thoughts at this moment:* Uh-oh. He's about to bring up The Other Half now. The bum.)

(*Author's retort to that observation:* Right you are, astute reading portion.)

All right, sorry about this, but here goes:

In the bad half of Koufax's career—i.e., the half that history has decided must have occurred during spring training—he was more like Jamie Easterly. Possibly Balor Moore.

Ready for Koufax's numbers in those other six seasons? Fasten your seat belts. How about a won-lost record of 36–40. And nearly 13 base runners allowed for every nine innings. And 5.3 walks per nine innings. And an ERA of 4.10, at a time when people still thought ERAs in the 4.00s were almost embarrassing.

He had so little idea where any pitch he threw was traveling that some of his teammates outright refused to take batting practice against him unless emergency life-insurance provisions were added to their contracts. His manager, the not-so-patient Walter Alston, often had the bullpen in five-alarm frenzy when Koufax pitched—*in the first inning.* And after the young left-hander's more unsightly outings, Alston's nerves would get so deep-fried it was often three weeks before he was ready to send Koufax back out there for more.

People chuckle as they look back on that period of Koufax's career now, of course—assuming they look back on it at all. It was just on-the-job training, right? And there were extenuating circumstances, too, right? Well, right. Because Koufax signed for a whopping $14,000 bonus, he fell under the mis-guided "Bonus Baby Rule." That dopey rule required the Dodgers to keep him in the big leagues for two years, whether the manager could stand watch-ing him or not. And that did nobody any good.

So if you want to shred those first two years right out of the argument, be my guest. But then what do we do about the next four? Koufax was only 32–34 in those four seasons, too. The ERA was still exactly 4.10. His walk rate was still 5.3 per nine innings. He still had just as many base runners around to keep him company.

Yeah, sure. Maybe he'd have been better if the manager had had any faith in him, if he'd gotten to pitch in a regular rotation, yada, yada, yada. Those rationalizations are out there. Who among us isn't at least a little sympathetic to Koufax's plight, knowing the kind of brilliance that was inside, just waiting for somebody to find a phone number for the genie who could unleash it?

But that brings us to the crux of a very tricky debate. Koufax may have been a victim of circumstance to some degree. He may have been cornered, by the Dodgers, into a position that made it impossible for him to succeed. But you know what he *wasn't*?

Invisible.

He had six tremendous seasons—in a *12-year* career. He also had six seasons that nobody wanted to put a frame around. Of all the pitchers in baseball who pitched as many innings as he did between 1955 and 1960, he had the second-*worst* ERA in the entire sport. Only the inimitable Chuck Stobbs (4.28) was worse.

sandy koufax

Played From: 1955–1966
Team: Dodgers
Career Record: 397 G, 165–87 W-L, 2.76 ERA, 2,325 IP, 1,754 H, 817 BB, 2,396 K

And remember, we're not talking about just a year or two of Koufax's career. We're talking about *half* his career. So, sorry. Much as this book would prefer to love and worship Koufax as much as the rest of you, we can't ignore That Other Half. Can't.

There's always going to be a romantic mythology that develops around the legend of any great athlete who is forced to retire young. We'd all love to know what might have been had somebody been futuristic enough to invent, say, Sandy Koufax surgery back then. But what might have been never was. So of all the left-handed starting pitchers in the Hall of Fame, not one piled up fewer wins than Koufax (165). There's a revealing, modern stat known as ERA-plus, which essentially compares a pitcher's ERA to his peers'. And in that funky category, Koufax ranks only 31st in history. It isn't just the all-time legends who are in front of him, either. Noodles Hahn, Mordecai "Three Finger" Brown, and even Tim Hudson outrank him.

But somehow, when those All-Century votes had finished rolling in, Koufax got more votes than *any* pitcher of the 1900s except Nolan Ryan. It's at that point, when stuff like that happens, that authors like us cease to be romanticists. You want romance? Go read Nora Roberts. You want to know how to get away with calling Sandy Koufax overrated? You've come to the right place.

The Rest of the Top Five

2. TOMMY JOHN

The good news is, John's name comes up in more ballpark conversations these days than any other pitcher of his time. The bad news is it's usually coming out of the mouth of an orthopedic surgeon. You have to admit it's actually an amazing feat in itself that John is now remembered more for his contributions to modern sports medicine than he is for those 288 games he won. But there's a message in there someplace. It's a tribute to John's adaptability and brainpower that we now refer to reconstructive elbow surgery as "Tommy John surgery." The guy did, after all, win 164 games after his career was pronounced dead. But it also took him 26 seasons to pile up his 288 wins. He was a top-three finisher in the Cy Young voting just two times in those 26 seasons. And his strikeout rate (only 4.3 per nine innings) is the lowest of any 200-game winner since World War II. So here's the deal: nice fellow. Terrific ligaments. But he's still overrated.

tommy john

Played From: 1963–1989
Teams: Indians, White Sox, Dodgers, Yankees, Angels, A's
Career Record: 760 G, 288–231 W-L, 3.34 ERA, 4,710⅓ IP, 4,783 H, 1,259 BB, 2,245 K

3. DAVID WELLS

There's something lovable about pudgy guys who survive in our modern sports world, where team fitness rooms are now the approximate size of Jennifer Aniston's house. And the Boomer didn't just survive. He pitched in the big leagues for 20 years. And won 230 games. And had an amazing knack for showing up in October, with six different teams. Now nobody is going to deny this guy had his moments (a perfect game, three All-Star Games and a trip to the mound in 1997 wearing Babe Ruth's actual cap). But the myth was even larger than the man—which wasn't easy. One of my math-major friends, a Bill James disciple named Lee Sinins, invented a stat for pitchers called "runs saved above average" (RSAA).

david wells

Played From: 1987–2006 (active)
Teams: Blue Jays, Tigers, Reds, Orioles, Yankees, White Sox, Red Sox, Padres
Career Record: 631 G, 230–148 W-L, 4.07 ERA, 3,281⅓ IP, 3,434 H, 677 BB, 2,119 K

Essentially, it just compares runs allowed to what an average pitcher would give up. Well, over the 13 peak years of Wells's career (1993–2005), only six pitchers won more games than he did. But 26 pitchers had a better RSAA rating—including Chuck Finley and Kevin Appier. In fact, the Boomer barely ranked ahead of Wilson Alvarez. So what do you call a man with stats like that, who also changed teams nine times in those 13 years? Overrated. Of course.

4. FRANK TANANA

Longevity is a beautiful thing. Almost as beautiful as being left-handed and breathing. So here's to Frank Tanana, a guy who managed to hang around the big leagues for 21 seasons, even though his shoulder disintegrated into chopped fettuccini by the time he was 24 years old. But here at Overratedness Central, we can only give so much credit for stuff like that. So as charismatic and hard-throwing and fast-talking as Tanana may have been over the first five full seasons of his career (1974–1978), a whole lot went on

frank tanana

Played From: 1973–1993
Teams: Angels, Red Sox, Rangers, Tigers, Mets, Yankees
Career Record: 638 G, 240–236
W-L, 3.66 ERA, 4,188⅓ IP, 4,063 H, 1,255 BB, 2,773 K

after that. And we regret to announce that the Tanana of 1979–1993 looked a lot more like, say, Larry McWilliams than he did like Steve Carlton. Over those first five seasons, Tanana averaged 16 wins a year. Over his final 15 seasons, he never won 16 in *any* season. Tanana was crafty enough to pile up 240 wins. And that's good. But he arrived at those 200 Win Club meetings with the lowest winning percentage (240–236, .504) of any 200-game-winning left-hander in history. And that's not so good. He's also the only left-handed pitcher ever to win 240 games without a 20-win season. There's something to be said for that, obviously. But there's something else we could call it: overrated.

5. BARRY ZITO

"Overpaid" isn't always the same thing as "overrated." But it works for Zito, who will now get paid as if he's a young Randy Johnson, thanks to the miracle of well-timed free agency. And he owes it all to: A) one spectacular Cy Young

barry zito

Played From: 2000–2006 (active)
Teams: A's, Giants
Career Record: 222 G, 102–63
W-L, 3.55 ERA, 1,430⅓ IP, 1,228 H,
560 BB, 1,096 K

season (23–5 in 2002), B) a ballpark in Oakland that made him look far more dominating than he really was, and C) an agent (Scott Boras) who put out a Why Barry Zito Makes Lefty Grove Look Like Glendon Rusch free-agency book that was longer than *Lord of the Rings*. But it sure was amazing how many people in baseball nominated him as "overrated" when they found out I was writing this book. "He's not overrated for reliability," one GM said. "But he *is* overrated if you think he's somebody who should pitch at the top of your rotation." Zito has never had a losing season. But guess what? Since that Cy Young season, he has fewer wins than Kenny Rogers and a lower strikeout ratio than Casey Fossum. So why is he getting paid more than those two guys put together?

The Most Underrated Left-Handed Starter of All Time

BABE RUTH

Is it safe to say a fellow was an underrated pitcher if your average living American can't quite recall that he ever threw a *pitch*?

Boy, as standards for underratedness go, it's tough to top that one.

Okay, so Babe Ruth went on to be known for attributes other than his left arm. It was a terrific little career move. Had he kept on pitching for a living, he'd have blown up his chance to be the most humongous baseball legend of the 20th century. So legend-worshippers everywhere can be grateful he didn't decide to devote his life to something as insignificant as perfecting his curveball mechanics. But had the Babe kept on pitching, something else would have happened besides that tragic loss of legendhood.

He also might have turned into The Greatest Left-Handed Pitcher Ever to Walk the Earth.

Have you ever taken a look at the Bambino's pitching stats? Let's just say they won't remind you of Hideki Irabu.

If Babe Ruth hadn't gone on to become the greatest slugger of the 20th century, he may well have developed into the greatest left-handed pitcher of all time.

Who's the only left-handed pitcher in Red Sox history to win at least 23 games in back-to-back seasons? The Babe, of course. Who's the only left-handed pitcher since 1900 to do that for *any* team before age 23? That would be...the Babe. How many left-handers have piled up back-to-back win totals like that, at any age, in the nearly nine decades since Ruth did it? Would you believe just five (Hal Newhouser, Carl Hubbell, Sandy Koufax, Mike Cuellar, and Wilbur Wood)?

All righty. Now that I've got your attention here, let's keep rolling.

The Babe led the American League in ERA in his first full season in a big-league starting rotation (1.75, in 1916). He was 21 years old at the time. It's nine decades later now. And he's *still* the youngest ERA champ in the history of the American League.

There were six seasons (1914–1919) in which Ruth's most common job description was "pitcher" (as opposed to "slugger" or, say, "Most Famous Human Being on Planet Earth"). How good was he? In those six seasons, he merely led every left-handed pitcher in the sport in winning percentage (.659) and fewest hits allowed per nine innings (7.07). That's how good.

From 1915 to 1918, when the Babe was devoting most of his attention to pitching (as opposed to, say, eating every food-like item in the nearest deli), he ripped off an ERA under 2.50 in all four of them. Oh, sure, that might seem like no big deal, seeing as how it was still the action-packed dead-ball era. But only one other pitcher in the American League matched that—a fellow named Walter Johnson.

Hey, speaking of Walter Johnson, you might have heard he was the greatest pitcher of the Bambino's era. Well, that might not exactly be true. He might have been the greatest pitcher of *anybody's* era. But the first seven times Ruth pitched against Johnson, here's how it turned out:

The Babe—six wins. Johnson—one win. And it would have been 7–zip if Ruth hadn't blown a shutout and a two-run lead in the ninth inning of that seventh game.

Johnson was totally in his prime in 1916 and 1917. Which meant that back then, your typical hitter thought it would be a lot more fun to enlist, go to war, and get shot at than to step in and hit against the Big Train. But take a look at how the Babe's two breakout seasons stacked up against Johnson's:

1916

Johnson: 25–20, 1.90 ERA, 290 hits in 369⅔ innings
Ruth: 23–12, 1.75 ERA, 230 hits in 323⅔ innings

1917

Johnson: 23–16, 2.21 ERA, 248 hits in 326 innings
Ruth: 24–13, 2. 01 ERA, 244 hits in 326⅓ innings

In other words, holy schmoly. Walter Johnson was the best frigging pitcher alive—and the Babe *out-pitched him.*

None of this even takes into account how the Bambino stepped it up when the Red Sox finally let him pitch in a few World Series games. (Which, incidentally, is something they didn't do in the 1915 Series—a snub Babe is undoubtedly still griping about to this day on whatever cloud he's hanging out at, in between scarfing down bratwursts.) All Ruth did in the 1916 and 1918 World Series was hang up 29⅔ consecutive innings' worth of zeroes. And that, friends, was a record that stood for 43 years, until Whitey Ford screwed up this paragraph of the book by breaking it.

That scoreless streak began, by the way, with one of the greatest World Series pitching gems ever: Game 2, 1916. Ruth allowed an inside-the-park homer in the first inning, then shut out the Dodgers from the second inning

babe ruth

Played From: 1914–1935
Pitched From: 1914–1919, plus
five games: 1920, 1921, 1930, 1933
Teams: Red Sox, Yankees
Career Record: 163 G, 94–46 W-L,
2.28 ERA, 1,220⅓ IP, 974 H, 441 BB,
488 K

through the (gulp) fourteenth. So how many other pitchers have won a four-teen-inning complete game in any round of any postseason? *None,* naturally.

In other words, the Babe was seriously dealing any time they gave him the ball. Before he'd even reached his 23rd birthday, he'd already had two 20-win seasons—a feat matched, at the time, by only three other pitchers in the 20th century (Christy Mathewson, Smoky Joe Wood, and the mysterious Al Mamaux). But it was about then that history was altered irrevocably—and by that we mean pitching history, not cursed-franchise history. Turned out Ruth had another pretty cool skill: every time he hit a baseball, it sounded like the army had just fired off another howitzer. So after he turned 23, he pitched in just five games the rest of his life (and won all five, naturally). Thus, we'll never know what kind of pitcher he might have been. He had 700 homers to hit. Not for the Red Sox, of course—but that's a whole 'nother book.

So the Babe's life may have turned in other directions. But he always reserved a spot in his heart for his fondest pitching memories (possibly because his stomach was usually filled up with other stuff he was also fond of). He apparently never felt he got enough accolades for his pitching. So even kidding him about it was always a really bad idea.

Allan Wood—author of the book *Babe Ruth and the 1918 Red Sox*—tells a story about how a bunch of players for the 1938 Dodgers made the bigggg mistake of giving their new coach, George H. "Bambino" Ruth, a hard time about his pitching career. Next thing they knew, Ruth was challenging them to take batting practice against him. (Little did they know he'd been secretly getting his arm in shape for a week.) According to Dodgers trainer Ed Froelich, Ruth threw BP to four of them for 10 minutes. They got exactly 10 balls out of the batting cage. In other words, the rest of those 10 minutes consisted of a whole bunch of foul tips, shanks, and hacks that hit nothing at all.

"I never saw anything like that before," catcher Babe Phelps later told Froelich. "He was moving the ball every which way it's possible to move the ball—down and in, down and out, up and in, up and out…darnedest thing I ever saw."

Well, of course. Because Ruth himself was the darnedest thing anybody ever saw. What *couldn't* he do? That's the question. Okay, so he probably wouldn't have made a great jockey at Pimlico. But now he can add this to his list of credentials: not just the greatest hitter of all time. Now, officially, the most underrated left-hander of all time.

The Rest of the Top Five

2. WARREN SPAHN

Have you read enough rants in this book yet about the All-Century Team voting? Okay, sorry. But here's another one: How the heck did The Winningest Pitcher of the Entire Live-Ball Era not get elected? Or, to put this another way, how the heck did The Winningest Left-hander in the History of the Universe not get elected? It took an act of divine intervention by a Special All-Century Panel for Undoing Fan Screw-Ups to get Warren Spahn on that team. And that, friends, is insane. Sandy Koufax got elected by the fans—and Spahn won almost

warren spahn

Played From: 1942–1965
Teams: Braves, Mets, Giants
Career Record: 750 G, 363–245 W-L, 3.08 ERA, 5,245⅔ IP, 4,830 H, 1,434 BB, 2,583 K

200 more games than he did (363–165). Yep, 200. Ponder that as you try to digest this man's career. You'll also need to ponder fun factoids like these: Warren Spahn won more games than Koufax and Fernando Valenzuela combined (338). Warren Spahn had more 20-win seasons (13) than Koufax, Steve Carlton, and Randy Johnson combined (12). Warren Spahn led his league in strikeouts more times (four) than Pedro Martinez (three), led his league in ERA more times (three) than Jim Palmer (two), led his league in innings pitched twice as many times (four) as Roger Clemens (two). And this guy did all that even though World War II cost him three years of his career. Luckily for him, he aged better than any human in history (except possibly Dick Clark)— pitching until age 44, throwing two no-hitters after he turned 39, and spinning off a 23-win season at age 42. So let's just say if you ever get a chance to vote some day in some All-Two-Century election or something, you'd better remember all this, or the publisher reserves the right to revoke your copy of this book.

3. STEVE CARLTON

Oh, no. Not *another* grievous All-Century oversight. Yeah, 'fraid so. And this time, no Special Committee to Look Out for Hall of Famers Who Treated the Media Like West Nile Mosquitoes stepped forward to rescue Steve Carlton. But maybe Carlton's exclusion from the All-Century fast lane should teach players everywhere a valuable lesson. Yukking it up with the media: good idea. Forgetting to speak to the media for an entire decade: bad idea. Not that Carlton would care much whether he made that team, you under-

steve carlton

Played From: 1965–1988
Teams: Cardinals, Phillies, Giants, White Sox, Indians, Twins
Career Record: 741 G, 329–244 W-L, 3.22 ERA, 5,217⅓ IP, 4,672 H, 1,833 BB, 4,136 K

stand, or whether this book considers him underrated, overrated, or downright irrelevant. This guy never even said thanks for his four Cy Young Awards. And come to think of it, once he did start speaking, he told us way more than we needed to know about the conspiratorial dangers of gamma rays and sinister bankers who were trying to take over the world. But forget all that. All you really need to remember is that the only left-hander in history who won more games than Carlton (329) was Spahn, and the only left-hander who won more Cy Youngs than Carlton (four) was Randy Johnson. So, obviously, he dominated the hitters better than he dominated a conversation.

4. LEFTY GROVE

(This time, I'm determined to make it through at least three sentences of this paragraph before even mentioning the All-Century Team, so wish me luck.)

lefty grove

Played From: 1925–1941
Teams: A's, Red Sox
Career Record: 616 G, 300–141
W-L, 3.06 ERA, 3,940 IP, 3,849 H,
1,187 BB, 2,266 K

The best-kept secret in baseball history is *not* the contents of Barry Bonds's medicine chest. It's that Lefty Grove was the greatest pitcher of the live-ball era, and nobody knows it. Certainly not the knuckleheads who allowed him to finish 18th—*that's 18th*—in the All-Century voting. (Oops. Only made it through two sentences.) All this freaking guy did was lead the league in ERA *nine* times, roll up the greatest winning percentage (.680) of any 300-game winner in history, and rip off the most stupendous three-year run of any pitcher who ever lived (79–15, with a 2.46 ERA, for the 1929–1931 A's). But somehow, he got fewer All-Century votes than Eddie Murray. Which proves only that it never pays to be dead.

5. TOM GLAVINE

Do you ever hear Glavine's name in those Greatest Active Left-Hander debates? Never. Ever. And that's a farce. Tom Glavine owns as many 20-win seasons (five) as Randy Johnson, David Wells,

tom glavine

Played From: 1987–2006 (active)
Teams: Braves, Mets
Career Record: 635 G, 290–191
W-L, 3.46 ERA, 4,149⅔ IP, 4,012 H,
1,399 BB, 2,481 K

and Barry Zito put together. He has unfurled more 200-inning seasons (13) than any left-handed pitcher in the last 30 years except Randy Johnson. Glavine also wouldn't know the disabled list from a grocery list. And he even has the highest career batting average (.186) of any pitcher in the DH era (1973–now) who made it to home plate as many times as he has. So who cares if the radar-gun operators spend the whole day yawning when he pitches. He is, after all, (how should we put this?) *left-handed*. Tom Glavine—as underrated as underrated gets.

CHAPTER 3

Relief Pitchers

The Most Overrated Reliever of All Time

LEE SMITH

In my tireless efforts to lend impeccable credibility to this book, I asked a retired starting pitcher if he had a nomination for the most overrated closer in history. There were instant indications I'd pushed the right button here.

"Yeah," he laughed. "All of them."

Turned out, he didn't *really* mean all of them. Just all closers who had saved a game in the last 20 years—the generation whose courageous assignment was often to get three outs before they gave up three runs. That's the generation that has made the save what it is today.

Namely, the most overrated stat in baseball.

So if the save is the most overrated stat ever, just think of all the spectacular choices that gives us in selecting the most overrated closer ever. It isn't quite "all of them." But it *is* a veritable buffet line. And after strolling past that smorgasbord for a long, long time, I've reluctantly concluded that the most overrated bullpen entrée ever is the man who used to be the leading save-collector in history, until Trevor Hoffman passed him late in the 2006 season—the always-affable Lee Arthur Smith.

Does that make Lee Smith a victim of guilt by association with the stat that defines him? Well, yeah. To some extent. After all, it isn't his fault that the category he became (ahem) the "all-time leader" in happened to be a category of such dubious merit. But here's why he got dragged into this muck, as opposed to the other 768 options for number one on this most-overrated list:

1) Let's first put into perspective what it means to be the (ahem number two) "all-time saves leader." We know it's not quite the same thing as being the all-time wins leader or the all-time strike-out leader or even the all-time balk leader—if only because, a century ago, there was pretty much no such thing as a save. And that, obviously, is Tony LaRussa's fault, for neglecting to be born yet so he could invent the three-out save, or just about any other kind of save. If Lee Smith had had to duke it out with "Three Finger" Brown or "Sea Lion" Hall for that (ahem number three) "all-time lead," that would be one thing. But holding the (ahem number four) "all-time lead" in a stat that, essentially, has barely existed for three decades makes a guy almost inherently overrated. Doesn't it?

2) But to show you the kind of magnanimous overrated-underrated chief justice I am, I'm willing to overlook Point Number One in its entirety. I introduced it only to deliver an important message— that we have no historical basis yet for determining what it means to be the (ahem number five) "all-time saves leader." Get back to me in 50 years on that one. But in the meantime, I'm actually a guy who believes, in general, that the value of closers is being underrated by the Hall of Fame electorate. So I'm not here to toss all closers not named Mariano Rivera into some giant dumpster. That would be hypocritical. I'm here to do exactly what I've done in all the other "overrated" sections of this book—merely divide what Lee Smith was from what he wasn't. And I'll start doing that approximately four words from now.

3) So was Lee Arthur Smith really as dominant as his one-time label as the (uh-oh, it's another ahem) "all-time saves leader" seemed to suggest? Alas, after careful study, I've been forced to conclude he

really wasn't. Oh, he could strike you out, all right. The guy did average almost a strikeout an inning over 18 seasons. And that tells you something. But his strikeout rate (8.73 per nine innings), by closer standards, was nothing extraordinary. In fact, it ranks behind the whiff rates of relievers like Ugueth Urbina, Armando Benitez, and Randy Myers—and just 10th overall, among members of the 200-Plus Save Club. You know, in case you hadn't thought much about this, there is a reason managers decide to use certain pitchers as closers and others to pitch the fifth inning of 11–2 games. Swinging and missing would be one of those reasons. So the old swing-and-miss skill set is more part of a closer's job

To be fair, Lee Smith's overratedness is more through guilt by association, and his penchant for earning saves—the most overrated stat in baseball.

description than it is an indication that any reliever is some kind of all-time great. Sorry. That's just the facts.

4) Okay, what about Smith's other numbers? Another big one to look at is Base Runners Allowed Per Nine Innings, or the much-trendier term "WHIP" (Walks and Hits Per Innings Pitched). Oops, he doesn't fare so hot there, either. He ranks 21st among the 200-Plus Save Club members in that department. His WHIP (1.26) even sits behind Rick Aguilera's, Dave Smith's, and Rod Beck's, among others. So if you're looking for Cooperstown-ish domination, you can't find it here, either.

5) But this book is all about fairness, so let's move along to one last indicator. Let's check a new-age stat known as ERA-plus. That one couldn't possibly be based on a more simple concept—how a pitcher's ERA compared with the average ERA in the time he pitched once you adjust it for the kind of ballparks he pitched in. Smith's career ERA-plus computes to 132, meaning it was 32 percent better than your average schmo. Which is good. But it merely ties him with Kent Tekulve and ranks him behind the likes of John Hiller, Roberto Hernandez, and Dan Quisenberry. Which means our man was clearly really good—but was he great? Well, Smith did pitch an awfully long time. So to be extra, extra fair, I decided to classify any season with a 150 ERA-plus as a "great" season. Smith had four of those in 18 years. But Doug Jones (right, Doug Jones) had seven of those "great" seasons. In other words, so much for that stat.

If you've read beyond the table of contents of this book, though, you know the agenda here is not to bash the winners of the Most Overrated competition until it's tough to tell their careers from, say, Scott Klingenbeck's. I admit I always liked Lee Smith. I found him funny and folksy and entertaining. And once, back when I worked for *The Philadelphia Inquirer,* I even wrote a column bashing the Phillies for not signing him to replace the irreplaceable Mitch Williams in 1994. (Instead, they traded for Doug Jones, whose own greatness I hadn't yet comprehended, clearly.)

I recognize that it took more work for Smith to pile up those 478 saves than just waking up from his nightly nap and heading straight out to the mound for the postgame handshakes. Heck, 18 years is a long time for any relief pitcher—make that any *pitcher*—to be effective and productive. And Smith was so durable and consistent, he was still making the All-Star team at age 37, two years before he was done.

lee smith

Played From: 1980–1997
Teams: Cubs, Red Sox, Cardinals, Yankees, Orioles, Angels, Reds, Expos
Career Record: 1,022 G, 71–92 W-L, 478 SV, 3.03 ERA, 1,289⅓ IP, 1,133 H, 486 BB, 1,251 K

He retired with more 30-save seasons (10) than any reliever of (sorry) "all time." He did pitch 90 innings or more for five straight years early in his career, back before Cheap Save–itis swept the land. And he is still the only reliever ever to trot out there 60 times or more in 12 straight seasons. But even a fun factoid like that last one isn't enough to make this man a living legend. After all, through 2006, the reliever with the second-longest 60-game streak ever was the not-so-legendary Mike Myers.

In other words, Lee Smith is a tough fellow to know what to make of. But I didn't just decide that 15 paragraphs ago. I decided it when my 2004 Hall of Fame ballot arrived in the mail and, after massive agonizing, he caused me to do something I've never done with any player on that ballot. Ever. I *stopped* voting for him. Normally, you see, I'm one of those voters with a rigid Hall of Fame voting philosophy. I give serious consideration to every legitimate candidate. I then ask myself the fundamental question, "Was this man a Hall of Famer or not?" And if I answer, "Yes," I commit to voting for him—not just that year, but every year he's on the ballot.

But in the case of Lee Smith, something revolutionary happened: I changed my mind. Oh, I'd changed a couple of nos to yesses over the years. But I'd never done that in reverse until this man had spent a year rattling around my subconscious. My initial inclination was to vote for (uh-oh) "the all-time saves leader." A year later, after ruminating on much of the information you've no doubt been enjoying so much in these last few pages, I decided I'd made a mistake. So when I call Lee Smith overrated, it's no random charge. In this case, he was even overrated by *me*.

The Rest of the Top Five

2. JEFF REARDON

Speaking of deposed "all-time" saves leaders, Reardon was once number one on that chart himself (with 367), until Smith blew by him. But this is another case where, if you look beyond the save numbers, Reardon wasn't the dominator you'd think he was. In his 11 seasons as a closer, he blew at least eight saves in *nine* of them. With 106 blown saves altogether, he doesn't even make the "all-time" top 50 in save percentage (converting just 77.6 percent). And his ERA-plus numbers rate below Rod Beck's or Mike Henneman's. So, in reality, the only department in which Reardon was truly the greatest of his generation was the thickest-beard standings. And much as we all admire a good whisker, that isn't enough to keep a guy out of the overrated bin.

jeff reardon

Played From: 1979–1994
Teams: Mets, Expos, Twins, Red Sox, Braves, Reds, Yankees
Career Record: 880 G, 73–77 W-L, 367 SV, 3.16 ERA, 1,132⅓ IP, 1,000 H, 358 BB, 877 K

3. DAVE RIGHETTI

Anybody who spends seven straight seasons closing for the Yankees is guaranteed to be: A) a back-page-of-the-tabloids regular, B) a subject of more talk-show calls than all the members of Congress put together, and C) the most famous (or infamous) closer in America. Well, that was Dave Righetti, from 1984 to 1990. In many ways, he had himself a heck of a career: won a Rookie of the Year award. Pitched a no-hitter. Even set (temporarily) the "all-time" single-season save record (with 46, in 1986). But here at Overrated-Underrated Headquarters, we're forced to peer beneath those numbers. We found 60 blown saves in just six years in one stretch, the lowest career save percentage (77.3) of any closer in the 250-Save Club, and way too many base runners (12.18 per nine innings) making for way too many scary saves. Righetti is a bright, personable man who became a terrific pitching

dave righetti

Played From: 1979–1995
Teams: Yankees, Giants, A's, Blue Jays, White Sox
Career Record: 718 G, 82–79 W-L, 252 SV, 3.46 ERA, 1,403⅔ IP, 1,287 H, 591 BB, 1,112 K

coach. But unfortunately, we're not permitted by the proper authorities to use those attributes as reasons to commute his overrated sentence.

4. BOBBY THIGPEN

How exactly can we describe what Thigpen represents in the annals of contemporary relief pitching? Is he the Roger Maris of relievers? The Earl Webb of relievers? The Kerry Wood of relievers? I'm not sure any of those work. So how about the Siouxsie and the Banshees of relievers—because this guy is one of baseball's epic one-hit wonders. Yes, Thigpen's 57-save season for the 1990 White Sox still stood as the "all-time" single-season record last time anybody checked. But

bobby thigpen

Played From: 1986–1994
Teams: White Sox, Phillies, Mariners
Career Record: 448 G, 31–36 W-L, 201 SV, 3.43 ERA, 568⅔ IP, 537 H, 238 BB, 376 K

surrounding that season, here's what you'll find: no other 35-save seasons, a 3.43 career ERA, an opponent batting average of .252, and a blown save for every four he converted. There's only one word for that, friends (and you can all sing along)—"overrated."

5. ARMANDO BENITEZ

When you write books like this, you always need someone to stand as the shining example of why numbers alone can't define who's overrated and underrated. So thank you, Armando Benitez. Numbers? You want numbers? Hey, Benitez can spew out numbers so pretty, you'll want to hang them in a gallery. Among all the pitchers in "history" with 200 saves, only Billy Wagner has a better strikeout rate (10.96 per nine innings), and only Wagner and Troy Percival beat him in lowest opponent batting average (.191). And

armando benitez

Played From: 1994–2006 (active)
Teams: Orioles, Mets, Yankees, Mariners, Marlins, Giants
Career Record: 699 G, 38–38 W-L, 280 SV, 2.95 ERA, 722⅓ IP, 492 H, 372 BB, 880 K

how about this: through 2006, Benitez had converted the same percentage of his career save opportunities as Dennis Eckersley (84.6). Well, if he's that good, how come folks in every city he's ever pitched in would rather volunteer for an appendectomy than see Benitez stomp in there in a big game? The numbers won't ever tell that tale. But a 2003 ESPN.com feature—pithily titled "Armando Benitez's Top 10 Meltdowns"—*that* tells it. Eight of those implosions occurred in either the last week of September or the postseason, by the way. Any more questions?

The Most Underrated Reliever of All Time

GOOSE GOSSAGE

There's one thing baseball authorities tend to look for in a great closer. And that, obviously, is facial hair. The bushier the better. So no wonder the Goose always looked so terrifying, stomping around out there with a Fu Manchu that would have obscured a small forest and sideburns longer than Yao Ming is tall.

Then he'd go, full torque, into his inimitable eight-cylinder windup, elbows flying, legs rocking, smoke foaming out of his eardrums, looking as if he were recoiling backward about 40 feet, all so he could unleash this never-ending supply of unhittable infernos. And that intimidating act led to a period of about 10 years, from the mid-1970s to the mid-1980s, where the phrase "Now pitching—Goose Gossage" was a synonym for "Drive home safely—because this game's *over*." When you took in the full breadth of Goose's hulking presence, you had to ask: who'd want to mess with *that* guy?

So any time Gossage's name comes up in a ballpark near me, I never feel any hesitation in uttering the phrase "most dominating relief pitcher ever." That's ever. As in ever. I don't care what name you care to bring up—Mariano, Billy Wagner, Rollie Fingers, Rob Dibble. The word was *ever*. I don't care what stats you want to cite—saves, ERA, WHIP, VORP, loose mustache whiskers per nine innings. Doesn't matter. That's my story, and I'm sticking to it. Most dominating relief pitcher ever. Ever.

I'll get to my own set of favorite Goose Gossage stats any sentence now, just to prove I'm not blabbering on here for the shameless purpose of merely making it through another chapter. But first, it's time for The Rant.

The Rant is presented to you from this personal perspective: I'm a Hall of Fame voter. I like and respect my fellow Hall of Fame voters. But when it comes time to vote on the Goose, what exactly is going on in their brain cells? The 2007 election marked Gossage's *eighth* attempt to collect his rightful Hall of Fame plaque. His eighth? Yep, his eighth. Anybody who had any idea what a Hall of Fame closer looks like would be asking why he even needed to make a *second* attempt, let alone an eighth.

What exactly is missing on this fellow's Hall of Fame qualifications sheet, anyhow? Longevity? Got it. Great-player aura? Got it. October brilliance (minus a couple of swings of the bat by George Brett and Kirk Gibson)? Got it. Played in New York? Got it. Hall of Fame facial hair? Got it. So what's the deal? Goose Gossage has it all. Except the plaque. Which makes him the most criminally under-supported Hall of Fame candidate of my lifetime. So there. You've now heard The Rant.

Goose Gossage, plain and simple, was the most dominating relief pitcher ever. End of argument.

Now here's why I'm always inspired to erupt into The Rant: I don't know what other people's standard for domination is. But here's mine: over the Goose's first 10 seasons as a closer, he had ERAs of 0.77, 1.62, 1.82, 1.84, 2.01, 2.23, and 2.27 twice. So that's eight seasons with ERAs of 2.27 or lower. That's as many seasons as Rollie Fingers and Trevor Hoffman combined.

goose gossage

Played From: 1972–1994
Teams: White Sox, Pirates, Yankees, Padres, Cubs, Giants, Rangers, A's, Mariners
Career Record: 1,002 G, 124–107 W-L, 310 SV, 3.01 ERA, 1,809⅓ IP, 1,497 H, 732 BB, 1,502 K

And if you were a right-handed hitter, you'd have had more fun on a chain gang than you had trying to hit Goose Gossage. These are the stats accumulated by the right-handed-hitting portion of the populace while facing Gossage over a period spanning all 22 seasons of his career: .211 batting average, .284 on-base percentage, .311 slugging percentage. After reflecting on those numerals, I thought: how can I make you astute readers understand how insane those numbers are? So I began looking at active hitters whose career offensive stats were in that neighborhood. I found a handful. They were all *pitchers*. In other words, the Goose spent 22 years making the greatest right-handed hitters alive *hit like pitchers*. Is that dominating enough for you?

When discussing Gossage, we are also required by the latest truth-in-book-writing laws to disclose that this man took on a workload, in his prime, that would have today's closers filing grievances every three days. He pitched at least 133 innings in relief in *three* different seasons, without being allowed to save 30 games in any of them. Want to compare that to your typical modern closers? Of the top 30 save-accumulators in the 2006 season, there were 14 who didn't even pitch *half* that many innings. Just for fun, I went back and looked at Gossage's first season as a closer (1975). He made 17 different appearances in which he got at least 10 outs—including four mind-blowing outings in which he went 5⅔, 7, 7⅓, and 7⅔ innings, respectively. In one of those games, he faced 34 hitters—in relief. That's a month in the life of Eddie Guardado.

Finally, here comes my favorite part of this Goose Gossage term paper. Let's compare him with Mariano Rivera, because there are incredible similarities. We'll begin with most seasons by a closer with ERAs under 2.30:

Gossage eight, Rivera seven. Okay, now let's give Mariano his due. Most seasons of 20-plus saves and sub-2.00 ERAs: Rivera seven, Gossage next with four. All right, how about most All-Star teams made by closers: Gossage nine (one as a starter), Rivera eight, Rollie Fingers seven. And since 2006 marked Rivera's 10th season as a closer, let's compare his theoretically incomparable decade with Gossage's first 10 seasons as a closer. Rivera saved many more games (408–254). But their ERAs are a wash (2.01 for Rivera, 2.06 for Goose). Gossage was by far the superior strikeout machine (8.52 to 7.66 per nine innings). And Gossage was more unhittable (6.39 hits per nine innings to 6.96). But the wham-bang, rest-my-case, grand finale is this: the Goose was able to unleash that domination while pitching (ready?) 267⅔ more innings. Whew.

I recognize that the Goose hung on way too long for some of these Hall voters' tastes, lowering his numbers from lunar-orbit altitude to merely satellite level. And granted, he couldn't take the ultimate hint that it was time to go—because he even pitched in Japan for a year. But I'll still argue that the tail end of his career was no worse than the final chapters of Dennis Eckersley's career. And nobody held it against the Eck. I'll even concede that, now that Bruce Sutter is in, Gossage *will* make it into the Hall of Fame one of these years. But anybody this great who had to suffer this sort of Hall of Fame indignation for this long at least makes life easier for us underrated-overrated authors. I've been trained now to know exactly what underrated looks like. And in this case, it looks exactly like a relief pitcher who forgot to shave for about seven years in a row.

The Rest of the Top Five

2. TREVOR HOFFMAN

If you read my comments about the dubious nature of the whopping save numbers piled up by Lee Smith and Jeff Reardon, you're probably asking: why are those guys overrated, but Hoffman, our new "all-time" saves leader, is underrated? Aha! I knew that was coming. And boy, am I ready for you. Obviously, you missed my point on those other pitchers. It isn't saves we're

trevor hoffman

Played From: 1993–2006 (active)
Teams: Marlins, Padres
Career Record: 821 G, 49–55 W-L,
482 SV, 2.71 ERA, 885⅓ IP, 675 H,
250 BB, 965 K

using as the measure of the man. It's the other stuff. And Hoffman blows those guys away on The Other Stuff. He has allowed nearly *three* fewer base runners per nine innings than another 400-save man, John Franco; almost two fewer than Smith; and more than 1½ fewer than Reardon. The batting average of opposing hitters against Hoffman (.208) is more than 40 points lower than the average against Franco and almost 30 points lower than the other two. And Hoffman kicks their butts in strikeout rate (9.81 per nine innings), too. But we can finish off this debate with this: Hoffman also beats Mariano Rivera in *every* one of those categories. *And* Hoffman's save percentage (89.6) is so good, he had virtually the same number of blown saves in his career (56) as Rivera (55) through the 2006 season—but in 70 more opportunities. In other words, Rivera would have to blitz through almost two full seasons without blowing one frigging save just to be able to say he has converted the same percentage as the great Trevor Hoffman. So is there *any* question that Hoffman is a Hall of Famer—or that this man is seriously underrated?

3. HOYT WILHELM

If I ever come up with a guide for how pitchers can become more underrated, one of the first pieces of advice I'd dole out would be: go to knuckleball

hoyt wilhelm

Played From: 1952–1972
Teams: Giants, Cardinals, Indians, Orioles, White Sox, Angels, Braves, Cubs, Dodgers
Career Record: 1,070 G, 143–122 W-L, 227 SV*, 2.52 ERA, 2,253 IP, 1,757 H, 778 BB, 1,610 K
(*196 saves before saves became an official stat in 1969)

school. If you almost never throw a pitch harder than 62 miles an hour, you're nearly guaranteed to increase your underratedness. And Wilhelm is Exhibit A. My ESPN.com colleague Rob Neyer calls Wilhelm the "greatest relief pitcher in history before managers decided what a relief pitcher is supposed to be." But it's funny how you never hear any big talk-show debates like: which closer would you rather have—Mariano Rivera or Hoyt Wilhelm? Too bad, because Wilhelm has it all—the most relief wins in history (124), the most games pitched in history (1,070), and the most spectacular senior-citizen period in history (52 wins, 115 saves, a 2.11 ERA, and 10 more big-league seasons after turning 40). He's the only reliever ever to spin off five straight seasons with a sub-2.00 ERA. And he's also virtually uncontaminated by life under the modern save rule. Finally, here's the extra-credit portion of this paragraph: you've got to love the fact that even though Wilhelm made just 52 career starts, one of them was a no-hitter. And (you should take notes here, because this will be coming up on a bar stool at some point in your life), he's also a human trivia answer. The question: name the only player in history to play 21 years, hit a homer in his first career at-bat and never hit another. So it's almost impossible to be more underrated than this guy.

4. BILLY WAGNER

Here's all you need to know (well, practically) about Wagner: he's 5'11" (according to his baseball card). He throws a baseball 100 miles per hour left-handed. And he's actually *right-handed*. All freaks of nature get extra underrated points. But Wagner might not even need them, since the batting average of all the hitters he'd faced in his career, through 2006, was an absurd .187. And how many relievers in the 200-Save Club can beat that? Correct answer: nobody.

billy wagner

Played From: 1995–2006 (active)
Teams: Astros, Phillies, Mets
Career Record: 654 G, 37–34 W-L, 324 SV, 2.38 ERA, 702⅔ IP, 468 H, 238 BB, 934 K

5. DAN QUISENBERRY

Relievers with trick pitches and funky deliveries never get their proper respect. And Quisenberry was both of the above—submarine-balling his gyrating sinkerballs with a delivery that made him look like a fellow who had just tripped over a hill, lost his balance, and, on the way down, decided to pick some flowers. But gaze behind the tricks and the funk and you find a closer who had seven dominating seasons in succession, wound up his career with the same ERA-plus as Walter Johnson had and did something no other closer has ever done—finish in the top three in the Cy Young voting four years in a row (1982–1985).

dan quisenberry

Played From: 1979–1990
Teams: Royals, Cardinals, Giants
Career Record: 674 G, 56–46 W-L, 244 SV, 2.76 ERA, 1,043⅓ IP, 1,064 H, 162 BB, 379 K

If the Quis Man wasn't underrated for all that, I'd include him anyway, just for being the most quotable reliever of all time. ("I have seen the future and it's much like the present, only longer.") I was once talking to him before a game when the security guard announced it was time for me to leave the clubhouse. Quisenberry promptly told the guard, "If he's got to go, I'm going, too." And out we went—into the stadium concourse, where we kept chatting for another 20 minutes, Quis in full uniform, as fans streamed by on the way to the hot-dog stand. Now *that's* underrated.

CHAPTER 4

Designated Hitters

The Most Overrated Designated Hitter of All Time

RON BLOMBERG

Might as well confess: I'm a National League kind of guy. So here are just a few of the inventions in history that I'd rank above the DH: Taxes. Telemarketers. The Clapper. Car air "fresheners." Spam. The relentlessly entertaining Big Mouth Billy Bass. And, of course, Carrot Top.

So if you're reading between the lines, you can safely conclude that, on my list of valuable contributions to modern American life, I'd place the designated hitter slightly above the FlingShot Flying Monkey but still below the Thighmaster.

Which leads us to how poor Ron Blomberg found his way into this chapter as The Most Overrated Designated Hitter of All Time. He was, in truth, a lot better at it than, say, Joey Meyer. But the whole darned DH concept is so overrated—except, possibly, for when David Ortiz heads for the plate with two outs in the ninth—we might as well trace this mess back to the man who started it all.

Oh, okay, Blomberg didn't really start it all. It's not like he's the one who woke up one day and said, "Let's see if we can make baseball more interesting— by allowing managers to catch up on their in-game nap time, by giving our customers more of those four and a half-hour games they've been demanding, and, most important, by making sure Catfish Hunter doesn't get near home plate with a bat, even if he tries to disguise himself as Reggie Jackson."

Yeah, it's true Blomberg didn't invent the DH. He merely happened to be history's first DH. Which probably makes him history's most famous DH. Which means he's really just a symbolic choice. He's overrated by association with baseball's most dubious idea since the Astros tried to grow grass inside the Astrodome.

To pick one particularly overrated DH would be unfair anyway, because designated hitting is such a strange line of work. No kid ever grew up dreaming of being a famous DH some day so he wouldn't have to waste his important allowance money on something as useless as *a glove*. And there has been just about no player ever who got to the big leagues as a DH and then did nothing but DH in his career.

Ron Blomberg, the first and most famous DH in history, batted an unimpressive .257 in that role.

So as I began sifting through the post-1973 DH population, looking for the *most* overrated DH, I ran into a massive catch-22. The men who did the most DH-ing (Edgar Martinez, Harold Baines, Hal McRae, Paul Molitor) got off the hook on a major technicality—i.e., they were all *good* at it. And the men who couldn't get the hang of it (Alan Wiggins, Butch Huskey, Dave Hostetler, etc.) were either allowed to move on to bigger and not necessarily better things or to become real, live, full-time players again.

Well, that didn't leave me with a whole lot of overrated options that made sense. What I found myself staring at was a long list of players who were legitimately good at other points in their careers—but eventually turned into run-of-the-mill, or at least overrated, DHs. Like Dave Parker. Or Reggie Jackson. Or Harmon Killebrew. You'll find those names later, filling out our Top Five list. But to label them the *most* overrated DH ever? I like to think I'm more humane than that.

So I'm dumping this fiasco in Ron Blomberg's lap. At least I know he can take it. If it weren't for the DH, he wouldn't be in the Hall of Fame, for instance. (Well, technically, *he's* not in there. But the bat he used to draw his historic designated walk for the Yankees, on Opening Day 1973, is in the Hall. So close enough.)

And if it weren't for the DH, he never would have become an official author, either. Blomberg published his autobiography, *Designated Hebrew* (co-written with Dan Schlossberg), in 2006, playing off the fact that the Yankees tried to promote him as The Great Jewish Hope when he was younger. I'd like to think I'll win a Nobel Prize for literature before Blomberg does. But he still put a darned entertaining book out there.

The fact that I even *read* it tells me he must be overrated in some way. Face it, it would have been a more effective use of my time reading Benjamin Franklin's autobiography than Ron Blomberg's. But because I did read it, I learned that:

1) Even Blomberg thought (at first) that the DH rule was "a big joke" that would undoubtedly get abolished "in a year or so."
2) He still gets to milk his First DH fame when he calls for restaurant reservations.

3) When his manager, Ralph Houk, informed Blomberg he would be the Yankees' first DH, he actually had to ask what the job entailed. (I'm not sure how Houk resisted the temptation to instruct him to set his glove on fire.)

4) When Blomberg got back to the dugout after his first at-bat and wondered what he was supposed to do now, Coach Dick Howser instructed him to go kill time by eating—advice Blomberg followed religiously for the rest of his DH career. Attaboy.

The record shows that while Blomberg may go down as a pioneer in DH-ing, he wasn't quite Edgar Martinez when given the chance to do it. He was a .321 career hitter, with a .391 on-base percentage and .509 slugging percentage, when he *didn't* DH. But in his 579 career at-bats in the line of work that made him famous, those numbers cliff-dived to a .257 average, .318 on-base, .425 slugging. Ah, the irony.

ron blomberg

Played From: 1969–1978
(Also played 143 games at 1B)
Teams: Yankees, White Sox
Career Record: .293 Avg., .360 On-Base Pct., .473 Slug Pct., 391 Hits, 52 HR

Luckily for Blomberg, pretty much nobody remembers that. Even more luckily, pretty much nobody recalls that the first time the Yankees ever had the first pick in the entire amateur draft (in 1967), they chose *him*—and advertised him as The Next Mickey Mantle.

Oops, so he wasn't quite the next Mickey Mantle. He wasn't even the next Mickey Hatcher. But Blomberg still got to carve out his own niche in baseball history, fluky as it may have been. It's been a tremendous niche for him. (Ask his favorite maître d's.) But for the rest of us, uh, not so tremendous.

Is there anything more bizarre about baseball than the fact that the two leagues don't even have the same rules? (Imagine one conference in the NBA using the three-point shot and the other not.) Screws up the World Series every darned year. Is it a stretch to blame that debacle on Ron Blomberg? Of course it is. But somebody had to be number one. And now it's his turn—again.

The Rest of The Top Five

2. DAVE PARKER

Okay, I'm warning you. The rest of this list is going to be a little schizophrenic, because almost everybody on it suffered from split-career syndrome. Like most of these other guys, Dave Parker had a lot more going for him during the non-DH sector of his career. As a right fielder, from the late 1970s to mid-1980s, Parker won a couple of batting titles and three Gold Gloves, led the league in slugging twice, won an RBI title, and once averaged more than 200 hits a year for *three years* (1977–1979). But that Dave Parker wasn't the guy who spent his last four seasons DH-ing in

dave parker

Played From: 1973–1991
(Also played 1,791 games in RF)
Teams: Pirates, Reds, A's, Brewers, Angels, Blue Jays
Career Record: .290 Avg., .339 On-Base Pct., .471 Slug Pct., 2,712 Hits, 339 HR, 154 SB

Oakland, Milwaukee, Toronto, and Anaheim. This Dave Parker had put on 50 pounds and had gotten himself implicated in a Pittsburgh cocaine trial. And even though this Dave Parker did drive in 97 runs for a 1989 A's powerhouse that won the World Series, the other numbers tell us all we need to know. Parker the right fielder: .297 career average, .347 on-base percentage, .487 slugging percentage. Parker the DH: .260, .306, .409. Among all players in history who made at least 2,000 trips to the plate as a DH, guess who has the lowest OPS (on-base plus slugging)? Yep, this guy. So he might have been a borderline Hall of Fame candidate as a right fielder. But as a DH, those RBI totals just camouflaged what he eventually became—overrated.

3. REGGIE JACKSON

Mr. October was an awesome slugger and a fabulous showman. But he was no Mr. DH. Sir Reginald really only turned to designated hitting late in life, as a member of the 1983–1986 Angels and 1987 A's, when he was trying to hang on long enough to climb the all-time home-run charts. But those were not his glory days. In 630 career games in DH Land, Reggie's slugging percentage was (yikes) just .406. That's 108 points lower than his .514 slugging percentage

reggie jackson

Played From: 1967–1987
(Also played 2102 games in OF)
Teams: A's, Orioles, Yankees, Angels
Career Record: .262 Avg., .356
On-Base Pct., .490 Slug Pct., 2,584
Hits, 563 HR, 228 SB

playing anywhere else. And according to Lee Sinins's *Complete Baseball Encyclopedia,* Jackson's .228 DH batting average and .738 OPS rank dead last among all men who spent more than 600 games as a DH. None of that tarnishes the rest of his thrill-a-minute career. But it sure does help us fill out our Most Overrated DH list.

4. STEVE BALBONI

If ever there was a player worth rooting for, based on his nickname alone, Steve "Bye-Bye" Balboni fit that mold even better than he fit in his uniform. He

steve balboni

Played From: 1981–1993
(Also played 630 games at 1B)
Teams: Yankees, Royals, Mariners, Rangers
Career Record: .229 Avg., .293
On-Base Pct., .451 Slug Pct., 714 Hits, 181 HR

arrived on the scene with the 1981 Yankees, his legend all but established by his nickname and three minor league home-run titles through that year. So you wanted this man to bop 50 homers a year, just to cement his place in baseball folklore. Unfortunately, real life—and those dastardly right-handed pitchers—just wouldn't cooperate. So while it may be Bye-Bye—not John Mayberry, Carlos Beltran, or anybody else—who still holds

the Royals' single-season home-run record (36, in 1985), Balboni's real claim to fame is this: only two other players in history—Rob Deer and Gorman Thomas—hit as many career homers as he did (181) despite a lifetime batting average (.229 in his case) that never even made it to .230.

5. HARMON KILLEBREW

harmon killebrew

Played From: 1954–1975
(Also played 969 games at 1B, 791 games at 3B, 470 games in OF)
Teams: Senators/Twins, Royals
Career Record: .256 Avg., .376
On-Base Pct., .509 Slug Pct., 2,086
Hits, 573 HR

Killebrew is Déjà Reggie all over again. For most of his career, The Killer was a feared Hall of Fame masher. But in 158 games as a DH at the end of his career, he was just a cool name to write on the old lineup card. How about this falloff: Killebrew's slugging percentage when he wasn't DH-ing was .519 (better than Willie McCovey's). His slugging percentage when he did DH, on the other hand, was only .346 (worse than Jerry Lumpe's). Now is it fair to take a 158-game chunk out of anybody's career and then use it to dump him into the Most Overrated bin? Of course not. I admit it. But there's just about no such thing as a *really* overrated DH. So somebody had to be number five on this list. And a guy with a minus-173-point DH effect on his slugging percentage left himself just a little too suitable for that honor. Sorry about that, Killer. I'll have to make it up to you in some other book.

The Most Underrated Designated Hitter of All Time

EDGAR MARTINEZ

If we ever sit around some night, discussing the 10 greatest hitters of the 1990s—as opposed to, say, America's 10 greatest airport baggage-claim areas—how long would it take until we got to Edgar Martinez?

He wouldn't be the first name brought up. (Barry Bonds, anyone?) He wouldn't even be the first name from his own *team*. (Kenneth Griffey Jr., anyone?) He might not (shudder) come up at all—unless we were holding this chat in a Starbucks at the summit of Mount McKinley.

Well, if I were leading this discussion (and come to think of it, I kind of am), here are the only names I'd toss out there ahead of Edgar's: Griffey. Bonds. Tony Gwynn. Mark McGwire (insert your optional raised eyebrow here). Sammy Sosa (ditto). Possibly Frank Thomas. And that's about it.

But if most of the rest of civilization were in charge of this session, I'm guessing we'd also hear all *these* names before Edgar Martinez entered the room: Jeff Bagwell. Mike Piazza. Chipper Jones. Larry Walker. Albert Belle. Craig Biggio. Roberto Alomar. Cal Ripken. Maybe even Mark Grace.

Hopefully, we wouldn't get all the way down to any Luis Polonias or Jeff Kings. But it wouldn't shock me—because Edgar Martinez might be the greatest hitter of our lifetimes whose name is on the tip of nobody's tongue (tongues located in the 206 area code not included).

So why is that, huh? This man was a two-time batting champ. In fact, he was the first right-handed-hitting, two-time American League batting champ since Joe DiMaggio. Edgar was also a former RBI champ (with 145 in 2000). He made seven All-Star teams. He's one of only four men in the last 70 years who can say he had back-to-back 50-double seasons. And he's one of just a half-dozen players since the 1940s who batted .320 or better at least six years in a row. (The others are Stan Musial, Wade Boggs, Rod Carew, Tony Gwynn, and Todd Helton—all of whom it's possible you've heard of.)

But Martinez's greatness had such a powerfully hypnotic effect on baseball fans everywhere, it apparently hypnotized them into forgetting everything he ever did. And I mean everything.

"Nobody even remembers the *best* game he ever had," said ESPN.com's brilliant Jim Caple—a fellow who clearly remembers it himself only because, miraculously, he lives in Seattle (and possibly because he covered that game).

So what *was* the best game Edgar ever had? Tell you what. I'll give you a minute. Comb through your brain cells. See if it's up there someplace. I doubt it. It did happen in October, though. That's one hint. It also came against the most famous franchise in baseball history. That's our last hint. All right, your answers, please.

Heh-heh. I know exactly what you're thinking: Game 5, 1995 AL Division Series. The Mariners trail the Yankees, 5–4, in the eleventh inning. The great Edgar Martinez then doubles in the tying *and* winning runs off Jack McDowell, dramatically ending the first postseason series the Mariners had ever won.

So that's it, right?...Heh-heh....Bzzzzzzz....Sorry, that's sooo incorrect. In fact, Edgar's greatest game was the game *before* that, Game 4: Mariners avoid elimination by charging back from a 5–0 hole. All Martinez does is hit a three-run homer to get them on the board, then crunch a *game-winning grand slam* off closer John Wetteland to finish it off. But, of course, it's like that game never happened.

"Everybody remembers Game 5, but *nobody* remembers Game 4," Caple said. "You'd think a guy who hits a grand slam and drives in seven runs against the Yankees would get a *little* attention. But he set a record for most RBIs in a postseason game against the Yankees—in a game in which the Yankees could have clinched the series—and *nobody* remembers it."

But that's our Edgar—the offensive machine America just plain forgot. To account for all that forgetfulness, you have to start with the geography factor.

Seattle is, after all, the one baseball town that's far from *everywhere*. But this man had other excuses for his anonymity, too—many of which had to do with those magnetic teammates he was always being eclipsed by.

"People always ignore Seattle," Caple said. "But if they *were* going to pay attention to Seattle, they weren't going to go any farther than Griffey or

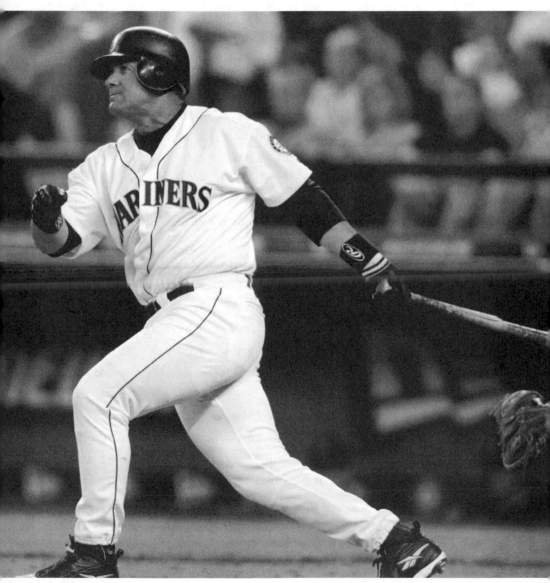

The last right-handed, two-time batting champ before Edgar Martinez? How about Joe DiMaggio?

A-Rod, or Ichiro [Suzuki], or Randy Johnson. If they were going to fly all the way out here, they sure as hell weren't going to do it to write something on Edgar."

The funny thing was, there may have been no easier Mariner to talk to than Edgar Martinez. But all the sparks flew out of the mouths of other men in that locker room. So they got the ink. They got the airtime. And the only folks who noticed Edgar were the people on the other team who never could figure out how the heck to pitch to him.

edgar martinez

Played From: 1987–2004
(Also played 563 games at 3B)
Team: Mariners
Career Record: .312 Avg., .418
On-Base Pct., .516 Slug Pct., 2,247
Hits, 309 HR

"Edgar was an advance scout's worst nightmare," said Bob Johnson, who scouted for the A's and Rangers in Martinez's era. "In his heyday, Edgar was the toughest guy to pitch to in the American League. He had no holes. He could do whatever he wanted with a bat. If you pitched him inside, he'd pull it. If you pitched him outside, he'd drive it down the right-field foul line. If he had to take a walk, he would. If he had to hit a fly ball, he'd hit a fly ball. If he had to hit a ground ball, he'd hit a ground ball. If he had to get a runner in from third, he did. He was the last guy you wanted up there with the game on the line, because there was no good way to get him out."

By the powers vested in me as the writer of this book, I'm ruling that that "heyday" lasted from 1991 to 2003. And if Edgar Martinez wasn't the greatest hitter alive for those 13 seasons, he was almost certainly the most dependable great hitter alive.

Only Bonds had a higher on-base percentage than Martinez (.428) in those 13 seasons. Just Gwynn, Walker, and Piazza had a better batting average than he did (.318). Only Biggio, John Olerud, and Jeff Bagwell fired more doubles than Edgar (451). But nobody was a more complete offensive force than he was.

Oh, he had his limits. No doubt about that. Not only was he not real fast, "he was very, very not fast," laughed Caple. But the man still scored 100 runs five times, including 121 twice. Defense over at third base wasn't what you'd call Martinez's forte, either—especially after he tore his hamstring in a 1993 exhibition game in noted baseball hotbed Vancouver. But because of that tear (and that non-forte), the greatest DH in history was born.

There really isn't much argument that Edgar is the King of the DHs, either. About the only other guys who are even in the debate are Paul Molitor, Hal McRae, Frank Thomas, and Harold Baines. And maybe, in a few years, David Ortiz could wipe them all off the board. But we'll get back to you on that when the sequel hits the presses.

Because all those men spent such different percentages of their careers at DH, it's hard to compare them. So we can't use the traditional totals, or "counting" stats, in this case. But Martinez tops them all (at least in their time as DHs) in career on-base percentage and OPS. And yes, that includes Frank Thomas, believe it or not.

Maybe the most complete statistic applicable to this situation, however, is a tremendous Bill James invention known as "runs created per 27 outs." And Edgar lands at number one in that stat, too. When the computer had finished spitting out that study, it told us that a lineup of nine Edgar Martinezes (in his DH years only) would have scored 8.82 runs per game. Among men who got 4,000 plate appearances as a DH, only Thomas and Molitor were even within two runs per game of Martinez. And he more than *doubled* a team of nine Dave Parkers (4.26).

The other new-age stat that's perfectly suited to measuring designated hitters is OPS-plus, which adjusts a player's OPS for both his home ballpark and the era he played in, then stacks it up against his peers. Martinez finished his career with a phenomenal 147 OPS-plus, meaning his numbers were 47 percent better than the average hitter of his day. He had eight seasons with a 150 or better. For comparison's sake, Molitor scored a 150 *once* and had a 122 for his career.

Alas, just because we've declared Edgar the best DH ever, that doesn't make him an automatic Hall of Famer. For a DH to make the Hall—especially a DH like Martinez, who didn't even spend one-third of his career playing the field— it's probably going to require astronomical numbers. And Martinez's 2,247 career hits and 309 homers aren't quite the orbit those judgmental Hall voters tend to look for. It's not his fault the Mariners didn't make him a regular until he was 27. But he'll pay the price.

The good news, though, is that we're waiving that price tag in this book. Heck, if they keep the guy out of Cooperstown, all that does is make him even more underrated. And who knew that was even possible, with a star who managed to keep his whole career as hush-hush as Edgar Martinez did?

The Rest of the Top Five

2. HAL McRAE

George Brett was always the big name on the marquee in Kansas City in the 1970s and early 1980s. But Hal McRae's intelligence, intensity, and Big Red

hal mcrae

Played From: 1968–1987
(Also played 478 games in OF)
Teams: Reds, Royals
Career Record: .290 Avg., .351
On-Base Pct., .454 Slug Pct., 2,091
Hits, 191 HR, 109 SB

Machine bloodlines helped him emerge as a leader and a difference-maker on a Royals team that made the playoffs seven times in 10 seasons from 1976 to 1985. And it didn't hurt that this guy was an extra-base-hit machine either. McRae finished in the top five in his league in doubles eight times. He blew past 80 extra-base hits twice (1977 and 1982). He won an RBI title (in 1982). He knew how to turn it on in October (batting .400 in four World Series, .294 overall in nine postseasons). And he would have edged Brett for the 1976 batting title if Twins left fielder Steve Brye hadn't misplayed Brett's final fly ball of the season into a controversial inside-the-park home run. So the Royals' decision to leave McRae off their 2006 Hometown Heroes ballot is a bigger mystery than the Bermuda Triangle. Let the record show that it may have been Ron Blomberg who became baseball's first DH—but it was Hal McRae who became baseball's first *great* DH.

3. TRAVIS HAFNER

What we have here is a fellow who would be a perfect candidate for one of those "Do You Know Me?" commercials. "Hello," Travis Hafner could say. "I DH for a living. And from 2004 to 2006, I had the best on-base percentage (.419) and OPS (1.030) in the whole American League. Albert Pujols and I were the only hitters in baseball with a .300 batting average, .400 on-base percentage, .500 slugging percentage, and 100 RBIs in all three of those seasons. And my *average* season during those three years was .308, 34 homers, 111 RBIs, 97 runs scored, 74 extra-base hits, and a .611 slugging percentage. Oh, and by the way, I'm

travis hafner

Played From: 2002–2006 (active)
Teams: Rangers, Indians
Career Record: .297 Avg., .402 On-Base Pct., .583 Slug Pct., 527 Hits, 118 HR

not David Ortiz. So do you know me?" Well, it would undoubtedly come as a major shock to Americans who don't live near Lake Erie that Travis Hafner was the answer to that question. But when you play in Cleveland instead of Fenway, you'd be amazed how easy it is to become more top secret than a CIA brief. At least, in Hafner's case, there's an up side to all that clandestine production: it turned him into a star in *this* book, anyway.

4. CHILI DAVIS

In case you're wondering, there has never been another great athlete—or great *anything*—named (or nicknamed) "Chili." I established this with the infallible Google Test. I Googled "Chili," and the only human being who came up in the first 200 entries (not counting the Red Hot Chili Peppers) was Chili Davis. So doesn't that *prove* this guy was underrated? Only three modern switch-hitters hit more home runs than the Chili Man (350)—Mickey Mantle, Eddie Murray, and Chipper Jones. Only three drove in more runs than Chili (1,372)—Mantle, Murray,

chili davis

Played From: 1981–1999
(Also played 1,184 games in OF)
Teams: Giants, Angels, Twins, Royals, Yankees
Career Record: .274 Avg., .360 On-Base Pct., .451 Slug Pct., 2,380 Hits, 350 HR, 142 SB

and Ted Simmons. And once this fellow discovered DH-ing, with the 1991 Twins, he became the best DH in the non-Edgar portion of the league. No DH in the '90s had more 25-homer seasons than Chili Davis (five). Only Martinez and Jose Canseco (five times apiece) slugged .500 in more seasons than Chili (four). So even though he only got his nickname because a friend in sixth grade ragged on him for a bad haircut that looked like it was cut around a chili bowl, he's more than the greatest Chili ever. He's also one of the most underrated DHs ever.

5. OSCAR GAMBLE

If there was a haircut wing of the Hall of Fame, Oscar Gamble would be the first inductee, because—and I don't make this claim lightly—he had The

oscar gamble

Played From: 1969–1985
(Also played 818 games in OF)
Teams: Cubs, Phillies, Indians, Yankees, White Sox, Padres, Rangers
Career Record: .265 Avg., .356 On-Base Pct., .454 Slug Pct., 1,195 Hits, 200 HR

Greatest Hair in Baseball History. I've seen planets smaller than this man's Afro. And that's a compliment. Back in the '70s, Gamble's spectacular 'fro was such a topic of conversation that pitchers used to joke that they wanted to throw at the guy's head just to see if the ball would stick to his hair. So how bizarre is it that the Big O had the best stretch of his career as a DH for the Yankees—a team whose owner made him clip off about nine feet of hair if he wanted to play? From 1979 to 1984, when Gamble finally found his niche as a platoon DH in New York (a span that includes a half-season with Texas), this man was the most dangerous DH in baseball. Among hitters who got to the plate as many times as he did in that time, the only two with a better OPS than Gamble (.903) were Mike Schmidt (.965) and George Brett (.929). And just three hitters had a better slugging percentage than Gamble (.518)—Schmidt (.569), Brett (.544), and Eddie Murray (.519). That, friends, is official Hall of Fame company. So obviously, the power of hair is overrated. But Oscar Gamble, that noted well-groomed DH? Clearly underrated.

CHAPTER 5

Catchers

The Most Overrated Catcher of All Time

BENITO SANTIAGO

In this short-attention-span kind of world we live in, it always pays to make a spectacular first impression. Well, there's one thing you have to say for the fascinating character that Benito Santiago was from Day One to Day Last: he rode that first impression all the way to the end of his line. Which comprised 20 seasons worth of stops.

Santiago's rookie season (1987) in balmy San Diego felt like one of those dramatic, we-interrupt-this-program announcements: "Your attention please. A star has just been born. Please locate all available neon lights so that we can spell his name so big and bright you'll probably need laser eye surgery."

Emperor Benito had some year, all right. He batted .300, with 18 homers, 53 extra-base hits, and (how 'bout this) 21 stolen bases—the fourth-most steals by any catcher, at the time, since 1916. He strung together an incredible 34-game hitting streak (still the longest by any rookie—and any catcher—in baseball history). He led the league in games and innings caught. He led all major league catchers in doubles, extra-base hits, batting, and stolen bases. And he became just the second catcher—joining only a future Hall of Famer named Carlton Fisk—to win a Rookie of the Year election unanimously.

Santiago also did all that with a certain style that had "spokesman for the National Hot Dog and Sausage Council" written all over him. He always seemed to be spinning, sprawling, dancing, and (especially) throwing the baseball someplace, anyplace. He loved to throw. He lived to throw. From his crouch. From his knees. From a sidewalk café in La Jolla. He was some spectacle, this Benito Santiago.

"He was the best I ever saw come into the league and just dominate in his first year," his manager that season, the not-so-easily impressed Larry Bowa, once told me.

It was that impression—that first impression—which clamped itself onto many a brain as Santiago careened through the rest of his career. By the time he was finished, he could spread out a list of lifetime achievements that would make you believe he was the Gabby Hartnett of his generation. Let's all take a deep breath now and review them:

Selected to five All-Star teams. Won three Gold Gloves and a Rookie of the Year trophy. Took home a National League Championship Series MVP award (2002 Giants). Compiled that historic 34-game hitting streak. Was one of eight catchers since World War II to have a 100-assist season. And finished number seven on the all-time list for most games caught (1,917).

But before you print Santiago's Hall of Fame ticket, it's time for this important announcement: *don't forget, you're reading the overrated section of this chapter.*

Uh-oh. So what does that tell you? If it doesn't tell you that the dreaded overrated killjoys who have made this book possible are back to punch a thousand holes in that attractive array of achievements, you're hereby ordered to go back to chapter 1 and start over until you get this concept down a little better.

All right, everybody ready? Let's start punching away.

In case you stopped paying close attention after the Emperor's Rookie of the Year press conference, those next 18 years of Santiago's career didn't all go like the first year. He never batted .300 again, for one thing—not in any season in which he got more than 29 at-bats, at least. He never even had another hitting streak as long as 15 games. And he had only one more season (1996)—out of nearly two more decades—where he reached or beat his

Benito Santiago burst onto the scene with a rookie year for the ages and then spent much of the next two decades hovering around mediocrity.

rookie totals in homers, RBIs, hits, runs scored, stolen bases, extra-base hits, or on-base percentage. Then, just when he was in the midst of a mini-resurgence in San Francisco, he wound up on the BALCO witness list. That piece of info is being passed along with no moral judgments. It's merely our own little public-service announcement.

But that's just for starters. If you look more closely at what Santiago accomplished that first season (and take a wild guess who did look), you'll be stunned to find he wasn't the offensive dynamo he appeared to be, even in his *best* year.

For starters, he enjoyed swinging the bat so much—at strikes, at balls, at seagulls, at an occasional low-flying traffic copter—that he drew just 16 walks in the whole 1987 season, in 572 trips to the plate. At the time, only three

National Leaguers in the expansion era (1961–1987) had made it into the batter's box that many times in one season and walked fewer times than that.

Then there were those 21 stolen bases. Definitely a dazzling number for a catcher. But pardon us for pointing out that, 21 steals or no 21 steals, nobody was getting the Emperor mixed up with, say, Tim Raines. Santiago swiped all those bases in large part because he was so determined to swipe all those bases. You could tell because he also got thrown out swiping 12 times. That's 33 SB attempts, if you're not calculating along with us here. And only two catchers in the entire live-ball era (John Wathan twice and John Stearns once) had displayed a greater urge to burglarize before Santiago came along.

benito santiago

Played From: 1986–2005
Teams: Padres, Marlins, Reds, Phillies, Blue Jays, Cubs, Giants, Royals, Pirates
Career Record: .263 Avg., .307 On-Base Pct., .415 Slug Pct., 1,830 Hits, 217 HR

Now, um, about that hitting streak. There's no such thing as a bad 34-game hitting streak, especially if it's a guy's first season in the big leagues. So let's get that straight. It's one darned fine feat. But…(sorry)…all hitting streaks are not created equal. And when the Elias Sports Bureau took a look at Santiago's streak, it found that: A) he walked only *twice* during the whole streak, B) he didn't work a single *unintentional* walk during the final 33 games, and C) his .346 batting average during the streak was the lowest (at the time) by any player who had ever hit in 30 or more in a row. Of course, that means he undoubtedly reached base less than any 30-game streaker in history—which does add to the degree of difficulty. So maybe that makes this a *more* impressive streak. Who knows?

That brings us to defense. Santiago always had a reputation as not just a great defensive catcher but as an *impact* catcher. And clearly, his arm was an intimidating force for a while there. Early in his career, other teams ran less on him than they did against other catchers. And in 13 of his first 14 healthy seasons, he nailed at least 30 percent of the runners who did try to steal on him. So I'm the first to acknowledge that this man had an arm that could launch the next satellite to Mars.

But…(sorry)…boy, did he like to head for the launch pad. Santiago spewed out 54 errors—almost all of them throwing errors—in his first three seasons alone. That's more than Elston Howard committed in his entire 14-year career.

So it took this fellow just three years to do something no catcher in the history of the sport had ever done—lead the major leagues in errors three years in a row.

It's one of those errors in particular—an all-time E-2 classic—that sums up Santiago's throw-aholic issues. The date: July 22, 1988. The situation: tie game, eleventh inning, winning run (for the Cubs) on second base. That winning run then scored on a wild pickoff throw by, uh, Guess Who—during *an intentional walk.* And the runner on second (Manny Trillo) happened to be *standing on the bag,* minding his own business, when Santiago got inspired to whoosh a misguided missile into center field. The Emperor's manager, Jack McKeon, wasn't too overjoyed by that sight, for some reason. But fortunately, the losing pitcher (Lance McCullers) figured out this wasn't all bad. "Hey," McCullers said, "at least we made *This Week in Baseball.*"

That wasn't exactly Santiago's last E-2, either. He went on to lead his league in errors in six of his first seven seasons. (The only year he didn't finish first, he broke his arm.) Had he just led one more time, he would have tied the legendary Ivey Wingo for most seasons overheating that "E" light on the scoreboard. Oh, well.

You think reputation can't carry a man a long way? Two of Santiago's three Gold Gloves came in seasons when he led the big leagues in errors. And in one of them (1989), he also led the majors in passed balls. How impressive is that trifecta?

Even the feat that seems to be Santiago's most glittering defensive achievement—the 100 assists he piled up in 1991—doesn't look quite so magnificent when you peruse it in slightly more detail. The Elias Sports Bureau determined that 30 of those assists came after third strikes he didn't catch. But that was nothing new. In a game in 1989, he once racked up seven assists—five of them after he forgot to catch strike three. When a guy can go that far out of his way to keep even the routine plays in baseball from looking routine, that's what the entertainment business is all about.

As someone who covered Santiago for a year in Philadelphia, I can personally vouch that he was indeed an entertaining guy. Maybe the pitchers weren't always so entertained. But the rest of the species found him engaging enough. And it's undeniable that he was one talented dude. But as Gary Carter told me once: "I don't want to downgrade Benito, because I have a lot of respect for his abilities. I just don't think he totally applies them."

Ooh. That's not good. So maybe that explains how a guy this skilled could hip-hop his way through 10 teams (counting the Reds twice). At least he was always good enough to find a team that would give him a try. Too bad he was usually undependable enough that eight of those 10 teams had seen enough after two years (or less).

Maybe that also explains how a fellow who wound up in the catching top 10 in career hits, homers, and games caught could be honored not with a Hall of Fame plaque but with *this* slightly different honor—the distinguished Most Overrated Catcher of All Time award. I admit I feel a pang of remorse for handing out this prize. But heck, it's Benito Santiago's own fault. If he'd just had the foresight to retire after that Rookie of the Year season, I'd have been happy to leave him out of this whole mess.

The Rest of the Top Five

2. RICK FERRELL

As you wander through the Hall of Famers' gallery in the sacred village of Cooperstown, New York, it's not good etiquette to blurt out remarks like: "What the hell is *this* guy doing in the Hall of Fame?" But when you're lounged out by a pool, reading a book like this, the rules are slightly different. So as we bring up the name Rick Ferrell, go ahead. Do it. Shout it out, loudly and proudly: "What the hell is *this* guy doing in the Hall of Fame?" Hey, glad you asked. Answer: ask the Veterans Committee. Ferrell appeared on the writers' ballot in three elections. In the first, he got one vote—as many as Burgess Whitehead. In the second, he got one vote—as many as Bing Miller (who, I'm pretty sure, was actually a big-band leader in the '40s). And in the third, Rick Ferrell got (yep) one vote—as many as Sibby Sisti. I won't even tell you who Burgess, Bing,

rick ferrell

Played From: 1929–1947
Teams: Browns, Red Sox, Senators
Career Record: .281 Avg., .378 On-Base Pct., .363 Slug Pct., 1,692 Hits, 28 HR

and Sibby were, because if you even had to ask, you made my point. I've heard people argue Rick Ferrell is the worst player in the Hall of Fame. I'm not sure they're right. But I *am* sure of this: he wasn't even the most dominating player in his own family. His brother, Wes, was a six-time 20-game winner. Rick, on the other hand, was a five-time league leader in passed balls. And ohbytheway, even though Wes was a pitcher and Rick was a "hitter," Wes out-homered his brother, 38 to 28—in 5,000 fewer at-bats. So you may ask why Rick Ferrell has a Hall of Fame plaque. But I bet you're no longer asking why he's now officially overrated.

3. MANNY SANGUILLEN

Remember earlier in this chapter, how we established that Benito Santiago seemed to think that working a walk was a crime that could get you 10 years in San Quentin? Well, Sanguillen made Benito look like Rickey Henderson. It isn't easy to go to bat at least 475 times in six straight seasons without walking more than 21 times in any of them. It's so tough, in fact, that only one man since 1900 has ever done it. If you guessed that man was Sanguillen, way to go. You're really getting the hang of this book.

manny sanguillen

Played From: 1967–1980
Teams: Pirates, A's
Career Record: .296 Avg., .326 On-Base Pct., .398 Slug Pct., 1,500 Hits, 65 HR

But if you lived in Pittsburgh in the 1970s, you're probably asking how this guy could get labeled as overrated, when he was a .296 lifetime hitter who caught every day for a Pirates team that went to the playoffs five times in six years. All right, here's how: because he got all those hits and still had a *lower* career on-base percentage (.326) than the league average (.331) in the era he played in. That'll do it every time.

4. CHARLES JOHNSON

We all love catchers who can throw. And catchers who can throw and hit home runs—we really love them. So no wonder there was a love affair going with Charles Johnson for a while there. Over his first five seasons, he nailed 43 percent of the runners who tried stealing on him. And there was a five-year period in the middle of his career (1997–2001) where he was one of only four catchers to average 20 homers a season. But even then, I used to hear general

charles johnson

Played From: 1994–2005
Teams: Marlins, Dodgers, Orioles, White Sox, Rockies, Devil Rays
Career Record: .245 Avg., .330 On-Base Pct., .433 Slug Pct., 940 Hits, 167 HR

managers call him the most overrated catcher in baseball. And after he cashed in on a 31-homer, salary-drive season in 2000, with a five-year, $35 million contract, he proved their point. Johnson never won another Gold Glove. (He won four in his first four seasons.) He also never hit much after that. (His career batting average the rest of the way was .238, even though he spent two years hacking away at Coors Field.) But Johnson's overrated signature was that he became the poster boy for two vintage salary-dump trades—the we'll-take-Mike-Hampton-off-your-hands-if-you-take-Charles-Johnson-off-our-hands deal that sent him from Florida to Colorado in 2002, followed in 2005 by the we'll-take-your-Byung-Hyun-Kim-headache-if-you'll-take-our-Charles-Johnson-headache swap that moved him to the Red Sox (who released him about three minutes later). Not to mention that he vetoed a midseason trade to the Dodgers in 2004 that would have made him the everyday catcher on a playoff team—because they wouldn't give him either an extension or a $350,000 housing allowance. Well, those housing bonuses may be overrated—but no more overrated than this guy.

5. RAY SCHALK

A friend of mine says there's only one reason Ray Schalk is in the Hall of Fame: he was a member of the Black Sox who wasn't in on the fix. And not only that—

ray schalk

Played From: 1912–1929
Teams: White Sox, Giants
Career Record: .253 Avg., .340 On-Base Pct., .316 Slug Pct., 1,345 Hits, 11 HR

he's rumored to have started a clubhouse mêlée with a couple of the bums who were. Technically, of course, that isn't why Schalk is in the Hall. He's in because he was viewed as the Pudge Rodriguez of his time—minus the offense, that is (all of it). Except for Roy Campanella, whose career ended early because of an auto accident, Schalk owns the fewest hits, runs, and homers of any Hall of Fame catcher, not to mention the lowest batting average (.253) and on-base percentage (.340). And how about this claim to fame: he has the worst slugging percentage (.316) of *any* Hall of Fame position player (plus five Hall of Fame *pitchers*). Noted catching authority Chuck Rosciam, who maintains the online Encyclopedia of Baseball Catchers, says Schalk is actually the most overrated catcher ever—and if it were up to him, he'd bounce Schalk out of the Hall and swap him for catching cult hero Wally Schang. Of course, Rosciam says, he'd call it "The Schalk-Schang Redemption." I'll never admit that I included Schalk in this book just so I could use that quote. But I won't deny it, either.

The Most Underrated Catcher of All Time

YOGI BERRA

One of the fun things about selecting the names that appear in this authoritative volume is zigging when you expect me to be zagging. Or is that zagging when you expect me to be zigging? Aw, whatever, I'm guessing the last guy you'd expect this book to be honoring as the most underrated catcher since Tsuyoshi Shinjo's heavily bruised great-grandfather invented the shin guard, is a man who:

1. spent his entire career as a really, really famous Yankee;
2. has been unofficially regarded, since the death of Joe DiMaggio, as "the Greatest Living Yankee"; and
3. is still starring in more TV commercials than A-Rod, even though some of them force him to spend prolonged time speaking with a duck.

Well, you know what? To have a fellow like Yogi Berra show up in a place like this might once have been as big a shock to me as it is to you—and even him. But the more I thought about Yogi and his raging national stardom, as America's most celebrated 80-something since possibly Lawrence Welk, I realized something pivotal:

About 98 percent of that raging stardom has to do with Yogi's reputation as some kind of crazy, quote-machinist combo of Benjamin Franklin, Will Rogers, Mark Twain, Steven Wright, and Gandhi.

Which means only around 2 percent has anything to do with the astounding stuff Yogi Berra did when he was actually playing baseball. And that, my friends, is what lit this particular book writer's lightbulb.

Our man Yogi fits into an underrated niche that consists, essentially, of only him: like some of his fellow All-Underrated luminaries, he definitely wasn't underrated when he played. But unlike those other men, time hasn't

Yogi Berra joins the underrated ranks because most people remember him today for his Yogi-isms and not for what he did on the baseball field, which was good enough for three MVP awards and 10 World Series rings.

forgotten him. It has only forgotten what he *did*. It can't, on the other hand, seem to forget anything he ever *said* (including the half of the stuff he said that he says he never said—or something like that).

Then again, who *can* forget it? After all, the future really ain't what it used to be. And you really can observe a lot by watching. And I can think of all kinds of places nobody goes anymore because it's too crowded. One of the highlights of a terrific *60 Minutes* piece on Yogi a few years ago was a montage of presidents, ex-presidents, and other statesmen quoting their favorite Yogi-isms. If you don't have a favorite of your own, well, you're making a very big wrong mistake.

But even that *60 Minutes* profile just reinforced our case here. Bob Simon's entire piece devoted two sentences to Yogi the ballplayer—and one of them was a telling remark about how easy it was to "lose sight of the fact that Berra was one of the greatest ballplayers of all time." Whereupon that's exactly what *60 Minutes* did.

That's not what this book is going to do, however. If somebody doesn't remind the world what a stupendous catcher Berra was, his entire career is liable to just vaporize some day and disappear, like sport's version of Atlantis. Can't let that happen. But we're well down that path to vaporization. There's new evidence of that every darned day.

"A lot of young people just know Yogi as that guy in the barber's chair, making the [Aflac] duck shake his head," says Dave Kaplan, director of the Yogi Berra Museum and Learning Center in Little Falls, New Jersey. "So when they walk through the museum, I think they're a little amazed when they see all his MVP plaques. And when they see all his [World Series] rings, they say, 'Oh, my God.'"

As well they should. No player who ever lived has as many of those rings as Yogi (10). And only one man (Barry Bonds) has more MVP plaques than Yogi (three). But people tend to gloss over those factoids way too fast, as if any old schlub who spent enough time loitering around the Bronx in the '50s and '60s was bound to accumulate all those rings and trophies. Coulda been Yogi. Coulda been Foster Castleman. It was a glory-by-association sort of thing.

Oh, yeah? Uh, guess again. Yogi Berra was *not* just another Yankee. Nowadays, in revisionist history, we think of DiMaggio passing the Ultimate Yankee torch directly to Mickey Mantle. But in real life, back in the day, that's not what happened. Joe D delivered that torch to Yogi, who later shoveled it over to Mantle. But in The Yogi Years, something unbelievable transpired. Something you never hear anybody talk about:

Between 1950 and 1956, Yogi Berra finished in the top four in the MVP voting *seven seasons in a row*. Right, *seven*. All right, now let's review all the other players in history who have done that. Oh, wait. There's *nobody*. Whaddayaknow.

Those MVP elections send a powerful message about what Berra represented to the Yankees dynasty during the most dominating period in any franchise's history (14 World Series visits in 16 years): it was the frumpy little 5'7½" catcher who was the centerpiece of the empire. Who knew?

yogi berra

Played From: 1946–1965
(Also played 148 games in LF,
115 games in RF)
Teams: Yankees, Mets
Career Record: .285 Avg., .348
On-Base Pct., .482 Slug Pct., 2,150
Hits, 358 HR

That's a concept that somehow got lost on about 99 percent of the earth's population—including George Steinbrenner himself. It was back in 1999, you might recall, that Steinbrenner summoned the courage to head for the Berra Museum to forge a peace pact with the Yankees legend who had not spoken to him for 14 years. While George was hanging around the gallery, he found himself transfixed by all the photographs of Yogi the ballplayer. It was almost as if the portraits those photos painted of *that* Yogi, and his place on those teams, banged on the door to Steinbrenner's brain and asked: "*Now* do you get it?" So no wonder the Boss turned to Berra at one point that day and said he always remembered that Yogi was a heck of a player—"but I never really knew what you meant to that team." Hey, join the club, George.

But we don't want to get too deep on you here. Whatever Yogi Berra brought to those teams in leadership and intangibility, he provided every bit as meaningful a contribution once the games started. In each of those seven MVP or near-MVP seasons, the numbers on Yogi's baseball card never dipped below 22 homers, 88 RBIs, or a .470 slugging percentage. No other player in the whole sport had seven seasons like that in those years. And just one other catcher in history has ever strung together that many seasons with stats that good: Mike Piazza. How about that?

Berra has admitted for years that he might even have had *better* seasons, too, if he hadn't given away so many at-bats with nobody on base. But those non-RBI situations apparently bored him. When the Yankees needed a big run knocked in, however, *that* got his attention.

He played in an age that hasn't presented us with the sophisticated batting splits we get on players today. But Dave Smith, founder of the invaluable retrosheet.org, kindly supplied us with the data Retrosheet has gathered on 79 percent of Berra's at-bats from 1950 to 1956. While we acknowledge that all precincts haven't reported, you don't need a degree from MIT to discern a trend from this spreadsheet:

Berra's average with nobody on base in those seven seasons: .258
With runners on: .318
With runners in scoring position: .314
In the late innings (seventh or later) of close games: .327

Get the picture? In only two of those seven seasons was his average *higher* than .257 with the bases empty. But in just one of those years (1951, when he hit .277) did he bat *lower* than .306 with men on base. Is that clutch enough for you?

We know, beyond that, that Berra is the only catcher who ever drove in more than 80 runs in 11 straight seasons (1948–1958)—and just Piazza (10 straight) has a streak even half that long. And stats aside, we also know how baseball men of that era talked about Yogi The Clutch-Meister. One of the great managers of the '50s and early '60s, Paul Richards (White Sox and Orioles), is quoted on the back cover of Berra's 1961 autobiography, saying: "I think he's one of the most dangerous late-inning hitters in baseball. It gets to be the seventh inning and I don't know how to pitch to him."

Hey, that's funny. The joke, in Berra's day, was that the best way to pitch to him was to throw one down the middle—because this guy had a reputation for hacking at everything between the George Washington Bridge and the Connecticut state line. But for a fellow who loved to let it fly, Yogi sure could find a way to make bat meet ball.

The legendary whiffin' magician Rob Deer struck out more times (456) in two and a half seasons (1986–1988) than Berra did in his 20 seasons (414). Berra had 13 straight seasons with at least as many walks as strikeouts. He had more *home runs* than strikeouts five times—including a mind-boggling 28-homer, 12-whiff season in 1950. And he had seven seasons (of at least 400 at-bats) in which he struck out no more than 25 times. The only man to do that since Yogi retired is a pretty decent batsmith named Tony Gwynn.

But how often do you ever hear about *any* of this nowadays? And if you ever do, it gets drowned out by the sound of that duck quacking. Well, welcome to our quack-free Yogi zone. Bill James has rated Yogi Berra as the greatest catcher in history. I haven't found anybody who doesn't place him in the top five. But now comes his most important honor yet—our prestigious Most Underrated Catcher of All Time award. And you know what? He doesn't even have to thank us for making this award necessary.

The Rest of the Top Five

2. TED SIMMONS

If there were a Hall of Fame for guys who have no shot at the Hall of Fame, Ted Simmons might be the first man admitted. All Simmons did in 21 seasons was drive in more runs than Johnny Bench, score more runs than Gary Carter and get more hits than Yogi Berra or Carlton Fisk (or any other catcher who ever played). But when the Hall of Fame votes were counted, those fellows got to work on their induction speeches. Ted Simmons got 17 stinking votes. So he was one and done on that ballot, never to return. I'm not sure whether Simmons deserved to get elected. But he at least deserved a long, hard look—after eight All-Star teams, seven .300 seasons, and eight years with at least 90 RBIs. Now was he Bill Dickey reincarnate when he slipped his hand inside a catcher's mitt? Ehhhh, let's not go that far. He did lead the league in passed balls three times, and by the end of his catching days, he couldn't throw out an elephant. But his caught-stealing percentages early in his career were surprisingly good. And

ted simmons

Played From: 1968–1988
(Also played 195 games at 1B, 279 games at DH)
Teams: Cardinals, Brewers, Braves
Career Record: .285 Avg., .348 On-Base Pct., .437 Slug Pct., 2,472 Hits, 248 HR

he was durable enough to lead the league in games caught three times (and catch at least 130 games four other years). So does that sound like a defensive résumé so abominable it should keep the *all-time hits leader* (among men who spent most of their careers catching) out of Cooperstown? Doesn't sound like it to this author. But it does sound like a man who is as underrated as any catcher who has never appeared in an Aflac commercial.

3. JOE TORRE

One of these years, Torre *will* end up in the Hall of Fame. Except it's going to be as a manager, not as a player. And you can make a heck of a case he's one of the rare men in history who deserves to make it for both of those lines of work. Should I be allowed to count Torre as a catcher? Maybe not, since he did spend close to two-thirds of his career without a face mask. But it's my book, so sue me. And whatever position he played, there's no doubt he was underrated when he occupied that batter's box for other reasons. Let's go back to our system for using a player's cra-adjusted

joe torre

Played From: 1960–1977
(Also played 787 games at 1B, 515 games at 3B)
Teams: Braves, Cardinals, Mets
Career Record: .297 Avg., .365 On-Base Pct., .452 Slug Pct., 2,342 Hits, 252 HR

and ballpark-adjusted OPS-plus to measure his career. If a "great" season is a year when that OPS-plus is 50 percent better than the average player and a "really good" season is a year when it's 25 percent better, Torre spun off two "great" seasons, six "really good" seasons, and only one year, out of 16 full seasons, in which he wasn't better than average. Add in an MVP award, nine All-Star teams, and a Gold Glove (as a catcher), and Torre has the look of a Hall of Fame something-or-other. And by that, I *don't* just mean manager.

4. GARY CARTER

If Gary Carter were still parked in his perennial spot outside the Cooperstown city limits, trying to figure out why the Hall of Fame party always seemed to start without him, he'd be number one on this list—even over Yogi. But just because he eventually got in, that doesn't change the farcical voting injustice that made this guy suffer through six elections first. I'm still waiting for a sane

gary carter

Played From: 1974–1992
(Also played 132 games in RF)
Teams: Expos, Mets, Giants, Dodgers
Career Record: .262 Avg., .335
On-Base Pct., .439 Slug Pct., 2,092
Hits, 324 HR

explanation of how Carlton Fisk breezed in on the second ballot, while Carter was still, inexplicably, getting just 33.8 percent of the vote on *his* second ballot. Please. Help me. Figure this out. These two men were contemporaries. They basically had the same career. Fisk's was longer. But Carter's was *better.* Fisk caught the most games in major league history. Carter caught the most games in National League history. Fisk made 11 All-Star teams. Carter made 11 All-Star teams. But here's where they diverge: Carter had more 100-RBI seasons than Fisk (4–2), had more 20-homer seasons (9–8), won more Gold Gloves (3–1), and started more All-Star Games (8–7). So if you can explain why Fisk made it to Cooperstown first, your next assignment is to explain Stonehenge.

5. ROGER BRESNAHAN

Roger Bresnahan was the first "modern" catcher elected to the Hall of Fame. He was the first catcher to use shin guards and a face mask. And he was once

roger bresnahan

Played From: 1897–1915
Teams: Senators, Cubs, Orioles,
Giants, Cardinals
Career Record: .279 Avg., .386
On-Base Pct., .377 Slug Pct., 1,252
Hits, 26 HR

Christy Mathewson's favorite catcher. Okay, now that we've got that out of the way, it's time to admit that isn't why he's in this book. He's in this book because it was a convenient excuse to tell the story of the only catching member of the Bresnahan family I actually know. That would be his great-nephew, Dave Bresnahan— aka Mr. Potato Head. Dave Bresnahan was no

Hall of Famer. But he'll always have a place in my personal Hall of Fame. I unanimously elected him in 1987, after he got ejected from a minor league game for attempting to pick a runner off third base—with a potato. How brilliant a move was that? Well, it fooled that runner. When the potato flew into left field, the guy took off for the plate, only to be tagged out via the seldom-seen hidden-potato trick. It was also brilliant enough to earn Dave Bresnahan a guest spot on the Letterman show. But unfortunately, it wasn't brilliant enough to keep Bresnahan from getting released the next day by his former employers, the Indians, for "jeopardizing the integrity of baseball." But, geez, did he really? "Steve Howe got five chances to play this game after using drugs," Bresnahan told me. "I was just trying to have some fun playing minor league baseball. We were 27 games out. I just figured, 'What the hell?'" Alas, it turned out to be the last throw of Bresnahan's career. But it's all worth it now, because his potato just landed—right here in this book.

CHAPTER 6

First Basemen

The Most Overrated First Baseman of All Time

STEVE GARVEY

A photo of Steve Garvey's intently focused face appeared on the cover of *Sports Illustrated*'s 1982 baseball-preview issue, next to the headline: "Is Steve Garvey Really Too Good to Be True?" Hey, thanks for asking. Some of us have been waiting more than two decades to answer that question. And I'd like to thank Triumph Books for the opportunity to blurt it out now, exclusively, in these very pages, after all these years:

Yesssssss.

The concept of separating myth from reality is what this book is all about, after all. And Garvey is another one of those perfect myth-versus-reality test cases. Actually, "perfect" might not be the right word here, because one of Garvey's nicknames, back in the day, was "Mr. Perfect." But his most common nickname was "the Senator." Both of those nicknames suggest that Garvey was a man with a carefully crafted image, which helped him become one of the most popular players of his generation. Alas, it's that popularity that has finally caught up with him, all these miles down the freeway, now that the overrated-underrated grand jury has convened to determine what the heck was up with *that*.

So do I really want to come off in these pages as one of those haughty, purist-type authors who would rip a guy for signing 8.6 trillion autographs? Or relentlessly chatting with his adoring public, which just might happen to result in a coincidental stampede to the All-Star ballot box? Or always finding time to provide his good friends in the news media a smile, a quip, and a sound bite? Nope. Sure wouldn't want to dump on a fellow like that. Fan-friendliness and media-friendliness are two of my all-time favorite concepts—especially if the alternative is, for example, Albert Belle trying to run over trick-or-treaters (several of whom were probably dressed up as interviewers) with his car.

Okay, so it's official. Autographs: good. Media cooperation: good. That's the position of this author, with no equivocation. And the author promises to quote that line on any future talk show where he's savaged for accusing his misguided Most-Overrated selections of shameless fan manipulation on the road to overratedness.

So let's get this on the record: I'm *not* accusing Steve Garvey of manipulating anybody for the sake of inflating his fame or fortune, or of decreasing the chances that a book like this would still feel like dissecting his career, long after he'd moved on to the pro-am celebrity-golfer phase of his lifetime. But some of his teammates sure did that. And whether they were right, wrong, or just jealous, Garvey's popularity definitely created a national buzz about him that overwhelmed what he was—and wasn't—as a baseball player.

There was lots to admire about what Garvey *was*, too. Anybody who would dispute that wouldn't know an RBI from an RPM. Hitting .300 seven times in eight years (1973–1980)—and "slumping" to .297 in the eighth year? A good thing. Leading his league in hits twice? A good thing. Five 100-RBI seasons in seven years (1974–1980)? Nothing bad about that. His MVP award in 1974? Way to go. His two All-Star Game MVP trophies? Very cool. His four Gold Gloves? A little shaky, but hey, he didn't vote for himself.

And here's the best section of Garvey's report card: the brighter the spotlight, the better he played. The man had a .393 career batting average in the All-Star Game, a .356 average in the LCS, and a .319 average in the World Series. He had a .550 career postseason slugging percentage—which tops Barry Bonds or Willie Mays, just to pick a couple of luminaries—and an .821 All-Star Game slugging percentage, which ranks among the five best ever.

Steve Garvey managed to become the face of baseball for a period of time in the 1970s, but statistics clearly show that he wasn't the player most people gave him credit for being.

So we know what you're thinking: What's overrated about a guy like that? Well, let's just say it's your ability to ask exactly the right questions at exactly the right time—so this book can segue into its fabled *on-the-other-hand* transitions—that makes all of us here admire our readership's intellect and curiosity. (Now you're probably also thinking: "Wait a second. This goofball just imagined that whole thing." But fortunately, we couldn't pick up on that thought.)

steve garvey

Played From: 1969–1987
(Also played 191 games at 3B)
Teams: Dodgers, Padres
Career Record: .294 Avg., .329 On-Base Pct., .446 Slug Pct., 2,599 Hits, 272 HR

All righty, here's what's overrated about Steve Garvey: if you look at those All-Star numbers and postseason numbers, you'd think this man was one of the most feared sluggers of his time, right? Well, at the very least, you'd think that, in 19 seasons, he would have had a .500 slugging percentage at least *once*. Wouldn't you? Nope. Never got there. You can say it was the age he played in, but more than 100 different players slugged .500 in at least one season during Garvey's career—from Oscar Gamble to Champ Summers to even alleged singles machine Ralph Garr. And one of Garvey's contemporary National League first basemen—Willie McCovey—had a *career* slugging percentage in the .500s. You can say it was all Dodger Stadium's fault, but Garvey's own teammates—Pedro Guerrero, Reggie Smith, and Dusty Baker—combined to have six .500-plus seasons while Garvey was a Dodger. So if you're scoring those feared-slugger points, it's Myth 1, Reality 0.

And what was the other side of the story when Garvey was averaging 201 hits a season from 1974 to 1980? It was what he did to make sure he got those 200 hits—or, more precisely, opted not to do. Such as: *take a walk* a couple of times a week. But walking wasn't Steve Garvey's thing. He averaged only 38 walks a season in that period—and averaged a mere 29 over the 16 full seasons in his career. One of his L.A. teammates, Jimmy Wynn, drew just about as many walks over the last five seasons of his career (468) as Garvey drew over all of those 16 seasons (472). Yeah, it's true that moneyball hadn't been invented yet. But decent on-base percentages were still legal. And of the 20 first basemen who got to the plate 4,000 times while Garvey was in the big leagues, only four had a lower on-base percentage than he did (.329).

Base running wasn't quite Garvey's specialty, either. In fact, he used his pervasive non-swiftness to do something that, essentially, can't be done: he had six different 200-hit seasons—without scoring 100 runs *in any of them*. No other player in the history of baseball has ever even approached that amazing feat. For that matter, nobody else has ever gotten beyond *two* 200-hit seasons without scoring 100 times at least once. I'll happily concede that no one ever asked Garvey to be a sprint champ. But you have to subtract at least a few points for base-clogging, don't you?

Then there was defense. What do we make of those four Gold Gloves? What do we make of his two other big leatherworking achievements—his NL-record 193-game errorless streak and his major league–record .9959 fielding percentage at first base? Oh, they tell you he was plenty sure-handed, and that beats the alternative. But scouts and his opponents used to laugh about how disinterested Garvey was in throwing the ball just about anywhere. He was always The Man to Bunt at for All Occasions, because no first baseman in modern times was ever more content to take the out at first base. So was that just a case of a player who knew he couldn't throw and played within his limitations? Or was it all part of the image protection program that his detractors thought consumed him? Heck, does it even matter anymore? I'm glad to give him the benefit of the doubt. But it still means his defensive reputation was as much about perception as reality.

Garvey even took pot shots from some people for extending his all-time National League iron-man streak (1,207 consecutive games) with pinch-hit cameos when anyone else would have missed time—with a pulled hamstring at one point, a hyperextended elbow at another. But I've looked carefully at that streak. And Garvey actually did less streak-padding than Lou Gehrig did in his day. So our judges have disallowed that line of hole-poking. The Streak goes into his Good Stuff column in this book.

If you've paid attention, you should give me credit for dropping lots of items in that Good Stuff column. I didn't have to, you know, but I'd be a knucklehead not to. In every one of these chapters, I feel the need to mention that "overrated" is a very different concept than "Biggest Stiff Who Ever Wore a Uniform." I can do that Biggest Stiff book some other time, maybe when I've decided I'm finally ready to find out what the Witness Protection Program is really all about.

The overrated half of this book, though, is designed merely to pop the bubbles of glitz that have wafted around certain players, for all kinds of reasons. It's safe to say Steve Garvey lovingly constructed his personal glitz bubble. And he built it well, because he had his talents down, limited as they may have been. He filled up the only parts of the baseball card most people even read back in his day—batting average, home runs, RBIs, and fielding percentage. So no wonder so many folks thought he was the greatest player of his time. Except he clearly wasn't.

So looking back on it, don't you wonder how he got elected to start seven straight All-Star Games (and nine altogether)? Don't you wonder why *he* was the first player to attract 4 million All-Star votes? Don't you wonder why *he* somehow seemed to evolve into the face of his sport, in the same era that gave us Mike Schmidt and George Brett and Joe Morgan? It's funny, though, how those three guys breezed into the Hall of Fame, while Garvey's vote total continues to sink. There's a reason for that. Now that we have other tools to evaluate players besides those old-fangled Triple Crown stats, it's becoming apparent there was actually less to Garvey than met the eye back when he was yukking it up on *The Tonight Show with Johnny Carson.*

That doesn't make Steve Garvey a bad dude. And it sure doesn't mean the Dodgers should have traded him for Pepe Frias. It just proves a point Bill James made many, many years ago, to the acclaim of just about no one at the time—that if you fed the right information into a computer "and asked it to pick the perfect overrated player, you would get—Steve Garvey." Hey, there's that word "perfect" again. Whaddayaknow. Turned out Garvey *was* perfect— perfectly overrated.

The Rest of the Top Five

2. ERNIE BANKS THE FIRST BASEMAN

Uh-oh. *This* paragraph has the makings of big trouble. I love Ernie Banks. Who doesn't love Ernie Banks? Everyone who has ever met Ernie Banks wants to take him to lunch, sit next to him at a ballgame, or, at the very least, make him commissioner. Beautiful human. Legit Hall of Famer. But this is where this book starts getting tricky. Like many great players, Ernie was a multi-position kind of guy. Nothing wrong with that. But the more you look at *his* multi-positionality, you find something funny going on. When he played a "defensive" position (shortstop), he was one of the best hitters

ernie banks at first base

Played From: 1953–1971
(Played 1,259 games at 1B, 1961–1971)
Team: Cubs
Career Record: .274 Avg., .330 On-Base Pct., .500 Slug Pct., 2,583 Hits, 512 HR

around. When he moved to an "offensive" position (first base), he forgot to keep hitting. As a shortstop, Banks averaged 37 home runs and 107 RBIs a year, with a .552 slugging percentage and .353 on-base percentage. But after a 37-homer, 104-RBI season in his first year at first base (1962), his seven full seasons after that averaged out to only 23 homers, 89 RBIs, .441 slugging percentage, and .307 OBP. He was the greatest offensive shortstop of his day. But at first? Eh, not so much. There have been 50 players in history who hit at least 200 homers as a first baseman. Banks ranks 50th in just about every sophisticated stat you can use to measure the offensive contributions of that group. So is it possible for a man to be underrated *and* overrated? Until about 20 sentences ago, you'd have thought that was a concept which made zero sense. Now, thanks to Ernie Banks, I only look like a minor knucklehead for suggesting it makes total sense.

3. CECIL FIELDER

Big Cecil was another guy we all wanted to pull for. He had to go to *Japan* to get somebody, anybody, to believe he could hit. Then headed back across the Pacific in 1990 to become baseball's first 50-homer bopper of the Post–George Foster Era (which also, thankfully, ended the Post–George Foster Era). After that, for a few years there, Big Cecil looked and felt like one of our greatest sluggers. But the more you look at those years (if you know where to look, at least), it becomes clear that this man, basically, hit home runs—and that was about it. Before you ask, "What about his RBIs?" we'll pre-answer:

cecil fielder

Played From: 1985–1998
(Also played 535 games at DH)
Teams: Blue Jays, Tigers, Yankees, Angels, Indians
Career Record: .255 Avg., .345 On-Base Pct., .482 Slug Pct., 1,313 Hits, 319 HR

guys who hit lots of home runs *always* drive in runs. They can't help that. Anyway, hear us out: from 1990 to 1996, Fielder out-homered everybody in baseball. But if we apply some of the more incisive, new-age stats to break down that period, here's where he ranked among hitters who got to the plate 2,000 times in that period: 38th in on-base plus slugging (behind Shane Mack!), 62nd in runs created per game (behind John Jaha!), 43rd in total average (behind Chris Hoiles!), and 67th in offensive winning percentage (behind Bernard Gilkey!). You can look up the definition of those stats some-place else if you need to. Or you can trust our big-picture interpretation—that they tell us just how limited an offensive force Cecil Fielder really was. Speaking of those limits, I'm still saddened that, after 1,096 games without stealing a base—which would have set the all-time career record for lack of base-burglarization—Fielder had to go and swipe his first in 1996, thereby un-breaking his own record. It was such a mind-boggling feat that when he called his wife after the game, her joyful reaction was: "Come on. You didn't steal no base."

4. TONY PEREZ

I voted for Tony Perez for the Hall of Fame. I don't regret that. I voted for him because no eligible player with as many RBIs as he has (1,652) had ever *not* made the Hall of Fame. And I voted for him because he had a certain presence that winners have—as a Big Red Machinist in the 1970s, and in Montreal, Boston, and Philadelphia after that. But the whole concept of overrated-underrated is relative. I might have mentioned that a few thousand times. And that's the only reason Perez is on this list. Tony Perez played

tony perez

Played From: 1964–1986
(Also played 760 games at 3B)
Teams: Reds, Expos, Red Sox, Phillies
Career Record: .279 Avg., .341
On-Base Pct., .463 Slug Pct., 2,732
Hits, 379 HR

with *great* players. That isn't his fault. But it also made his run-producer rep-utation possible. In his 10 seasons as a regular in Cincinnati (1967–1976), he drove in 90 or more runs every single year. But he also did it for a team that was more than just the best offensive team around. Only one other team in the National League (the Pirates) was within 575 runs of the Reds in that decade. So as much as Perez elevated them, they elevated *him*. They elevated a .279 lifetime hitter, who slugged .500 in only three of 23 seasons, all the way to Cooperstown. I'm not one of those people who think Tony Perez doesn't deserve to be there. I just recognize that he was as lucky to be around his Hall of Fame teammates as they were to be around him.

5. GIL HODGES

I may never be allowed to cross the Brooklyn Bridge again after writing this paragraph, because Hodges was as icon-ish in Brooklyn in the 1950s as Pelé was on the streets of Rio de Janeiro in the 1970s. But I'll refer you to that Tony Perez section just to the north of this one. Gil Hodges was a gentleman, a leader, and a folk hero on the much-revered Brooklyn Dodgers of the 1950s. We admire him for all of that. But on these pages, we don't debate leadership or gentlemanliness. We don't even want anybody who once idolized Hodges to renounce his idolatry half a

gil hodges

Played From: 1947–1963
(Also played one game in 1943)
Teams: Dodgers, Mets
Career Record: .273 Avg., .359 On-Base Pct., .487 Slug Pct., 1,921 Hits, 370 HR

century later. What we debate is whether the actual, real-life career of the baseball player matches up with the folklore. And in this case, the answer is: not quite. Hodges never finished in the top five in his league in the MVP voting. He made the top five in slugging percentage only twice in 18 total seasons, 14 full seasons. He hit just five homers in 131 postseason at-bats. And among all first basemen with as many career home runs as he hit (370), only one (Andres Galarraga) ranks lower in runs created per game. If Tony Perez is in the Hall of Fame, I have no problem with Hodges being in there, too—especially if you give him extra points for defense and managerial miracles ('69 Mets edition). But it *is* possible to be a Hall of Famer *and* overrated. So sorry. You Gil Hodges Fan Clubbers can't use *that* argument to counter this one. Just put my photo up at all the toll booths on the Verrazano Narrows Bridge. I earned it.

The Most Underrated First Baseman of All Time

HANK GREENBERG

I'll get to the topic du chapter, Hank Greenberg, in a moment. But first, let's take a step back to help you understand the always-informed thought process that ping-pongs through my brain as I select the men whose names will be included in this important contribution to the annals of baseball literature (or, in just a few more weeks, to the book section of overstock.com).

Here in the Underrated Wing of Overrated-Underrated International Corporate Headquarters, we use certain gauges to measure the underratedness of our tragically underappreciated subjects. And what better gauge to use than Hall of Fame voting—the ultimate measuring stick (theoretically) of a player's talent and legacy?

Judging from the blogs I've run across in my cyberspace flights, many caring people out there have a better understanding of the chemical composition of Super Glue than they do of Hall of Fame voting. But if you can't figure out *modern* Hall voting, good luck unearthing any logic whatsoever in the bizarre voting that went down back in the '40s and '50s. Which brings us back to The Man, Hank Greenberg.

Jimmie Foxx (seven elections) coasted into Cooperstown compared to Hank Greenberg. Joe DiMaggio (four elections) was just about rubber-stamped compared to Hank Greenberg. Carl Hubbell (three elections) was practically unanimous compared to Hank Greenberg.

Hank Greenberg, ladies and gentlemen, was one of the greatest hitters who ever lived—yet it took him *nine* shots to get elected to the Hall of Fame. Yup, *nine*. Even if you toss out 1945, when he got three votes before he'd even retired, the guy still had to suffer through eight elections to get his own plaque. Unbelievable.

But that's just one tip-off that the greatness of Greenberg got lost on our hero-conscious land. He was also left off the All-Century Team—another massive outrage. And he almost didn't make it onto the ballot when Tigers fans voted for their favorite Hometown Heroes in the summer of 2006. Sheesh, who would have been on there ahead of him—Jim Walewander?

It took Hank Greenberg, one of the greatest hitters of all time, an astounding nine tries before he was voted into Cooperstown.

So how could this be, huh? True, Greenberg hasn't played a game in close to 60 years, which has slightly limited his *SportsCenter* exposure. But on the scale of men who played baseball in Detroit before the invention of Al Kaline, Greenberg's career has had many more ripple effects than (just to pick one of his exalted Tigers teammates) Boots Poffenberger's. Just since the mid-1990s, Greenberg has been the topic of three books and one highly acclaimed movie. And that's three more books and one more movie than Charlie Gehringer has had devoted to him lately, in case Charlie's heirs hadn't noticed.

Greenberg remains a hot topic largely because he was one of the most significant Jewish athletes in the 20th century. But, inexplicably, what has been overshadowed in all these examinations of his character and heritage is this:

hank greenberg

Played From: 1933–1947
(Also played 1 game in 1930)
Teams: Tigers, Pirates
Career Record: .313 Avg., .412 On-Base Pct., .605 Slug Pct., 1,628 Hits, 331 HR

This guy was a big-time masher. About as big as they get, in fact.

Where do we start laying out what a stupendous hitter Hank Greenberg was? How about this: his .605 *career* slugging percentage ranks number six in history among men who came to the plate as many times as he did. Ahead of him, you'll find only five nobodies named Babe Ruth, Ted Williams, Lou Gehrig, Jimmie Foxx, and Barry Bonds.

Get your attention yet? Thought so. All right, try this: there's an old Bill James stat known as "runs created per 27 outs." The idea is to measure how many runs per game a team of nine Hank Greenbergs would have scored. The answer, according to our handy-dandy computer, is 9.65. That's one run more than a team of nine Honus Wagners. It's two more than a team of nine Frank Robinsons. It's three more than a team of nine George Bretts. How about *that?* Greenberg ranks seventh all time in that department, trailing only Ruth, Williams, Gehrig, Bonds, Foxx, and Rogers Hornsby. But what really caught my eye was the four players immediately *behind* Greenberg: Mickey Mantle, Ty Cobb, Stan Musial, and Joe DiMaggio. Ever heard of any of them?

I could keep throwing numbers like that out there. But this is about more than decimal points. Hank Greenberg was also a two-time MVP and the only man who ever made a dramatic run at both of the most exalted records of his time—or, possibly, anybody's time. Those would be Ruth's 60 homers and Hack Wilson's 190 RBIs (which we now know, upon recount, should have been 191). What makes those assaults especially spectacular is that Greenberg made them in two *different* seasons. He barely missed Wilson's RBI record (with 183) in 1937. In 1938 he got within two homers of Babe Land. But there was even more to those sensational seasons than those gigundous numbers would suggest.

Let's just say that, in the world he lived in, a sizable chunk of the population didn't want to see a Jewish man break either of those records. So some eyebrow-arching stuff happened along the way. For instance: the Indians mysteriously moved their season-ending series with the Tigers in 1938 into the canyon that was Municipal Stadium, instead of the more homer-friendly League Park. (Official reason: because Municipal Stadium held more fans.) Hank Greenberg could have spent the final 48 years of his life grumbling about stuff like that. But the classier way to go was to take a higher road: a road on which he was so determined to fight in World War II that he asked to retake his physical after he failed the first one. A road on which he was one of the first major leaguers to stand up for Jackie Robinson. A road in which he never stopped battling for the sporting principles he believed in while allowing society to work out its pesky cultural hang-ups on its own.

So how does a man like this somehow fade into the background when we debate the greatest hitters ever? Good question. Probably the easiest answer is that even now—in the new, improved, sabermetrically aware world we live in—we still tend to look at the wrong benchmarks. We want to see 500 homers and 1,500 RBIs and 3,000 hits from our "all-time greats," because somewhere along the line, we learned those were The Magic Numbers that mattered. And no matter how many times we try to hit the Reprogram button in our noggins, it never works.

Well, Hank Greenberg had "only" 331 home runs and 1,276 RBIs when he retired (at age 36). But if those numbers cause any one of you to conclude that he must have been a lesser player than Fred McGriff or Jose

Canseco, the only decent retort is: it's a good thing you started thumbing through this book.

Greenberg had four and a half seasons (1941–1945) disappear out of his career while he was off fighting for truth, justice, and the right of all Americans to listen to World Series games on their crackly Philco radios. He missed virtually all of another season with a fractured wrist, after a collision at first base that some people suspected might not have been an accident. So even though he arrived in the big leagues to stay in 1933 and played until 1947, Greenberg racked up 500 at-bats in only seven seasons—out of a 15-season career window. So if you measure his career with the standard "totals," that doesn't work so hot.

That's why he's one of those men who make us veer off into the always-shaky world of What-Might-Have-Been totals. Unfortunately, Nostradamus wasn't available to help with this book, so this is all guesswork. But if you apply even conservative averages of Greenberg's prewar and postwar production to those war years, he would zoom past 500 homers and 2,000 RBIs, and he'd be approaching 2,500 hits. If you give him back all the seasons he lost to World War II and injuries, *and* factor in that he retired young, he's in the 600-Homer Club and maybe close to 3,000 hits.

Now let's try to digest the context of those numbers. There's only one man in the 600-Homer, 3,000-Hit, 2,000-RBI Club—Hank Aaron. There are only two men in the 500-Homer, 2,500-Hit, 2,000-RBI Club—Aaron and Ruth. Even if we concede that Ted Williams would have joined them if his own off-to-war adventures had never happened, that's one illustrious group to be drinking tall ones with.

Unfortunately, the real world isn't capable of yanking those numbers out of either our imaginations or our calculators and imprinting them *on* the *Complete Baseball Encyclopedia*. But we underrated-overrated authors aren't bound by anybody's rules except the ones we choose to apply. (Sorry about that, real-world admirers.) By our rules, there's a very special honor we can bestow on men like Hank Greenberg who got screwed by that nasty real world: Most Underrated First Baseman of All Time. Except for the fact that no cash or trophy is part of that package, does it get any better than that?

The Rest of the Top Five

2. WILLIE McCOVEY

The stuff that makes people underrated usually is none of their doing. In Stretch McCovey's case, it definitely wasn't his fault that he wasn't even the most famous *Willie* on his own team. (If you don't know who was, you're disqualified from reading the rest of this paragraph.) There also wasn't much McCovey could have done about the fact that the Giants happened to develop two Hall of Fame first basemen at the same time. (Okay, we'll help you with this one: Orlando Cepeda was the other.) That forced McCovey to play part-time or get stuck roaming the outfield for five ridiculous seasons (1960–1964) *after* he'd already won a Rookie of the Year award. So this poor guy was 27 before he finally got to play his real position every day. And he still went on to set the all-time National League record for home runs by a left-handed hitter (521) until that Bonds fellow broke it. And set the NL record for grand slams (18). And become the first player in history to terrify managers into intentionally walking him 40 times in one season. Usually, when the other team fears a hitter that much, it tells you all you need to know about him. So what do we know about Stretch McCovey? Boy, was he underrated.

willie mccovey

Played From: 1959–1980
(Also played 257 games in LF)
Teams: Giants, Padres, A's
Career Record: .270 Avg., .374 On-Base Pct., .515 Slug Pct., 2,211 Hits, 521 HR

3. JEFF BAGWELL

If you're The Greatest Player in the History of Your Franchise—anybody's franchise (all right, Devil Rays not included)—the world should always recognize what you are. But I'm not sure enough people in our world recognized what Bagwell was in Houston before his right shoulder turned into tortellini and blew up his career. You know what Jeff Bagwell was? A Hall of Famer. That's what. How many first basemen besides Bagwell ever hit 400 homers *and* stole 200 bases? Uh,

jeff bagwell

Played From: 1991–2005
Team: Astros
Career Record: .297 Avg., .408 On-Base Pct., .540 Slug Pct., 2,314 Hits, 449 HR, 202 SB

none. How many other first basemen ever spewed out six straight seasons of 30 homers, 100 RBIs, and 100 runs scored? Two (Lou Gehrig and Jimmie Foxx). How many other other first basemen since 1900 have scored *and* driven in more than 1,500 runs? Two (Gehrig and Foxx again). Now add in defense (a Gold Glove) and leadership (ruled his clubhouse like the Lion King). And what have you got? One of the most underrated players of his era. Period.

4. DICK ALLEN

This one is for all the kids who grew up in Philadelphia in the 1960s, worshipping Dick Allen, and couldn't figure out why the grown-ups around them

dick allen

Played From: 1963–1977
(Also played 652 games at 3B, 256 games in LF)
Teams: Phillies, Cardinals, Dodgers, White Sox, A's
Career Record: .292 Avg., .378 On-Base Pct., .534 Slug Pct., 1,848 Hits, 351 HR

used to boo the guy until their vocal cords exploded. I was one of those kids. And Allen was the first baseball player I can remember who caused this thumping sensation in my chest any time he unfurled his humongous 42-ounce bat. Because when he waved that bat, I knew he might launch a baseball over the roof, over the billboards, over the flagpole, even over the monstrous Ballantine scoreboard at old Connie Mack Stadium. And who knew that was possi-

ble? Not us kids. We didn't care that this guy couldn't throw, couldn't conform, couldn't be managed. We just loved watching him swing that massive bat. From 1964 to 1974, only one player in the entire sport had a higher slugging percentage than Dick Allen—Hank Aaron. So how tragic is it that Allen didn't possess enough self-discipline to have a career as long and glorious as Aaron's? Aw, don't ask. Unlike most of our underrated heroes, it *was* Allen's fault that he finished his career with "only" 351 homers (and "only" one MVP award). He was the Albert Belle of his generation, and that's no compliment. But this is my book. So I no longer worry about The Other Side of Allen's story. Not now. This is for those kids. And this is for my mother, who inspires me every day—and helped inspire this item, by phoning me on the day of Allen's final Hall of Fame election (in 1997) to ask: "How'd Dick Allen do?" After I reported, "Mom, he didn't make it," my own dear old mother replied: "He didn't have the numbers, Jayson." And she was right. As always. He didn't. But he had enough star power to make this book, at least.

5. TODD HELTON

Now that Bagwell has packed it in, Helton might be *the* most underrated active player. Yeah, sure, sea level does happen to be located 5,000 feet below that ballpark in Colorado he plays in. But look at it this way: Helton became an everyday player in 1998. Over the next nine seasons, he led the sport in batting average, doubles, extra-base hits, and times reaching base. Only Bonds had a higher on-base percentage. Only Derek Jeter and Vladimir Guerrero got more hits. And

todd helton

Played From: 1997–2006 (active)
Team: Rockies
Career Record: .333 Avg., .430 On-Base Pct., .593 Slug Pct., 1,700 Hits, 286 HR

before you start on the altitude factor, I'd just like to retort, "Denver, Schmenver." Bet you didn't know Helton's *road* average (.294), on-base percentage (.393), and slugging percentage (.507) are higher than Paul Konerko's or Johnny Damon's (among others). Underrate *that*.

CHAPTER 7

Second Basemen

The Most Overrated Second Baseman of All Time

STEVE SAX

If you're anything like me, you're no doubt constantly amazed by all the dumb stuff that sticks to your brain for way too many years, for no apparent reason. How does that work exactly? Does the body somehow manufacture small quantities of Velcro that inadvertently attach themselves to random thoughts and memories? And then, next thing you know, your brain membranes are stuck with them forever?

Well, it looks now as if I'm stuck with Steve Sax for the rest of my lifetime. Not all of him, thankfully—especially the part of him that might cause me to try tossing a crumpled up sheet of book notes into the wastebasket and have it land instead in my next-door neighbor's microwave. But Steve Sax's rookie year? It's still up there. So how'd I get sentenced to living with *that* for life?

It's all because the first major baseball award I ever got to vote on was National League Rookie of the Year, 1982. Steve Sax won that award, you might recall. But even if you don't recall, we're about to rehash it anyway. And before you regard this as clear proof I've lost my sanity—venting about a Rookie of the Year vote I didn't agree with *a quarter of a freaking century later*—let me explain.

It was way back then that I shrewdly detected that the overrating of Mr. Stephen Louis Sax had officially begun. And not a moment too soon.

He played in Los Angeles, the home base of several television cameras and a place where overrating (more commonly known as "hype") is a way of life, much like traffic and sushi. And he played for the most garrulous manager in the history of garrulosity, Tommy Lasorda. Sax also played for a team that had already produced the previous three National League rookies of the year, incredibly enough. And he played for the defending World Series champs—replacing Davey Lopes, a high profile everyday force for four Dodgers World Series teams, at second base and at the top of the lineup.

So in a season that produced what is now regarded as the greatest crop of rookies in any season in the 1980s, no rookie was more visible than Steve Sax. And I'm convinced, to this day, that's why he won.

After a long and thorough review of the candidates that year, I voted for someone else. I voted for a man whose own second-base career turned out okay, you might say. That someone was Ryne Sandberg. Here was my thinking:

Sax scored 88 runs that year. But Sandberg scored 103 (fifth-most in the league)—for a Cubs team that scored fewer runs than the Dodgers. Sandberg also drove in more runs (54–47) and hit more home runs (7–4).

Sax batted .282 to Sandberg's .271. But Sandberg had 45 extra-base hits to Sax's 34. Sax did steal more bases (49–32). But he also got thrown out stealing more times (19) than all but three players in the league—and (ohbytheway) had a worse stolen-base success rate (72.1 percent) than Sandberg (72.7).

But the biggest separator of those two, for me, was defense—never exactly Sax's specialty *de la casa*. Sandberg, playing third base for the only season in his career, had the second-*best* fielding percentage in the major leagues. Sax, meanwhile, made 19 errors and had the *worst* fielding percentage of any second baseman in the big leagues who played 130 games or more.

So I cast my first-place vote for Ryne Sandberg. He later thanked me for it—since it was the only vote he got. Sax, on the other hand, got nine first-place votes. So the Dodgers had themselves yet another Rookie of the Year. And I got a scar on my brain out of it that still hasn't healed up. I'm still asking: anybody got a cure for brain scars?

I remain positive, all these years later, that I got that vote right. And I have a video I can show you of Sandberg's Hall of Fame induction to prove it. But I need to assure you that I wasn't warped enough to hold that election against Steve Sax for the next thousand years—or until I could write a book to get it off my chest. C'mon, folks. Give me a little more credit than that. It's just that that Rookie of the Year election made me more aware than ever what an asset it could be for a guy to show up in a place like L.A. with a little talent and a winning smile—and then let the hype machine take over.

You won't hear me denying that Steve Sax was a very useful player for a decade or so. From 1982 to 1992, he was number four in the whole sport in stolen bases (behind only the sprint-relay team of Rickey Henderson, Tim Raines, and Vince Coleman). He was also fourth in hits (behind the Hall of

Despite his colossal defensive liabilities, and introducing Steve Sax Disease to the game of baseball, the poor-throwing second baseman was revered by fans in L.A. Photo courtesy of Getty Images.

Fame threesome of Wade Boggs, Sandberg, and Cal Ripken). And if you peruse Sax's career in the encyclopedia, you'll notice he batted over .300 three times, got over 200 hits twice. So this is the point in every one of these chapters where I'm compelled by federal overrated-underrated regulations to make the following announcement:

Just because this fellow wound up in the overrated section of this chapter, it doesn't mean I think he'd have been better off selling pots and pans on QVC.

No, I recognize exactly what he did well. But I also recognize he didn't do it as well as most folks seemed to think. This man made *five* All-Star teams (as many as Jeff Kent). He even batted leadoff for one of the most storied collections of All-Stars of all time—Mr. Burns's ringer-studded Springfield Nuclear Power Plant team on a 1992 episode of *The Simpsons*. But was Steve Sax really that kind of player? He was a leadoff hitter who never scored 100 runs in any of his 14 seasons. And, in a related development, he was a leadoff hitter with a lifetime on-base percentage of .335 (lower than Luis

steve sax

Played From: 1981–1994
Teams: Dodgers, Yankees, White Sox, A's
Career Record: .281 Avg., .335 On-Base Pct., .358 Slug Pct., 1,949 Hits, 54 HR, 444 SB

Alicea's!). So face it. This man wasn't quite Rickey Henderson.

But remember, offense was the part Sax was good at. What's really tough to ignore is the part he wasn't so good at—since you can find it documented on about a dozen blooper tapes. From 1982 to 1992, the prime of Sax's career, he wasn't merely the worst second baseman in baseball by a little bit. He was the worst second baseman in baseball by a margin as long as the Ventura Freeway.

He committed 30 more errors at second in that span (183) than his next-closest cohort (Juan Samuel). And just one other second baseman besides Samuel was within 50 (yes, 50) of him. (That was Willie Randolph, who was 46 back.)

Don't ask me why a man who could smoke a 95-mile-per-hour fastball up the gap couldn't master the art of throwing a baseball 75 feet to first base. I forgot to go to medical school, or to get that Ph.D. in psychology, so I don't understand what happened to Steve Sax. But something short-circuited between his mind and his shoulder. So for years, routine throws to first were a good bet to land anywhere from Lasorda's lap to Louisiana. And it led to everybody's favorite Tommy Lasorda story—one so good we have to retell it here:

Back in those days, the Dodgers had Pedro Guerrero—never confused with Brooks Robinson himself—playing third base. So one day, Lasorda asked Guerrero what went through his head when he was out in the field in the ninth inning of a tie game.

"The first thing I'm thinking," Guerrero said, "is I hope they don't hit the ball to me."

"So, Pedro," Lasorda replied, "what's the second thing you're thinking?"

"The second thing I'm thinking," Guerrero laughed, "is I hope they don't hit it to Sax, either."

There sure were a lot of Dodgers fans who could relate to *that* thought. But as ugly as it sometimes got out there on the infield clay of Chavez Ravine, Sax remained many of those same fans' favorite player. Which is great. I'm happy for him that people could be so empathetic, so willing to overlook the defensive debacles that kept unfolding in front of them. It restores our faith in the human spirit.

But it's also a made-to-order blueprint for how to show up in a book like this under the heading: "Most Overrated Second Baseman of All Time."

Just to verify that billing, I talked with one of my favorite scouts about where Sax ought to land in this book's overrated rankings. He barely hesitated.

"He's *gotta* be number one," the scout said. "He played pretty much his whole career with the Dodgers [eight seasons] and Yankees [three seasons]. So that almost has to make him overrated right there. And he's the brand name for ineptitude at his position. Steve Sax Disease is like Tommy John Surgery. When Mackey Sasser—or anybody who can't throw straight—comes along, what has he got? He's got Steve Sax Disease. When you're the definition of defensive ineptitude, how can you *not* be overrated?"

Oh, it's possible, I suppose....Just not in this chapter.

The Rest of the Top Five

2. BOBBY RICHARDSON

Other than marrying Lucille Ball, there was no better way to become an instant famous person in the 1950s and 1960s than to be a Yankee. And

bobby richardson

Played From: 1955–1966
Team: Yankees
Career Record: .266 Avg., .299 On-Base Pct., .335 Slug Pct., 1,432 Hits, 34 HR

Richardson was one of the lucky Americans whose Yankeedom did wonders for lifting his profile. Over his 10 seasons as a famous Yankees regular, Richardson played in the World Series seven times, made seven All-Star teams, and won five Gold Gloves and a World Series MVP award in 1960 (even though his team *lost* the Series). It was great work if you could get it. But while Richardson was a smooth fielder and had two terrific World Series with the bat, a look back at The Rest of His Story makes it clear he wasn't quite as stupendous a player as you might think if you just checked out his trophy case. He never walked more than 37 times in any season. Even though he often hit at or near the top of the order, his career on-base percentage was only .299. (Mickey Mantle, not coincidentally, had two seasons of 40-plus home runs, but *fewer* than 100 RBIs, while hitting behind Richardson.) Richardson had just two above-average offensive seasons in his whole career. And, if you use an old Bill James stat known as "offensive winning percentage," you'll find that a lineup of nine Bobby Richardsons (with an average pitching staff) would have had a winning percentage of (yikes) .391 over those 10 seasons—at a time when his team's actual winning percentage was almost 200 points higher than that (.581). So is it safe to say that if he'd had exactly the same career for the Senators or the Cubs, he might not have been quite as universally renowned? Um, it is in *this* book.

3. WALLY BACKMAN

Fact: the 1986 Mets were one of the best, and most charismatic, teams of the division-play era. Fact: everybody on those 1986 Mets ought to send Bob Stanley and Bill Buckner a Christmas card every year for the rest of their lives. Fact: just about every player on the 1986 Mets who didn't pitch for a living is probably overrated in some way, shape, or form. Which brings us to Wally Backman, the gritty little dirtball who was Lenny Dykstra's cohort in top-of-the-order mayhem for that team. There was a lot to love about Backman in 1986, especially in the epic NLCS against Houston, when he scored or drove in *four* game-tying or go-ahead runs in the ninth inning or extra innings.

wally backman

Played From: 1980–1993
(Also played 111 games at 3B)
Teams: Mets, Pirates, Phillies, Mariners
Career Record: .275 Avg., .349 On-Base Pct., .339 Slug Pct., 893 Hits, 10 HR, 117 SB

But while Backman played chunks of 14 seasons in the big leagues, he never had that kind of impact again on any team. He was, in fact, just a platoon player, a switch-hitter whose career average batting right-handed was (gulp) .165, and one of the least reliable defensive players of his time. In the three seasons he got to play 100 games at second (1984, 1985, and 1986), 17 second basemen in the big leagues played as many games in the field as he did. None got to fewer balls than Backman did, and the only three in that group who had a worse fielding percentage all handled at least 500 more chances out there. So while we all love our dirtballs, we also love to overrate our dirtballs. Sorry about that, Wally.

4. DON ZIMMER

When a man spends more than half a century in baseball, he becomes a walking, talking slice of sporting folklore. And that's Don Zimmer, one of the most recognizable people in the whole darned sport. Just the thought of Zimmer, sitting in the Yankees dugout wearing a combat helmet after taking a foul ball off that debonair face of his, can make you chuckle. But all the chuckles, the folklore, and the visibility Zimmer inspired in his coaching days may have led you to overlook the temptation to check out his playing career. And if that's

don zimmer

Played From: 1954–1965
(Also played 288 games at SS, 375 games at 3B)
Teams: Dodgers, Cubs, Reds, Mets, Senators
Career Record: .235 Avg., .290 On-Base Pct., .372 Slug Pct., 773 Hits, 91 HR

true, it's a good thing for him. This guy spent 12 years in the big leagues and didn't have even *one* season in which his numbers beat the league norm. His career offensive winning percentage was a frightening .328—meaning a team of nine Don Zimmers would have had an average record of (gulp) 53–109. And when he retired, his .235 lifetime batting average was second-worst only to the immortal Rabbit Warstler among all non-catchers in the entire live-ball era who got to the plate as many times as Zimmer did. So why doesn't he rank even higher on this list? In part because he spent half his career playing other positions. And in larger part because he was never the same after suffering one of the worst beanings in baseball history, at a time when he was leading the American Association in home runs in 1953. Anybody who was knocked unconscious by a baseball for nearly two weeks has to get a whole bunch of we'll-never-know-what-might-have-been points. Even in seemingly heartless books like this one.

5. JULIAN JAVIER

Any time you run across that phrase "slick-fielding second baseman" a voice should thunder out of the heavens, speaking the two words that sum up what

julian javier

Played From: 1960–1972
Teams: Cardinals, Reds
Career Record: .257 Avg., .296 On-Base Pct., .355 Slug Pct., 1,469 Hits, 78 HR, 135 SB

that phrase really means: "can't hit." But in Julian Javier's case, not many people noticed back in the 1960s, because Javier was shrewd enough to be one of the Cardinals' *best* hitters the only times most people in America got to see him—in the 1967 and 1968 World Series. He batted .346 in those two World Series. So

he was looked at as such a star for much of his career, he was the only NL second baseman besides Bill Mazeroski to be selected to start the All-Star Game in multiple years (1963 and 1968) in the 1960s. But it's time for the Overrated Fact-Checking Police to step in here. In reality, Javier *couldn't* hit. He still owns the second-lowest career on-base percentage (.296) among all second basemen in the live-ball era who came to bat as many times as he did. And it would be a shock to legendary GM Bing Devine—who once called Javier the greatest defensive second baseman in Cardinals history—to learn that Javier actually ranked *last* in fielding percentage among the 23 men who played at least 700 games at second between 1960 and 1972. So apparently, it wasn't all Mazeroski's fault that Javier never did win a Gold Glove—or that he sneaked into the wrong half of this chapter.

The Most Underrated Second Baseman of All Time

CRAIG BIGGIO

Way back in our introduction, this book laid out, in that invaluable way it will soon be noted for (or not), a foolproof 10-step plan for How to Become More Underrated. If you zipped right by it because you wanted to check out the big names in the other chapters first, feel free to U-turn and read it now. No problem. I'll wait.

Hey, welcome back. Wasn't that worth the detour? Now back to our regularly scheduled programming.

Craig Biggio didn't follow all 10 of those steps—possibly because he was 19 seasons into his career before this book hit the shelves. But as much as any active player, he lived by the principles that embodied that foolproof plan.

You want central time zone worship? This man played every darned second of his career in Houston, which still hasn't figured out a way to get itself relocated to either coast.

You want a player who was overshadowed by other stars? Heck, he played with Jeff Bagwell, Lance Berkman, Moises Alou, Luis Gonzalez, Richard Hidalgo, and Steve Finley—all of whom commanded at least as much national hoopla as Biggio did. And it wasn't the lineup that ever seemed to be the face of the Astros, anyway. It was all those pitchers: Roger Clemens, Roy Oswalt, Andy Pettitte, Randy Johnson, Billy Wagner, Brad Lidge, Mike Hampton, Mike Scott, Darryl Kile. And we haven't even gotten to Jose Lima yet. So it was easy to forget Craig Biggio was around some of those years.

You want those always-helpful height issues? Biggio mastered them nicely, too. He could have grown an extra inch and made it to 6' even. But he understood, even during puberty, that that one little inch might eliminate him from consideration by important literary volumes like this one.

You want a guy who begs for a pay cut? Hold on now. Who ever expected anybody to follow *that* advice? But Biggio came as close as any big-time player you'll run across. Four times in his career, he took less money one season than he'd made the year before. And in January 2003, he even signed a two-year extension which deflated him from a $9.75 million salary in 2003 to $3 million in each of the next two years. Sheez, not only has this guy done all that to stay with the only team he's ever played for. But in his two decades, you know how many times he even went so far as to file for free agency? How about *once* (in 1995)? Not even bothering to flirt with the Yankees may not have done much to pump up his checking-account balance. But it definitely did wonders for his underratedness rankings.

You want a man who avoided October? Okay, Biggio didn't quite do that. His teams did make the playoffs six times. But this fellow appeared in 2,564 regular-season box scores before he played in his first World Series game in 2005. That was more than any player in the whole World Series era (1903–present). So how poetic was that?

Biggio's unmatched selflessness in a selfish era in Major League Baseball—taking pay cuts and changing positions no less than four times during his career—helped land him on the underrated list.

Finally, you want intangibles? We'll give you some serious stinkin' intangibles. What other seven-time All-Star (Non–Pete Rose Division) was willing to change positions four times (from catcher to second base to center field to left field and then back to second base) during his career, mostly because his team's lineup worked better if he made those moves? Okay, so Carlos Beltran and Willy Taveras had something to do with those final two relocations. But we don't recall, say, Derek Jeter being willing to budge more than six inches after Alex Rodriguez showed up.

So what we have here is a player who has spent his career skating along two trails that don't always run parallel. One is leading him to the Hall of Fame. The other dragged him into this very chapter in this very book. So he can head for the window and cash that daily-double ticket any time he's ready.

Oh, it's not as if Biggio has played his whole career incognito. The Astros showed up in October enough to assure that your average *Baseball Tonight* viewer knew his name, and could even spell it. But how many of those folks realized they were watching one of the all-time greats at his primary position (i.e., the position that didn't involve shin guards or mad sprints around the outfield)? Remarkably few.

But that's what Craig Biggio is, you know—an all-time great. By the time he's finished, the only men in history who accumulated more hits than him while spending most of their careers playing second base will be Eddie Collins (3,315) and Nap Lajoie (3,242). And in case those names don't bring back any vivid memories, it might be because they were both doing some of their best baseball work during World War I.

Of that same group of men who logged most of their time at second base, only Jeff Kent—a middle-of-the-order force, not a top-of-the-lineup engine-starter—is going to wind up with more home runs. And no player in National League history has hit more home runs leading off games than Biggio (who did that for the 50th time in 2006).

Biggio might also wind up in the top five on the all-time doubles list. And when he retires, *every* player ahead of him in runs scored and extra-base hits will be a guy with a plaque in scenic Cooperstown, New York.

It's amazing how all that has been going on, right in front of our own eyeballs, over the last two decades, and so few of us caught on to what we were witnessing. But that can happen to those semi-anonymous stars in the "wrong" town, in the "wrong" time zone. All of a sudden, you look up on the scoreboard or peruse the daily notes blitz, and the powerful names that men like Craig Biggio start passing on those historic lists begin to wallop you across the brain until you say, "Whoa."

craig biggio

Played From: 1988–2006 (active)
(Also played 427 games at C,
216 games at CF)
Team: Astros
Career Record: .283 Avg., .367
On-Base Pct., .436 Slug Pct., 2,930
Hits, 281 HR, 410 SB

I had a fascinating talk with Biggio himself about this one day in 2006. He'd just whooshed by Cal Ripken in doubles—and Hank Aaron was next. *Hank Aaron.* So Biggio did something modern players almost never do: he actually looked up Aaron's numbers, to see if that might make this feat compute any easier. And as he was staring at Hank Aaron's career, he thought of himself, about to pass the legendary Hammerin' Hank in *anything*—doubles, autograph shows, total sweatsocks laundered, whatever. And Craig Biggio had to admit: "It gives you goosebumps."

It may be true that he wasn't passing Aaron in the kind of extra-base hit Aaron became most noted for. But for a guy like Biggio, doubles fit right into his underratedness formula. If you're known for hitting home runs, you're always in danger of making somebody's overrated list (even this one). If you want to be underrated, you do stuff like hit 50 doubles in back-to-back seasons. (Biggio is one of only four men to do that since the 1930s.) And roll up 50 doubles and 50 stolen bases in the same season. (Biggio's 50–50 season in 1998 made him the first player to do that since Tris Speaker, who did it in 1912.)

Or you make it through an entire season without hitting into a double play. (Biggio is still the only player since the dawn of 162-game schedules to pull that off.) Or, while you're avoiding those double plays, you *don't* avoid many fastballs boring in on your elbows. (Somehow, Biggio has managed to get hit by more pitches than any player in history—and still gone on the disabled list just once in his whole career.)

I've seen this man play enough to recognize that, at his peak, he may not have been as dominating as Joe Morgan, or as dazzling a worker in the second-base leather shop as Roberto Alomar. But Craig Biggio was still scoring 100 runs at age 38, and still hitting 20 homers at age 40. And he hustled his butt off to first base every time he put a ball in play. That's not something you can say about every guy who hangs around this many years.

Dependability and durability are qualities we sometimes take for granted—when, in fact, they're the most valuable ingredients to look for in *any* athlete. But when a player's best qualities are the ones the public notices least, it's good to know there are still some people paying attention—particularly if they happen to be people writing books on the most underrated players of all time.

Unfortunately, as this book was heading for a printing press nowhere near you, Biggio was about to do something with the potential to blow his safe haven in the Underrated Hall of Fame to smithereens—i.e., get his 3,000th hit. And apparently, there was nothing any of us involved in this project could do to stop him. But that doesn't change the first 19 years of his career—when only Barbara Bush, Lyle Lovett, several million other Texans, and a few off-kilter hit-by-pitch junkies seemed to notice what Craig Biggio was up to.

He was laying the groundwork for his journey to Cooperstown *and* to these last few pages. And even that was more underrated than most folks gave him credit for.

The Rest of the Top Five

2. BOBBY GRICH

If you thought the only role air conditioners played in modern baseball history was to keep the temperature in domed stadiums under 147 degrees, you obviously don't know the story of Bobby Grich. Just before spring training in 1977, the American League's greatest second baseman tried to carry an air conditioner up the stairs to his new apartment—and the air conditioner won. Grich blew out his back, needed surgery, and was never quite the same spectacular defensive force again. But this was still one seriously

bobby grich

Played From: 1970–1986
(Also played 159 games at SS)
Teams: Orioles, Angels
Career Record: .266 Avg., .371 On-Base Pct., .424 Slug Pct., 1,833 Hits, 224 HR, 104 SB

multitalented guy. He won four straight Gold Gloves. He set records (since broken) for best second-base fielding percentage in a season (.997) and a career (.984). He led his league in homers and slugging in 1981. He joined Joe Gordon as the only AL second basemen in the 20th century to have a 30-homer, 100-RBI season (in 1979). And his combination of power, plate discipline, and defense made him, in Bill James's words, "a hidden star." Grich was so well hidden, in fact, he lasted just one year on the Hall of Fame ballot (with 11 measly votes), never to return. So he won't be heading for Cooperstown. But the good news is that snub did wonders for his standing in this book.

3. ROGERS HORNSBY

You're no doubt asking how a man who is almost universally regarded as the greatest second baseman ever could wind up on a list like this. Good question. It would have been impossible—if the Cardinals hadn't left Hornsby off their entire five-man Hometown Heroes ballot in the summer of 2006. The point was to choose the Greatest Cardinal in History, so it wasn't easy to keep a player this legendary off the ballot. Granted, the five men who displaced him were Bob Gibson, Stan Musial, Albert Pujols, Ozzie Smith, and Lou Brock. So at least Hornsby wasn't beaten out by Stubby Clapp. Nevertheless, there *had* to be a place for an All-Century Team member who once batted .402 *for five years* (1921–1925). And had the highest career batting average in National League history (.358). And led the league in slugging *nine* times (second only to Bambino Ruth). And had a .434 career on-base percentage (topped, since 1900, by just Ted Williams, Ruth, Lou Gehrig, and Barry Bonds). Yeah, well, guess not. But Hornsby can play on our All-Underrated Heroes Team any time he wants.

rogers hornsby

Played From: 1915–1937
Teams: Cardinals, Giants, Braves, Cubs, Browns
Career Record: .358 Avg., .434 On-Base Pct., .577 Slug Pct., 2,930 Hits, 301 HR, 135 SB

4. JEFF KENT

Much like the way Craig Biggio's numbers are now surprising folks who weren't paying attention, it's going to come as a shock to many people some day that The Best Offensive Second Baseman Since Hornsby has been hanging around us since the early '90s. And that man is...no, not D'Angelo Jimenez, but Jeff Kent. Who's the only second baseman in history with eight 100-RBI seasons? Kent. Who's the only second baseman in history with six 100-RBI seasons in a row? Yep, Kent. Who's the only second baseman to crank out nine straight seasons with at least 60

jeff kent

Played From: 1992–2006 (active) (Also played 116 games at 1B, 157 games at 3B)
Teams: Blue Jays, Mets, Indians, Giants, Astros, Dodgers
Career Record: .289 Avg., .356 On-Base Pct., .504 Slug Pct., 2,189 Hits, 345 HR

extra-base hits? Right, Kent. (The next-longest streak ever is only *four*.) Who's the only second baseman since Hornsby with a .500 career slugging percentage? Right again. It's Kent. And who's the all-time home-run leader among the 3 billion second basemen in history? Yessir, it's Jeff Kent. Obviously, Kent's no Mazeroski-esque magician with the glove. And there's some kind of message in the fact he has played for six different teams. But if you've never thought of Kent as a potential Hall of Famer, feel free to start reevaluating the minute you finish this sentence.

5. JOE GORDON

In books like this, we love men who evolve into One-Man Trivia Factories. And that's Joe Gordon. Which Yankee won the American League MVP award in 1942, in a year Ted Williams won the Triple Crown? No, not Joe DiMaggio. It was Gordon. Who was the only AL second baseman in the 20th century to hit at least 29 homers and drive in at least 90 runs in back-to-back seasons? Even if we gave you the hint that he did it in Cleveland,

joe gordon

Played From: 1938–1950
Teams: Yankees, Indians
Career Record: .268 Avg., .357 On-Base Pct., .466 Slug Pct., 1,530 Hits, 253 HR

you'd probably guess Roberto Alomar or Carlos Baerga. But it was, in fact, Joe Gordon (in 1947–1948). And if we asked you to name the seven second basemen in history to make at least nine All-Star teams—and we told you the first six were Alomar, Rod Carew, Ryne Sandberg, Joe Morgan, Billy Herman, and Red Schoendienst—we're betting you'd guess Bill Mazeroski or Jackie Robinson for the final spot. But that answer, too, is Joe Gordon. And those aren't even Gordon's greatest trivia claims to fame of all. His best bolt is: name the only managers in history ever traded for each other? Answer: Joe Gordon for Jimmie Dykes (in *mid-season*, in 1960). Anybody with all that going for him *had* to make this book. Don't you think?

CHAPTER 8

Third Basemen

The Most Overrated Third Baseman of All Time

GRAIG NETTLES

Now that you're nearly halfway through this book, it seems like a safe time to reveal one thing you *won't* find in it. Sorry, you won't be reading any 10-step plans for how to become more *overrated*. There's a real simple reason for that, too. Who the heck needs 10 steps? You only need one step:

Become a Yankee.

When you're writing a book like this, it would be easy to plop a Yankee onto the top of every Most Overrated list. You realize that, right? Yankees have everything you're looking for when you're awarding such an important honor—too much hype, too many rings, too much money, too much air time, too many Victoria's Secret models sitting behind the dugout. It's all there—like trolling the world's longest salad bar.

So I hope all you readers—and, especially, all you professional book reviewers—will take note of how much restraint I've shown so far in avoiding the greatest temptation any overrated-underrated author can possibly face. Think how many more non-Yankees have appeared in these overrated lists than Yankees. It's a miracle. It could be the most spectacular feat witnessed in literary circles since the release of *A Tale of Two Cities*.

Graig Nettles was a magician with the glove—never better than in the 1978 World Series—but his offensive numbers are either somewhat inflated by Yankee Stadium's short porch in right or just not that impressive (batted .235 or lower in nine different seasons).

Now I want you to keep that in mind as I lay out the case for Graig Nettles as the most overrated third baseman of all time. I'm not picking on the Yankees. I've gone out of my way not to pick on the Yankees. And I would never, ever resort to a cheap stunt like that just to make America's 918 million official Yankee-haters purchase this book (although they're welcome to purchase away; operators are standing by).

I understand Graig Nettles was a mini–cult hero in the 11 seasons (1973–1983) he spent as a Yankee. Matter of fact, he's still a mini–cult hero to people who loved that group of Yankees. I still hear from those people once in a while, trying to explain why they think Nettles got screwed by Hall of

Fame voters, why he was better than Brooks Robinson, why in many ways he's one of the Yankees' all-time greats.

Well, Graig Nettles had his moments. No denying that. And some of those moments came in the biggest games he played in his life. (Feel free to sit back and play that 1978 World Series video right now. Go ahead. I understand.) This man unfurled some of the most memorable October defensive plays any third baseman has ever made. He won a home-run title. He's seventh on the all-time Yankees home-run list (pretty dazzling list). He's first on the American League's all-time third-base home-run list (another attractive list). And he was always a witty son of a gun. (His requiem for Sparky Lyle—"from Cy Young to Sayonara"—is right up there, for me, as the most inspired quote of the 1970s.)

So you don't have to explain to me that Nettles was a fun guy to watch and a fun guy to have as a teammate. Just because I think he's overrated doesn't mean I would ever have advised George Steinbrenner to trade him, even up, for Phil Mankowski. Hopefully, you've caught on by now that when I suggest that someone is overrated in this book, I'm not requesting that he refund all his salaries or seek asylum in Madagascar.

In fact, I'd appreciate it if most of the overrated population in these pages would consider it a compliment (as opposed to, oh, launching a major Smear Stark campaign). To be considered the most overrated anything, you have to be good enough to be rated at all. That's a vital concept to keep in mind— and one you should take into account strongly before hitting the send button on your "what a dope you are" emails.

In Graig Nettles's case, I just happen to see all sides of this. So I'm uniquely qualified (mostly because I'm the only one writing this book) to separate what Nettles was great at from what he was not so great at, in that distinguished voice of reason I'm trying to perfect as quickly as possible.

As an offensive force, Nettles was great at aiming for the ever-inviting right-field fence at Yankee Stadium. It was his goal in life to launch as many balls as he could into that neighborhood, and it was a goal he pursued, and realized, with awesome precision.

"He used to use a bat with a very thin barrel," says one longtime scout. "And you know why? He had the philosophy that he'd rather swing and miss than hit a foul ball. He tailored his swing for that right-field porch, so any-thing he made contact with had a chance to go out. He wanted that small barrel because it took away a lot of pop-ups and foul balls. It was all about pulling home runs in Yankee Stadium. Have you checked his home and away numbers?"

Well, heck, of course. I've checked *every* number (the ones that help me make this argument, anyway). And during Nettles's career as a Yankee, he hit 141 of his 250 homers at home. His batting average was 30 points higher at Yankee Stadium than it was on the road. His slugging percentage was nearly 90 points higher at The Stadium. His on-base plus slugging (OPS) was more than 100 points higher. So it wasn't merely being a Yankee that made him seem like a more imposing hitter than he actually was. It was also being a left-handed-hitting Yankee in Yankee Stadium.

Because Nettles did win one home-run title (in 1976), he had a reputation as a dangerous thumper. But here come some facts: he hit 30 homers or more just twice in 22 seasons (20 full seasons). He never had a .500 slugging per-centage in any full season. Of all the members of the 300-Homer Club, Nettles's career OPS (.750) ranks *second lowest* in history (behind—or is that above?—only Gary Gaetti's .741). And while Nettles's fans want us to dismiss his batting average, that's tough to do. He batted .235 or lower in nine differ-ent seasons. And of the men in that 300-Homer Club, only Dave Kingman and Greg Vaughn had lower lifetime batting averages than Nettles (.248).

But just to show I'm trying my best to be reasonable here, let's adjust his numbers to the era he played in and the ballparks he got to hit in—with an adjustable stat known as OPS-plus. We're going to say an OPS-plus of 150 (50 percent better than the average player) constitutes a "great" season. And an OPS-plus of 125 (25 percent above the norm) would be a "really good" season. In 20 full seasons, Nettles had no "great" years and only two "really good" years (as well as one with an OPS-plus of 124). Now let's stack that against the other third basemen of his day.

Sal Bando had two "great" seasons and five "really good" seasons. Ron Cey had no "great" years but seven "really good" years. Bill Madlock had two "great" seasons and six "really good" seasons. George Brett had three "great" seasons and

10 "really good" seasons. And the gold standard—Mike Schmidt—had 10 "great" years and three "really good" years (or, since all three were in the 140s, three "really, really close to great" years).

So if you'd like to argue that Nettles was one of the best offensive players of his time, you can give it a try. But all those facts don't help. And I haven't even mentioned the game in 1974 when he broke his bat and a bunch of Super Balls flew out of it. (Oops. I just did.) I have no idea what to make of that little "incident." But that never looks good on anyone's compendium of offensive credentials.

graig nettles

Played From: 1967–1988
Teams: Twins, Indians, Yankees, Padres, Braves, Expos
Career Record: .248 Avg., .329 On-Base Pct., .421 Slug Pct., 2,225 Hits, 390 HR

Of course, the folks who argue Nettles's Hall of Fame case always start with defense. And well they should. Using "defensive win shares" as his grading curve, Bill James has awarded Nettles an A– defensive rating—the same mark he gave Brooks Robinson. Which gives credence to the rationale that since Nettles was "just as good" as Robinson defensively and a better hitter, Nettles should be in the Hall of Fame, too.

I've heard dumber Hall of Fame arguments. I'll say that. But hold on. Did Nettles truly drive the old glove train as skillfully as Brooks Robinson? Robinson smokes him in "range factor" (chances per nine innings), 3.17 to 2.98; in fielding percentage, .971 to .961; and in Gold Gloves, 16 to 2. And a scout who saw both of them in their prime says, "It's no contest. Robinson covered balls over the line *and* to his left. And nobody made the play coming in on the ball better than Brooks Robinson. Graig Nettles's range, I think, was highly overrated. I used to see him dive for balls that would go by him a step and a half to his left, and everyone would go crazy—but I'd say, 'What was he diving for?' So Brooks, to me, had great overall range. Nettles had to cheat more."

It would be dumb, though, to spend any more space than that running down Nettles's glove work. That would constitute piling on. It might even border on complete insanity. Graig Nettles was a massive defensive upgrade on Butch Hobson or Toby Harrah or Howard Johnson. That's for sure. So if the guy wasn't quite Brooks Robinson, big whoop. That just gave Nettles something in common with the rest of the human species. There was, after all, only one Brooks Robinson.

Yet the Graig Nettles cult is always trying to lump him in there with Robinson and always trying to paint him as the American League's Mike Schmidt with the bat. So why is he overrated? *That's* what I'm talking about. Put a good player on the Yankees at the right point in Yankees history, and he's exactly what you get—reputation inflation. There's no overratedness like Yankees overratedness. And it's our sad duty to inform Graig Nettles and his fans he has just been tried and convicted of that unfortunate offense.

The Rest of the Top Five

2. PIE TRAYNOR

Anybody with a name like Pie ought to be on the All-Pastry Team, not the All-Overrated Team. But the more you look back on Traynor's career, the more you wonder if this guy was the elite player he was, uh, cooked up to be. He was the only third baseman elected to the Hall of Fame by the baseball writers in their first four decades of balloting. He was chosen as the greatest third baseman of all time when baseball picked a 1969 All-Centennial Team. He made the All-Century Team ballot in 1999. And he sneaked onto the Pirates' list of five Hometown Heroes finalists in 2006 ahead of a man who got 3,152 hits— Paul Waner. But does the Pie Man really deserve to be that legendary? Not according to this book, he doesn't. Yeah, he was a real good defensive third baseman. Yeah, he hit .300 10 times and drove in 100 runs seven times. And yeah, in 17 seasons, the most times he ever whiffed was 28. But if you examine that OPS-plus stat I used to compare Nettles to his contemporaries, Traynor's offensive reputation looks downright half-baked. He had just one "really good" season in his whole career (in 1923, when his OPS-plus was exactly 125). But in the same era, his own teammate Waner had 12 "really

pie traynor

Played From: 1920–1937
Team: Pirates
Career Record: .320 Avg., .362 On-Base Pct., .435 Slug Pct., 2,416 Hits, 58 HR, 158 SB

good" or "great" seasons *in a row.* And Eddie Collins, the best third baseman of the 1910s and 1920s, had 16 of those seasons. So call me, cough-cough, crusty if you want, but when you take all that out of the oven, this Pie starts looking more overrated than Boston cream.

3. BOB HORNER

Suppose all you knew about Horner was that: A) he never spent a day in the minor leagues, B) he's the only American-born player ever to win a Rookie of the Year award without a stop off in the minors, C) he had a .499 career slugging percentage, and D) he's one of just a half-dozen players in the division-play era to hit four home runs in one game. You'd think, "Whoa, that guy must have been one of the great sluggers of modern times." Nope, he was actually one of the great disappointments of modern times. He never hit

bob horner

Played From: 1978–1988
(Also played 330 games at 1B)
Teams: Braves, Cardinals
Career Record: .277 Avg., .340
On-Base Pct., .499 Slug Pct., 1,047
Hits, 218 HR

more than 35 home runs in a season, never drove in 100 runs in *any* season, never led his league in any offensive category, and batted .091 in his only postseason (1982). Granted, on any given swing of the bat, Horner could whomp one a long ways. But on any given swing of the bat, he was also a decent bet to pull a rib-cage muscle. His career was one gigantic string of nonstop injuries and other mishaps—at least some of them tied to the fact that he wasn't exactly a fitness freak. So for Horner to have landed in the big leagues so fast and still wind up with only 218 career homers defines him as a guy who never lived up to the buzz that hovered over him for most of his career.

4. GARY GAETTI

If Gaetti could just have cloned his 1987 season for the next decade or so, he'd be headed for Cooperstown, not this dubious list. Now *that* was a season: 31 homers, 109 RBIs, a Gold Glove, an ALCS MVP award, and a World Series parade. That's the Gary Gaetti a lot of people remember. But by the time this man was done, after 20 seasons, the Rest of the Story sure wasn't as picturesque as the warm glow of 1987, his four Gold Gloves, and his 360 career homers

gary gaetti

Played From: 1981–2000
(Also played 138 games at 1B)
Teams: Twins, Angels, Royals,
Cardinals, Cubs, Red Sox
Career Record: .255 Avg., .308
On-Base Pct., .434 Slug Pct., 2,280
Hits, 360 HR

would suggest. In fact, of all the players in history with that many home runs, *not one* had a lower lifetime OPS than Gaetti (.742). Only two (Dave Kingman and Joe Carter) had lower career on-base percentages than Gaetti's .308. And just the aforementioned Graig Nettles had a lower career batting average or slugging percentage than Gaetti (.255 and .434, respectively). Oh, and one more thing: there are only seven players in the Thousand More Strikeouts Than Walks Club—but Gaetti barely missed that one, too (1,602 whiffs, 634 walks). He is, I have to admit, yet one more guy I don't enjoy lumping with the overrated crowd, because Gary Gaetti is one bright, likeable, amiable guy. But can that help him escape overrated purgatory? Guess not.

5. HOWARD JOHNSON

I'd love to love HoJo, just for being the most famous player ever with the same name as a hotel chain. (And that's official. Phil Hiatt had spelling issues. And Dave Hilton only matched up his last name.)

howard johnson

Played From: 1982–1995
(Also played 273 games at SS,
217 games in OF)
Teams: Tigers, Mets, Rockies, Cubs
Career Record: .249 Avg., .340
On-Base Pct., .446 Slug Pct., 1,229
Hits, 228 HR, 231 SB

I'd also love to love HoJo for the other good stuff he had going for him. Bet you didn't know that, aside from members of the Bonds family, he's the only National League player ever with more than two 30-homer, 30-steal seasons. (He had three of them.) And unless you're president of the Ripper Collins Fan Club, I'm positive you didn't know that HoJo and the Ripper (1934) are the only switch-hitters ever to lead the NL in homers. (Johnson did it in 1991.) So how'd he tumble into the overrated half of this chapter? Hey, did you get stuck in the hot-dog line at Shea in the top of *every* inning of HoJo's career? This man could light that "E" light faster than the stadium electrician. Of the 86 men in modern history who played 1,000 games at third base, Howard Johnson finished dead last in career fielding percentage

(.929). And besides that 30–30 Club, HoJo joined one other club in 1991—the 30–30–30 Club (Homers, Steals, and *Errors*). That's one club that doesn't need to rent out Carnegie Hall for its meetings—since Howard Johnson is the *only* member.

The Most Underrated Third Baseman of All Time

RON SANTO

Only about 500 people in the world get to vote in the Baseball Hall of Fame election. I'm one of them. So I'm always aware, when I hold that ballot in my hand, that this is about more than a list of names. This is about lives and legacies. Those lives, those legacies, are changed forever by the results of those elections.

So from the day that ballot arrives in the mail to the day I fill it out, those names, those lives, those legacies grab a little chunk of my brain and hold on so tight, you'd think they were stamped on a winning Powerball ticket. They pinball around up there for weeks—until I've finished the momentous debate that revolves around every one of them: Yes or no? Hall of Famer or not?

I've learned, in a decade and a half as a voter, not to answer that question too quickly. And I know exactly who taught me that lesson.

Ron Santo.

My first year as a Hall voter was 1989. Santo's name was on that ballot. I left the box next to his name unchecked. Little did I know it would be a life-altering experience. (Author's note: all my life, I've been waiting to type a line like that. It just sounds so *book*-like. Didn't Dustin Hoffman's character teach a whole course on "Little Did He Know" in *Stranger Than Fiction*? I'd better alert him. Okay, now back to our story.)

At the time, Santo hadn't played a baseball game in 15 years. His prime had come and gone long before I started covering baseball. So because it was my first year as a voter and I had the Hall of Fame fate of 30 players to weigh, I zipped past Ron Santo faster than I should have. I took a quick look at his numbers, but what I really did was something I've never allowed myself to do since: I went by first impression. A voice up there said Santo was only the fourth-best player on a Cubs team that never won anything. So how could he be one of the greatest players ever to play his position?

This is the logic hundreds of voters used for years to rationalize not voting for Ron Santo. But I admit now that I used it myself before I'd ever seriously thought it through. I didn't even know I'd done that until a couple of weeks later.

Ron Santo, conspicuously absent from the Hall of Fame, excelled on defense and put together an offensive streak of eight straight seasons with at least 25 homers and 90 RBIs. Before today's era of inflated numbers, only two other players accomplished that feat from the end of World War II to the end of Santo's career: Willie Mays and Hank Aaron. Photo courtesy of Getty Images.

So how did I figure it out? Well, let's just say it's not usually a good sign when talk radio changes your mind about anything—sports, politics, even your favorite lasagna recipe. But in this case, I was cohosting a talk show about the Hall of Fame when a caller began grilling me on why I hadn't voted for Santo. The more I explained myself, the more he thought my logic made less sense than Borat. So he decided to write me a letter, laying out the case for Santo with depth and passion. I'm still glad he did.

Here's what I know now about Ron Santo that I didn't know then:

1) It *is* possible to be the "fourth-best player on your own team" and still be a Hall of Famer. It's not as if Santo was the player/GM of the Cubs. He didn't arrange to be on the same club as Ernie Banks, Billy Williams, and Ferguson Jenkins. It just happened. There may be quotas on how many anchovies you can import from France. But there are no quotas on how many Hall of Famers can play on one team. So the only question is whether Ron Santo was a great player at his position in his era—not how his own greatness related to his teammates' greatness. But before I get to that question, let me remind the skeptics that it was Santo—not Banks, not Williams—who hit cleanup for those Cubs teams, from his third full season in the big leagues (1963) through his 11th (1971). And there was a reason for that. "Anytime things started to get tough," says Dodgers GM Ned Colletti, who grew up a Cubs fan in the 1960s, "you'd find yourself hoping it was Ronnie's turn to bat."

2) Ron Santo was almost certainly the greatest all-around third baseman of his time. Name *any* other third baseman from the 1960s you would rather have run out there than Santo. Maybe Brooks Robinson, if you ate a lot of crabcakes. And there's a case to be made for Ken Boyer, a similar player whose Cardinals teams at least finished first once in a while. But I'd still take Santo. Of the 23 third basemen who got to the plate 3,000 times during Santo's 15 seasons, he led all of them in homers, RBIs, runs scored, extra-base hits, walks, and times reaching base. Only Dick

Allen and Eddie Mathews outslugged him—but Allen was so awful defensively, he had to be moved to first base, and Mathews was done as a full-time player by the mid-1960s. Finally, let's put Santo's eight straight seasons of at least 25 homers and 90 RBIs in perspective. From the end of World War II through the end of Santo's career, only two players at *any* position had streaks longer than that: Willie Mays and Hank Aaron. This was not an age where 40-homer, 125-RBI seasons were as prevalent as bad sitcoms. So the only fair way to evaluate Santo's numbers is from the perspective of *his* time, not our time.

3) Ron Santo was even more underrated defensively than he was offensively. I didn't figure that out right away, either. By the time I became a voter, Mike Schmidt had broken all of Santo's National League glove-story records. And Brooks Robinson, who played in Santo's era, probably needed to add a floor to his house to hold all his Gold Gloves. So if you were someone like me, who hadn't seen Santo leather it up, you had no idea how good he was. But that's why I now make sure to take a closer look at *everyone* who appears on the Hall of Fame ballot. During the time Santo was in the big leagues, he not only led all third basemen not nicknamed "Brooksie" in assists, double plays, and total chances. He set or tied National League records for most years leading the league in every one of those categories. He won five straight Gold Gloves, in an age when the only other third baseman who did that was Robinson. So he didn't just have a *good* glove. He was the dominant glove man in his league at his position.

4) We shouldn't be keeping Ron Santo out of the Hall of Fame just because his team was allergic to October. No team in most of our lifetimes has been more creative in finding ways to avoid the World Series than the Cubs. But that didn't keep Jenkins, Banks, or Williams from barging into Cooperstown. So what's the excuse for using that argument to keep Santo out? The only reason to factor that in is that poor Ron Santo never got the opportunity to use that stage to show the masses how good a player he was. And

that had a lot more to do with the guys who pitched for his team than with the third baseman who would have given up deep-dish pizza for life to win it all just once.

It's now more than three decades since Ron Santo played baseball for the Cubs. He's still as beloved a figure as anybody who has *ever* played for the Cubs. In part, I know, that's because he became the voice of the Cubs. But there is more to that phenomenon than a radio microphone.

Santo may have been "the fourth-best player" on those Cubs. But really, says Ned Colletti, "he was the leader of those clubs. Yeah, he had Williams on one side of him and Banks on the other side, so he was protected in that lineup. But *he* also protected *them.* If you want to win, you have to have players who lead. And nobody

ron santo

Played From: 1960–1974
Teams: Cubs, White Sox
Career Record: .277 Avg., .362 On-Base Pct., .464 Slug Pct., 2,254 Hits, 342 HR

on those teams played harder, competed harder, or cared more than he did. They wouldn't have been the same team without him. He defined the personality of the club. He was the one everyone looked to."

Even after he took off that uniform, not even the men who were still wearing those uniforms could possibly have cared more whether the Cubs won or lost than Ron Santo. There is a classic scene in *This Old Cub,* the riveting documentary on Santo's life, that takes us back to the final week of the 1998 season: Cubs left fielder Brant Brown dropping a ninth-inning fly ball with the bases loaded. The Cubs losing a game in Milwaukee, 8–7, that they once led, 7–0. And the voice on the radio—Ron Santo's voice—is summing up the moment in two eloquent words: "Oh, nooooooooooooooooooooo." After the game, Santo's partner, Pat Hughes, heads for the clubhouse. What he finds, he says in the film, is "something that probably has not ever been seen before in a big-league clubhouse. I saw the *manager* trying to cheer up the *broadcaster* after the game."

All right, I know the compassion many of us feel for Ron Santo—at that moment, at every moment—has nothing to do with whether he's underrated or not. But I've already established that the guy was one of the great all-around talents of his time. His real story, though, is about something larger than that.

For a lot of people in this world, the Cubs are a walking laugh track, a Comedy Central compendium of collapses and calamities and bad billy-goat jokes. But there's a human side to that tale. And no one embodies it more than Ron Santo. All those great seasons. All that passion. For all those years. And now here he is, in his midsixties, still waiting for his just reward. He has had to have both legs amputated because of diabetes, a condition he battled his whole career. He has survived cancer and a quadruple bypass. There isn't much more he asks out of life. Just to see the Cubs win a World Series one stinking time. And to have his amazing lifelong dedication to his team and his sport recognized by the Hall of Fame.

Many years ago, a talk-show caller convinced me to look at Ron Santo's career from a different, more enlightened place. Hopefully, this tiny slice of baseball literature will cause a lot more people to do the same.

The Rest of the Top Five

2. EDDIE MATHEWS

Okay, how many people out there are aware that Eddie Mathews is one of the two or three greatest third basemen who ever played baseball? Fifty? Eighty? A couple of hundred, tops? It isn't many. That's for darned sure. And that's a bigger mystery than the Loch Ness Monster. Mathews leads all retired third basemen not named Mike Schmidt in homers, RBIs, OPS, extra-base hits, home-run ratio, and slugging. He leads all retired third basemen, period, in runs scored, 40-homer seasons (four), and .600-slugging-percentage seasons (three). And if you adjust Mathews's numbers to the parks and era he played in, he climbs over Schmidt, George Brett, Wade Boggs, and every third baseman in history in funky, adjustable stats like offensive winning percentage, runs created above average, and runs created above (his) position. So explain to me, please, how Mathews got left off the All-Century Team and needed *five*

eddie mathews

Played From: 1952–1968
(Also played 112 games at 1B)
Teams: Braves, Astros, Tigers
Career Record: .271 Avg., .376 On-Base Pct., .509 Slug Pct., 2,315 Hits, 512 HR

elections to make it into the Hall of Fame, huh? I don't care if this man played with Hank Aaron or Hank Williams. Eddie Mathews was so great, he shouldn't have been capable of being overshadowed *or* underrated.

3. DARRELL EVANS

What Bullwinkle Moose is to animation addicts, Evans is to underrated lovers everywhere. If there's such a thing as an underrated idol to these people, that's Darrell Evans, king of the underrateds. Bill James, in fact, once described him as "the most underrated player in baseball history." Obviously, I don't quite agree with that, or I'd have placed Evans number one on this list, imprinted his face on the cover and probably let him coauthor a few chapters. But I totally agree that Darrell Evans has been massively underappreciated. It's always dangerous to play the

darrell evans

Played From: 1969–1989
(Also played 856 games at 1B, 253 games at DH)
Teams: Braves, Giants, Tigers
Career Record: .248 Avg., .361 On-Base Pct., .431 Slug Pct., 2,223 Hits, 414 HR

comparison game, but here goes: Evans hit more home runs (414) than Duke Snider or Al Kaline. He had a higher OPS (.792) than Pete Rose or Cal Ripken. He had a higher on-base percentage (.361) than Eddie Murray or Don Mattingly. But somehow—probably because he became a first baseman/DH midcareer—this man got lost in somebody's shuffle. He got eight stinking votes in his only Hall of Fame election. So you'll never find him in Cooperstown. But he's the mayor of Underratedtown.

4. KEN BOYER

You'd be dead wrong if you thought Ken Boyer qualified for this underrated list simply because he was part of the least-heralded set of Tremendous Big-League Brothers ever. He actually had kind of an unfair advantage on that front—since he was one of 14 kids and one of *six* brothers who played pro baseball. So come to think of it, the Boyer brothers should have out-homered the Aaron brothers and DiMaggio brothers combined, shouldn't they? Nevertheless, bet you didn't know that Ken and Clete Boyer are still the only brothers in history to hit 150 home runs or more apiece. Trot that one out there at the old sports bar some night. But that's not why Ken

ken boyer

Played From: 1955–1969
(Also played 111 games in CF)
Teams: Cardinals, Mets, White Sox, Dodgers
Career Record: .287 Avg., .349 On-Base Pct., .462 Slug Pct., 2,143 Hits, 282 HR, 105 SB

Boyer's underrated time has come. It has come because this guy was a great do-it-all player, and nobody remembers that. Boyer and Ron Santo were the only third basemen in history to rip off at least seven straight seasons of 20-plus homers and 90-plus RBIs. And *both* of them did it while winning at least four Gold Gloves in a row. Well, if that doesn't impress you as much as it's intended to impress you, how 'bout this: the only other players to run off concurrent Gold Glove and 20–90 streaks that long at *any* position are Willie Mays and Andruw Jones. So I guess we can now rest *this* case.

5. SCOTT ROLEN

I always get this sense that people look at Rolen and think he somehow hasn't achieved all he was supposed to achieve. Huh? By the year 2015, unless he

scott rolen

Played From: 1996–2006 (active)
Teams: Phillies, Cardinals
Career Record: .285 Avg., .375 On-Base Pct., .515 Slug Pct., 1,454 Hits, 253 HR

tears 14 ligaments after crashing into FredBird, we'll be looking at this man as one of the greatest third basemen since the invention of third base. First off, brace yourself for this bulletin: Scott Rolen is on the road to becoming the best defensive third baseman of all time. Yeah, he has to win a slew of Gold Gloves to catch Brooks Robinson (who collected 16). But an ex-teammate of Robinson's told me once, "If I had to take one of them, I'd take Rolen." And Mike Schmidt, who won more Gold Gloves (nine) than any third baseman in National League history, says he has no doubt that Rolen is "better than I was." So that's that. And offensively, while Rolen can definitely be Mr. Streaky (see: World Series, 2004), he's piling up some serious numbers. By the end of the 2006 season, when he was still only 31, he'd climbed to within 110 extra-base hits of George Brett and within 107 homers of fifth place on the all-time third-base home-run list. If he maintains his .515 career slugging percentage, he'd rank number three among all third basemen on that chart, too. So that, ladies and gentlemen, does *not* constitute underachieving on his end. It constitutes underrating on our end.

CHAPTER 9

Shortstops

The Most Overrated Shortstop of All Time

PHIL RIZZUTO

Holy cow. I've done it now. It's times like this when writing this book gets way tougher than it probably looks from your beach chair. If all I had to do was pick the most underrated and overrated players in, like, the Federal League, I wouldn't care who the heck I called overrated. Let the great-great-great-grand-children sue me. But this is different.

I'm like just about everyone in our beautiful land who has ever had the pleasure of running into Phil Rizzuto, or listening to him make people laugh uproariously in a stadium press room, or just catching his one-of-a-kind broadcasting act on four decades' worth of Yankees telecasts. I always really, really liked the guy. How could anybody not like Phil Rizzuto? In New York, over the last half century, the Scooter might have been more popular than Mickey Mantle, Derek Jeter, Walt Frazier, Phil Simms, Toots Shor, and the pastrami distributor for the Stage Deli put together.

Holy cow. There was never any baseball-watching experience since the dawn of baseball-watching that was remotely like trying to follow Rizzuto's stream-of-conscious roller-coaster ride during the course of one ballgame. Here are just a couple of priceless highlights, as imparted by the brilliant book of Scooter verse, *O Holy Cow!*

- MAY 31, 1987—RON CEY FACING TOMMY JOHN
  "Oh, that's gone!…Holy cow!…Watch the—Look at the
  Penguin!…It's not gone.…I was watching him run.…Wait a
  minute.…When he hit it.…That was the funniest run I've ever
  seen."
- JULY 10, 1992—YANKEES SHORTSTOP ANDY
  STANKIEWICZ BATTING
  "And he hits one in the hole.…They're gonna have to
  hurry.…They'll never get him.…They got him.…How do you
  like that.…Holy cow.…I changed my mind before he got
  there.…So that doesn't count as an error."

Well, if that didn't count as an error, then can we get you to promise that this half of this chapter shouldn't be counted as any form of hatchet job on the Scooter? There is nothing personal about this selection, and there is nothing personal about the way it's written. Here's the spirit with which it *is* being written:

One thing that those of us who love baseball happen to love about it most is that we can debate it pretty much 24/7. And we'd debate it 25/8 if that were allowable. We debate everything about it. Everything. From who's the greatest center fielder ever to who's the worst-looking relief pitcher ever. Everything.

And there's no debate that gets us going more than this debate: "Who's a Hall of Famer and who's not?" That debate is matched only by its first cousin: "Who's not in the Hall who should be—and who's in the Hall who shouldn't be?" It's when the cousin shows up in the debate room that Phil Rizzuto tends to arrive about four seconds later.

Because I care about Rizzuto the human being, I've never been angry, outraged, or even unhappy that he finally made it into the Hall of Fame, 40 years after he stopped playing. Sheez, it was worth it for the induction speech alone. (Actual quote 20 minutes into the speech: "All right. This is it. Oh, no. Wait a minute—I forgot my whole career as an announcer.")

But this is where it comes time to face up to reality. And the reality is this: Phil Rizzuto is about as borderline a Hall of Famer as you can locate within the Cooperstown city limits.

In his 15 years on the baseball writers' ballot, he never got within 150 votes of being elected. He had to spend a whole decade on the ballot before he even cracked 100 votes in *any* election. He also never got more votes in any election than two shortstops of his generation—Pee Wee Reese and Marty Marion (neither of whom was ever elected by the writers). Then, after Rizzuto made it onto the Veterans Committee ballot, it took him another 13 years until he finally picked up enough votes to collect his plaque.

So if Rizzuto was a Hall of Famer, the writers who covered him never saw it. How do you ignore that fact of life? You can't. Now here come more facts of life:

Rizzuto got fewer hits (1,588) than any Hall of Fame shortstop in the live-ball era. Among "modern" Hall of Fame shortstops—men whose careers began from the 1940s onward—he's the only one who didn't rack up either

Phil Rizzuto, shown scoring in a game against the Red Sox, is one of the most borderline Hall of Fame inductees in the history of the process.

150 home runs *or* 150 stolen bases. Of the 19 men who played at least 750 games at shortstop during the 1940s and 1950s—*his* generation—he ranked only eighth in that group in batting average, seventh in on-base percentage, and 13th in slugging percentage.

Even if we apply some new-age sabermetrics to this analysis, that doesn't help, either. According to Lee Sinins's *Complete Baseball Encyclopedia*, a lineup of nine Phil Rizzutos, playing with an average pitching staff, would have compiled a winning percentage of only .494. And if we rank all shortstops of the 1940s and 1950s to see how many runs they created compared to the average shortstop, Rizzuto lands way down in 14th place (behind even Solly Hemus and Johnny Logan).

But you know what? There's no need to belabor this case. It's been made: with the bat, Rizzuto was just another guy in the lineup. I've heard all the tales about the little stuff he did—the bunts he laid down, the big bases he stole, etc. Even if we give him credit for being a greater force than the sum of his numbers, there is no way to argue he had Hall of Fame offensive stats or skills. I wish there were. Really.

phil rizzuto

Played From: 1941–1956
Team: Yankees
Career Record: .273 Avg., .351 On-Base Pct., .355 Slug Pct., 1,588 Hits, 38 HR, 149 SB

That means all his Hall credentials have to come from other parts of the game. Well, the Scooter was a terrific defensive shortstop. That's a given. In his book *Win Shares,* Bill James gave him an A+ as a defender—the same grade he gave Ozzie Smith. But remember, it was Marion, not the Scooter, who was regarded as the greatest defensive shortstop of Rizzuto's era. And other shortstops covered more ground. Of the nineteen 500-assist seasons by shortstops in the 1940s and 1950s, none were turned in by Rizzuto (whose career high was 458). So as good as he was, he was never Ozzie. He was never what Mazeroski became at second base. He was never the brand name for shortstop excellence.

Nevertheless, the Scooter was, without debate, a leader on a succession of tremendous teams—teams that went to nine World Series and won seven of them. And he did have two back-to-back seasons (1949–1950) that were so stupendous, he won an MVP award in one (1950) and finished second in the other. So obviously, the writers of his era saw there was more to the man than the stats on his baseball card.

But wait a minute. Holy cow. I almost forgot. Most of those very same writers never thought he was a Hall of Famer. What were those huckleberries thinking, anyway? Oh, wait. They apparently were thinking a whole lot more clearly than the Veterans Committee insiders who eventually did elect Rizzuto to the Hall, after relentless lobbying by his pals all over the game.

Being a Yankee, of course, comes with a phenomenal set of perks, at no extra charge. And by that, I don't mean all the pasta and parmigiana you can eat at Mama Leone's. It's actually pretty obvious what I mean. Being a Yankee can transport you to places you'd never go if you were, say, a Brewer. Being a Yankee can transport you all the way to the Hall of Fame induction stage. Being a Yankee can magically make people think you were a greater player than you really were. And when you reach the point where people decide you were a greater player than you really were—even if the word "great" can be used to describe you at any level—you know what happens next.

You wind up in a book like this, lumped in with the Most Overrated club. Being the relentlessly nice guy that I am, I took no joy in placing anybody in the Most Overrated half of this volume. But I can honestly say I felt worse about including Phil Rizzuto than anyone else in here. Am I a softy or what?

The Rest of the Top Five

2. MAURY WILLS

For one magical season, Wills was as disruptive and electrifying as any base-stealer has ever been. Look over his stat line from 1962 sometime. It's quite a sight—104 stolen bases, only 13 times caught stealing and 130 runs scored in a season in which he reached base only 261 times and got just 29 extra-base hits. That, friends, constitutes some big-time havoc-raising. It was baseball's first 100-SB season of modern times, and a season in which Wills broke Ty Cobb's single-season record of 96 steals, which had survived nearly half a

maury wills

Played From: 1959–1972
Teams: Dodgers, Pirates, Expos
Career Record: .281 Avg., .330 On-Base Pct., .331 Slug Pct., 2,134 Hits, 20 HR, 586 SB

century. There's only one problem with having a year like that, you know: you can't slap a frame around it, hang it in a museum, and quit. So even though many people's image of Wills froze in 1962, he stuck around for a whole 'nother decade. But he never scored 100 runs again, and only once stole more than 53 bases.

He never did walk much or learn to rope a ball up the gap, either, so his career on-base (.330) and slugging (.331) percentages are flat-out unsightly. But that one season was apparently enough to cement his reputation as a game-changer and a leader of the stolen-base revolution, because he averaged 112 Hall of Fame votes a year for 15 years. Well, luckily, the Overrated-Underrated Watch Force was paying attention. So this is where we step in to make sure you understand exactly what Maury Wills really was: A) a one-dimensional player who didn't do much with his only dimension after that one historic season and B) as overrated as any player of his time.

3. BUCKY DENT

Some people have their 15 minutes of fame. Bucky Dent rode one swing of the bat to a whole lifetime of fame. Okay, so maybe it hasn't been a watch-

bucky dent

Played From: 1973–1984
Teams: White Sox, Yankees, Rangers, Royals
Career Record: .247 Avg., .297 On-Base Pct., 321 Slug Pct., 1,114 Hits, 40 HR

out-for-the-paparazzi-and-run-for-governor, Arnold Schwarzenegger–esque kind of fame. But it's still pretty staggering for a man who played 12 seasons and never hit 10 homers, stole 10 bases, or scored more than 57 runs in *any* of those seasons. I'll be happy to concede that Dent was a very reliable glovester and did win a World Series MVP award in 1978. But

that doesn't change the fact that few players in history did less to earn their household-name-for-life trophy than Bucky Dent did. He's living proof that if you're wearing the right uniform (Yankees, of course) and you hit the right wind-blown fly ball in the right ballpark (Fenway) on the right day (one-game AL East playoff, 1978), and that fly ball just happens to inflict decades' worth of pain on the right set of cursified fans (Red Sox, naturally), you, too, can grow up to be famous—and appear in this very book.

4. LUIS APARICIO

A friend of mine was talking to a general manager one day about this book. And the first words out of that GM's mouth were, "You know who's *really* overrated? Luis Aparicio." So there. At least you know it's not just me. On one hand, Aparicio *wasn't* overrated down at the leather shop. He won nine Gold Gloves, the most by any shortstop ever till Osborne E. Smith came along. But his reputation as an offensive force, on the other hand? Nearly as over-inflated as Refrigerator Perry. To see that,

luis aparicio

Played From: 1956–1973
Teams: White Sox, Orioles, Red Sox
Career Record: .262 Avg., .311 On-Base Pct., .343 Slug Pct., 2,677 Hits, 83 HR, 506 SB

though, you have to look beyond Aparicio's nine straight stolen-base titles, still the most in history, because he also owns another historic streak. He's the only everyday player ever to run off 13 straight seasons with an on-base percentage under .325. Want to get a feel for how hard that second streak is to compile? No active regular player finished the 2006 season with a streak longer than *one* year in a row. Yet even though he never scored 100 runs in any of his 18 seasons and he batted .300 just once, Aparicio was still considered one of the best leadoff hitters of his time. But, in reality, that tells you as much about his time as it does about him. The guy did play in an age when leadoff men had never read *Moneyball.* Just because he was a product of his era, however, doesn't mean he wasn't eligible for this list. It just kept him from ranking number one. That's all.

5. SHAWON DUNSTON

When you write a book like this, people just about stand in line to give you advice on how to select your candidates. Here's the advice one veteran coach gave me: "If a guy was a first-round draft pick, he's automatically overrated." The name Shawon Dunston didn't specifically come up, but it could have. In the first 35 years of the not-so-great June baseball draft, only three shortstops were taken with the first pick in the whole darned draft. One was Dunston (1982). The others were Alex Rodriguez (1993) and Chipper Jones (1990).

shawon dunston

Played From: 1985–2002
(Also played 242 games in OF)
Teams: Cubs, Giants, Pirates, Indians, Cardinals, Mets
Career Record: .269 Avg., .296 On-Base Pct., .416 Slug Pct., 1,597 Hits, 150 HR, 212 SB

Well, if A-Rod and Chipper were overrated, they were sure as heck a lot less overrated than Dunston, otherwise known as That Guy the Cubs Drafted When They Should Have Taken Dwight Freakin' Gooden. Dunston had two spectacular talents: 1) He could throw a baseball harder than 90 percent of the pitchers he played behind, and 2) he was one of the greatest hitters who ever lived—at avoiding walking. He somehow drew fewer walks in 18 seasons (203) than Barry Bonds drew in *one* season (232, in 2004). He's the only player in the live-ball era who had *three* seasons (of at least 350 plate appearances) with under 11 walks per year. And he had the worst strikeout-walk ratio (1,000 whiffs, 203 walks) of all time. We expect extraordinary things from our number one picks. And it doesn't get much more extraordinary than that.

The Most Underrated Shortstop of All Time

BARRY LARKIN

As you meander into the upbeat half of this chapter, look around you. Is there an expired credit card lying nearby? An empty candy wrapper? Maybe a business card from that salesman you blew off yesterday afternoon? Grab it now. Why? Because you'll want to stuff it into this page as a bookmark.

And why the heck is that? Because you'll be hunting for this section again in 2010, when Barry Larkin appears on his first Hall of Fame ballot. You'll want to commit the next couple of pages to memory—word for word, if you like—so that when you get into one of those Hall of Fame arguments that always seem to be busting out of your car radio or your frosted mug around Hall election time, you'll be ready.

Ready for what? you ask.

Ready to explain why Barry Larkin is a Hall of Famer, even though only about 11 people outside of the great metropolis of Cincinnati appear to realize it.

You can start with this tale: back in 1990, when Larkin was leading the Reds toward a World Series parade at age 26, ever-opinionated Cardinals manager Whitey Herzog was asked the kind of question we sportswriters love to toss around when we're killing time (which is pretty much *all* the time).

"If you were starting a team right now," Herzog was asked, despite the unlikely possibility he'd be allowed to start his own team in the middle of an actual season, "which player would you start it with?"

Whitey Herzog's insightful reply: Barry Larkin.

That was not, by the way, the only logical answer. There would have been about 50 other players most Americans would have expected Herzog to nominate first. Such as: Barry Bonds, Ken Griffey Jr., Mark McGwire, Tony Gwynn, Roger Clemens, Greg Maddux, Matt Williams, and Ryne Sandberg (to name eight). So that was one reason the choice of Barry Larkin should have hit you like a sledgehammer to the kneecap. The other big reason, though, was this:

Herzog's own shortstop, at the time, happened to be a man named Ozzie Smith.

It was Ozzie, after all, who was baseball's most famous and most beloved shortstop. So what does it indicate—even now—that Smith's own manager thought some other team's shortstop was his sport's number one franchise player?

Well, it could indicate that the Wizard might have been one for his last 37 at the time. But what it really indicates is that people inside the sport recognized that, even before he'd reached his prime, Barry Larkin was a special player.

Okay, here's another story. On June 28, 1991, Larkin crunched three home runs in the first five innings of a game against the Astros. All three homers came off the same pitcher—my good friend Jim Deshaies. That was a long, long, long time ago, friends. But it's a funny thing. To hear Deshaies talk about those three home runs, you would think he'd just finished trudging off the mound that day and was only now beginning to twist the shower knobs.

"He hit one to left, one to center, and one to right," Deshaies reminisced. "And he hit one off all three pitches I threw—fastball, slider, and curve."

But that's not even the part of that day Deshaies remembers best. The part he can't forget is that before the game a reporter from *USA Today* handed him a player survey, asking him to select the starters for the All-Star Game and other assorted honors.

"Not only did I pick Barry as the All-Star shortstop," Deshaies said. "I voted for him as the best player in the league. Then I went out and tried to prove myself right. It didn't make me look too good as a pitcher. But I looked a lot better as a scout."

Oops, he was too late for that, because it was the scouts—not the pitcher-scouts—who were the first to know about Barry Larkin. Eventually, though, everybody caught on. Ozzie may have been the fan favorite. But inside baseball, Larkin was long regarded as the National League's preeminent shortstop.

It's hard to imagine how much more Barry Larkin might have accomplished if he'd not had such bad luck staying healthy.

He came along after Cal Ripken but before the dawn of the Nomar–A-Rod–Jeter Age of Big-Bopper Shortstops. So Larkin played in an era where the standards for what constituted a superstar shortstop changed radically between his first game in the big leagues and his last. But the best way to describe him is that he was a slice of all the generations.

He wasn't your classic masher—but he did have a 33-homer season (1996). He topped 50 extra-base hits five times. And his .815 career OPS (on-base plus slugging) is almost indistinguishable from Miguel Tejada's.

Larkin wasn't a Jose Reyes kind of speedballer, either. But he *was* the only shortstop to steal 50 bases in any season in the 1990s. He was also the first shortstop to join the 30-Steal, 30-Homer Club (1996). And when he tried to swipe a base, he was so good at it, the umpires called him safe 83.1 percent of the time—the sixth-best percentage in history among players with at least 200 stolen bases.

Larkin may not quite have been Ozzie Cloned in the field—as if anybody was in the history of the solar system. But he did reel in three Gold Gloves in a row (1994–1996) after the Wizard decided it was okay for somebody else to win a few.

And unlike Nomar and A-Rod, Larkin never won a batting title. But he might have—if he hadn't blown out his elbow in one of baseball's harebrained relay-throw competitions before the 1989 All-Star Game. At a time when he was batting .342.

The truth is, Larkin might have done all kinds of cool stuff—beyond those 2,340 hits, 379 steals, and 198 homers—if he hadn't been one of the American Medical Association's favorite patients. This guy visited the disabled list almost as many times (14) as he visited Kentucky. Over 19 seasons, he injured assorted fingers, toes, elbows, shoulders, knees, ankles, and hamstrings. He hurt his back, his neck, his Achilles tendon, and his groin. So what part of his body didn't short-circuit on him at one time or another? His navel?

His health luck was so bad, in fact, he even hurt himself one day in 1992 while he was in the *on-deck circle*. How'd that happen? Home-plate umpire Terry Tata saw a bat lying on top of the plate as Larkin's teammate Bill Doran, was heading home to score on a single. So Tata whipped the bat out of the way—and bonked Larkin in the ankle with it. Once it was established that Larkin was going to live, Doran told Tata: "Next time, just let *me* step on the bat and break my ankle. Don't be hurting *Barry.*"

That quip, amusing as it was, delivers a message about what Larkin meant to the men he played with. He had such a presence, and such a quiet ferocity, in the way he played, he was to those Reds teams what Derek Jeter later became to the Yankees. Which explains how Larkin won an MVP award in 1995 with only 15 homers and 66 RBIs. Those aren't your classic MVP numbers. But to evaluate Barry Larkin, you always had to look beyond the standard stats, anyway.

barry larkin

Played From: 1986–2004
Team: Reds
Career Record: .295 Avg., .371 On-Base Pct., .444 Slug Pct., 2,340 Hits, 198 HR, 379 SB

Just as you can't measure what Jeter brings to the dance floor by counting up how many home-run trots he makes, you need to know where to look to properly gauge Larkin's greatness.

Let's start with accolades. Three Gold Gloves. One MVP award. More All-Star teams (12) than any shortstop in history except Ozzie and Ripken. Ten Silver Sluggers. And he won both major off-the-field awards that honor character and contributions to the real world—the Roberto Clemente and Lou Gehrig awards.

But the best way to put Larkin's career in its rightful perspective is to stack it up against what other shortstops were doing in the era in which he played. As Aaron Gleeman, of the always-incisive Hardball Times website, pointed out after Larkin retired, very few shortstops have ever outperformed their contemporaries like Larkin did.

Larkin's career batting average—over 19 seasons, remember—was .295. The average shortstop in that time hit .256. That's a difference of 39 points—or 15 percent.

Larkin's career on-base percentage was .371. The average shortstop's OBP was .317. So Larkin beat that by 54 points—or 17 percent.

Larkin's career slugging percentage was .444. The average shortstop slugged .361. So that's an 83-point gap—or 23 percent.

And that brings us to OPS (on-base plus slugging). Larkin (.815) was 137 points—or 20 percent—better than the average shortstop of his day (.678).

The only two shortstops of the last three decades who had an OPS that much better than their peers' were A-Rod (31 percent) and Garciaparra (25 percent), both of whom moved to other positions before end-of-career declines shrunk those gaps. Anybody notice any names that *weren't* on that list? Yep, Larkin even outperformed Ripken, who beat the average by just 18 percent. And the next-closest National League shortstop—Dave Concepcion—topped the competition by only 8 percent. So *that's* domination.

Because Larkin sustained that success for so long, an amazing statistical gizmo known as Lee Sinins's *Complete Baseball Encyclopedia* informs us that Larkin created 488 more runs during his career than the average shortstop. Know where that ranks in the history of baseball? How about *third*—behind only Honus Wagner and Arky Vaughan. Among shortstops who started their careers since the end of World War II, just seven other men even got *halfway* to 488.

So is Barry Larkin a Hall of Famer? Why would we even debate it for longer than, like, a minute and a half? After Larkin retired, I asked a longtime National League pitcher if *he* thought Larkin belonged in the Hall of Fame. He just started laughing.

"If you were in gym class and you had to pick a shortstop, and your choices were Phil Rizzuto, Ozzie Smith, Pee Wee Reese, or Larkin," the pitcher said, "you'd take Barry Larkin, wouldn't you? Heck, you'd take him and not even think twice. You'd take him and think, 'Boy, that was an *easy* decision.'"

So is Barry Larkin the most underrated shortstop of all time? That decision was just as easy.

The Rest of the Top Five

2. DEREK JETER

Best I can tell, the world is made up of two kinds of people. There are the folks whose computer programs or anti-Yankees genetic makeup tell them that Jeter is the most overrated athlete since the creation of our species. Then there are the rest of us. I actually thought about claiming that Jeter is number one on this most-underrated list, just to make my point to the millions of you

derek jeter

Played From: 1995–2006 (active)
Team: Yankees
Career Record: .317 Avg., .388
On-Base Pct., .463 Slug Pct., 2,150
Hits, 183 HR, 249 SB

who vociferously think otherwise. But I couldn't even convince myself to go that far. Nevertheless, Jeter, to me, embodies why someone had to write a book like this. We all need to recognize that there are elements of greatness which numbers can't quantify. And the essence of Jeter's greatness can't be measured by his zone rating, his OPS, or any of the other stuff his critics keep grumbling about. What makes Derek Jeter great is that he's one of those special human beings who lives for The Big Moment and knows precisely what that moment looks like when he sees it materializing beneath the light towers. (Think it's a coincidence that this man has hit .400 or better in eight different postseason series?) It's that quality which enables him to feed off all the Yankees nuttiness that reduces other guys to Fettuccini à la A-Rod. And the people who don't get that are the same people spouting the most irrelevant argument of all time—that if Derek Jeter were a Royal or a Devil Ray, he'd be just another player. If you've ever even thought that, boy, have you missed the point. Derek Jeter doesn't merely *happen* to be a Yankee. He's the *heart* of the Yankees. And if you don't comprehend why that's a big deal, I'd like to thank you for helping me justify one more paragraph in this book.

3. ERNIE BANKS AT SHORTSTOP

If you could have sworn it was only a couple of chapters ago that this same book was calling Banks overrated, there's good news. That's *not* because you consumed too many pitchers at happy hour. It's because Derek Jeter isn't the only great player who proves a guy can be thought of as both underrated *and* overrated. But nobody proves that better than Ernie Banks. Since we told you at one point how he was an overrated first baseman, it's only fair that we make it up to him by reminding you how underrated he was as a shortstop. Back in the 1950s, shortstops weren't supposed to bop 40 homers a year. In Banks's time as a

ernie banks at shortstop

Played From: 1953–1971
(Played 1,125 games at SS,
1953–1961)
Team: Cubs
Career Record: .274 Avg., .330
On-Base Pct., .500 Slug Pct., 2,583
Hits, 512 HR

shortstop, in fact, the average National League shortstop didn't even average *10* homers a year. So now try to digest what it meant back then that Mr. Cub cranked 40 home runs *five times* in *six years*, between 1955 and 1960. How many times had all the other shortstops in history hit 40 before Ernie did it? Correct answer: *zero*. Sheez, how many shortstops have even done it *since*, for that matter? How about two—A-Rod (six times) and Rico Petrocelli (once)? So if you've ever wondered how a man could win back-to-back MVP awards for two teams (the 1958 and 1959 Cubs) with sub-.500 records that finished a combined 33 games out of first place, now you know. Because Ernie Banks was one of the greatest shortstops of anybody's time.

4. OMAR VIZQUEL

Vizquel is yet one more player who can ignite the epic he's-overrated–no-he's-underrated tug o' war that has made this book the surefire best seller it's destined to be (assuming all the other publishers in America forget to publish any other books for the next year or so). His critics blab on about how he's no Ozzie defensively. (And who *is*, exactly?) And with the bat, he doesn't fit with the new generation of mashing shortstops, either. But Vizquel is another guy whose career can't be judged by sabermetrics alone.

omar vizquel

Played From: 1989–2006 (active)
Teams: Mariners, Indians, Giants
Career Record: .276 Avg., .342 On-Base Pct., .360 Slug Pct., 2,472 Hits, 73 HR, 366 SB

Is it some kind of mirage that he's won 11 Gold Gloves—a trophy collection topped by only two infielders in history (Brooks Robinson and Ozzie)? And even if he can't touch the Wizard in range factor, name any infielder *ever* with better hands than Vizquel's. He's the only shortstop since 1900 with *eight* seasons of more than 135 games played and fewer than 10 errors. (Next-closest: Ripken, with three.) And how 'bout this: in three of those seasons, Vizquel made *five* errors or fewer. All the other shortstops who have ever trotted out there have had three seasons like that *combined*. Meanwhile, you might want to check his offensive numbers again, because Vizquel has a realistic chance to wind up as (gulp) the all-time leader in hits *and* runs among men who spent their whole careers playing shortstop. So if you'd like some time to rework your he-ain't-that-good data, we can review all the stuff he couldn't do at his Hall of Fame induction.

5. ALAN TRAMMELL

A true confession: I don't vote for Trammell for the Hall of Fame. Which is one reason he doesn't rank higher on this list. But I'm still allowed to think

alan trammell

Played From: 1977–1996
Team: Tigers
Career Record: .285 Avg., .352
On-Base Pct., .415 Slug Pct., 2,365
Hits, 185 HR, 236 SB

he's underappreciated—possibly even by me. Think about this: suppose Cal Ripken had just had the good sense to spend his whole career at third base. Would we look at Trammell as the greatest American League shortstop of his era? Of course, we would (assuming Robin Yount goes down as a two-position hybrid). Now granted, that's a ridiculously moot point, since Ripken didn't exactly cooperate. But it's still true. Trammell won four Gold Gloves (more than all but five shortstops in history), so you know he caught the ball. And offensively, he ranks in the top five among post–World War II shortstops in OPS, slugging, on-base percentage, home runs, and RBIs. I can even get all futuristic on you and check his runs created compared to the other shortstops of his era—where he's second only to Ripken. So why don't I vote for him? Because some of those numbers come from the sheer accumulation of 20 respectable seasons, only one of which (1987) qualified as truly great. But Trammell's biggest problem is that, like a lot of the best players of the 1980s, his numbers look worse in comparison to today's big boppers than they did at the time. And that's an injustice I can only fight by including him on this prestigious Most Underrated list.

CHAPTER 10

Left Fielders

The Most Overrated Left Fielder of All Time

LOU BROCK

Thanks to the dubious miracle of nationally publicized email addresses, I've learned something about the ardent, tenaciously loyal baseball fans of St. Louis:

Don't mess with *their guys.*

In St. Louis, I've come to understand, *their* Cardinals take on a special sacred status, similar—but not identical—to Moses after he parted the water, Joan of Arc after she helped liberate France, and Johnny Damon after he de-cursified Red Sox Nation. We're talking love, worship, devotion ... and willingness to dye their bodies red from hair to toenails. That sort of thing.

And if those of us who don't have a vat of red dye handy should fail to love *their guys* as much as they do, uh-oh. Then, obviously, we hate them. We're out to get them. And we're conspiring with all the other media types on earth to hate them. Obviously.

Those emails come flying in, by the dozens, by the hundreds, when we write the wrong thing or say the wrong thing. And by that, I don't mean *ripping* one of *their guys.* I mean merely not loving them enough. Like if we suggest Albert Pujols is only the *second*-best player in the league instead of

The Very Best, for instance. (*Emailer alert:* the previous sentence was hypo-thetical and not intended for literal consumption.) Then, we hate them. Obviously.

So before I tread delicately into the rest of this chapter, can I say, for the record, that I do not hate, nor have I ever hated, St. Louis, the Cardinals, Cardinals fans, Cardinals management, Cardinals concession stands, Cardinals grounds-crew members, the College of Cardinals, Ryan Adams's backup band (Ryan Adams & the Cardinals), or actual birds that even resemble a cardinal? In truth, I greatly admire the whole scene. All that passion for one team, in my sport? It isn't possible to hate that. Is it? I'll confess that, as mascots go, I'm not wild about FredBird. But please forgive me for that. I beg you.

And now I'll also ask you to forgive me for the choice of Lou Brock as number one on this overrated list. What I'll mostly ask, though, is that you hear me out on this. Theoretically, we're so deep into this book that I should have firmly established by now what overrated is and isn't. Hopefully, I've proven that overratedness is a fuzzy concept that doesn't have to represent an insult. In part, in fact, it's actually a compliment, because it means many millions of ordinary citizens have a high opinion of the fellow they're overrating. So when I say a guy is overrated, it's not the same thing as saying he should have been a clarinet player, not a baseball player. Not even close.

You can be a great player and still be overrated. You can be a Hall of Famer and still be overrated. This book is more about dividing myth from reality than it is about defining who's a legend and who couldn't wash Lou Gehrig's socks. If you haven't caught on to that by now, either I've failed in my mission or you've been listening to way too much talk radio.

So I'm glad to give Lou Brock credit for everything he was as a baseball player. He was the all-time stolen-base champ once (with 938), before Rickey Henderson dethroned him. And he was the single-season stolen-base champ in the pre-Rickey era, too (with 118, in 1974). I happily salute him for both of those feats. Maybe his most impressive achievement is one almost nobody talks about—swiping 50 bases or more 12 seasons in a row. It's proof that Brock took forever to wear down, that he kept those legs pumping long after most base stealers began picking their spots. I don't minimize the value of that, believe me.

And unlike many players known for their legs, Lou Brock's idea of hitting didn't consist of trying to beat out three 42-foot squibbers every game. This man didn't get 3,023 hits by accident. Of the 10 players in history with at least 700 stolen bases, only Henderson and Ty Cobb got more extra-base hits than Brock (776). He gets points for that, too.

For all the speed that enabled Lou Brock to become the most prolific base stealer the game had ever seen, you would think he would have been able to play left field a little better.

Two other claims to fame have also stoked Brock's reputation. One was that he was on the right end of one of the most lopsided trades in history—the 1964 deal that sent him from the Cubs to the Cardinals for a package led by pitcher Ernie Broglio (whereupon Brock became a Hall of Famer and Broglio won seven more games the rest of his career). The other was Brock's three sensational World Series (1964, 1967, and 1968). The everlasting image of Lou Brock is of a man with a .391 career World Series batting average, who crammed 14 stolen bases, four homers, and 16 runs scored into 21 Series games. As everlasting images go, that'll work.

But you're no doubt asking: when do we start saying stuff like "on the other hand" and "yeah, but?" Well…um…now, as a matter of fact.

On the other hand (see, told ya), in baseball we latch onto our magic numbers. Sometimes we latch onto them with a little more reverence than we should. And Lou Brock gives us a great excuse to examine one of the most magical numbers—3,000 hits.

Look, there are no lousy players in the 3,000-Hit Club. But that doesn't mean everybody in it is Ty Cobb, either. So take a closer look at that club. Here's what you'll find:

Of the 25 club members, Brock ranks *last* in OPS (on-base plus slugging percentage). How'd that happen? Because he didn't walk much *or* hit many home runs. That's how. Only Pete Rose (a far more feverish count-worker) had a lower slugging percentage than Brock. Only Roberto Clemente (who never walked and got "only" 3,000 hits on the nose) reached base fewer times than Brock. Just Cal Ripken Jr. and Robin Yount—two men who spent much of their careers at a premier defensive position, shortstop—had a lower on-base percentage than Brock.

This would be a good time for all you Lou Brock fans to protest that none of those numbers factor Brock's base-stealing talents into the equation. Valid protest. So let's bring a Bill James statistic, runs created, into our discussion, because it *does* take stolen bases into account—but also deducts for strikeouts and times caught stealing.

So guess what? We used our favorite statistical gizmo—Lee Sinins's *Complete Baseball Encyclopedia*—to examine all the Mr. 3,000s in that department. And Brock actually fared even worse.

Sinins invented a variation on runs created known as runs created above position (RCAP), which compares how many runs a player created with the number created by an average player at his position in his era. Unfortunately, not only does Brock finish last in this group in RCAP, he'd need a telescope to see *next-to-last.*

The computer estimated that Brock created only 56 more runs during his career than the average outfielder, believe it or not. That's 186 runs lower than the next-lowest name—Dave Winfield. There's no other gap even close to that large between any other two names anywhere on the list.

lou brock

Played From: 1961–1979
(Also played 240 games in RF,
115 games in CF)
Teams: Cubs, Cardinals
Career Record: .293 Avg., .343
On-Base Pct., .410 Slug Pct., 3,023
Hits, 149 HR, 938 SB

Wait. Don't start pounding away on those emails yet. Can we talk this out first? This isn't some nit-picky attempt to dump on Lou Brock by comparing him to The Greatest Hitters Who Ever Lived. It just gives us more insight into the stuff nobody noticed that Brock didn't do. That's all.

Here's more: there are 62 outfielders in the Hall of Fame. Brock had the lowest on-base percentage (.343) of all of them. But only two of those 62 struck out more times than Brock did (1,730)—Reggie Jackson and Willie Stargell. At least those two guys combined to hit 1,038 homers, so there was a decent rationalization for all that whiffing.

Brock, however, hit only 149 home runs and led off for most of his career. He was even regarded as the greatest leadoff hitter of his generation. So isn't it slightly shocking that the quality of his at-bats wasn't a little better than this? He was a leadoff man who struck out more than Mickey Mantle but walked less than Mark McLemore. That isn't quite how you'd design the ideal leadoff monster in the lab.

But we've actually spent too much time here breaking down Brock's offensive issues. In reality, his only serious black mark as a player was that his glove wasn't gold.

"When he first came up with the Cubs," said one longtime scout, "I said, 'This guy's so fast, why isn't he playing center field?' But the more I watched him, the more I realized he just didn't have good defensive instincts. He never anticipated. He never got jumps. He didn't have that feel you need to play defense."

And that's a fact of life we don't need any statistical creations you never heard of to prove. Lou Brock led either all the outfielders or all the left fielders in his league in errors *nine* times. Over his 11 peak seasons, from 1964 to 1974, he averaged 13 errors a year—and committed nearly 50 more errors than any other outfielder in the whole sport. Even more puzzling, if you compute his range factor (his total chances per nine innings), he somehow covered less ground than the average left fielder—and he might have been *the fastest man in the game.*

"There's a difference between how you use speed on the bases and how you use it in the outfield," said the same scout. "When you steal bases, you're running in a straight line. But in the outfield, you're chasing balls over your head, balls on angles. So you need that instinct. The thing about Lou Brock was, he didn't have that ability to adjust."

In a perfect world, where people don't debate stuff like overrated and underrated, there would be no reason to care about this now, more than a quarter century after Brock's last game. We'd conveniently forget *everybody's* shortcomings and just wax on forever about all the things they were great at. But one of the best parts of being a real sports fan is that we never stop debating *anything*. That's what makes a book like this possible.

So it's also what makes it possible for books like this to describe players as great as Lou Brock as overrated—but only in a myth-versus-reality way. Remember that. It doesn't mean I don't love him, you, all past and present Cardinals fans, future Cardinals fans who have neglected to be born yet, and, okay, even FredBird. Just doing my job here, writing a book that will inspire you to think and debate for many pleasurable hours and days and weeks to come. Got that? Great. Now start typing those emails.

The Rest of the Top Five

2. JOE CARTER

All right, so I come from Philadelphia. And yes, Joe Carter once inflicted voluminous pain on the city of Philadelphia with one of the most famous

World Series home runs ever bashed (Game 6, 1993). But that's a minor coincidence that has zilch to do with his presence on this overrated list. That presence has more to do with the opportunity Carter presents to explore what an overrated stat RBIs can be. In the 12 seasons from 1986 to 1997, Carter drove in 100 runs 10 times. Once upon a time, he no doubt thought all those 100-RBI seasons would be his Hall of Fame entry pass. Instead, he got 19 votes—not even enough to keep him on the ballot, let alone get him elected.

joe carter

Played From: 1983–1998
(Also played 624 games in RF, 432 games in CF, 308 games at 1B, 175 games at DH)
Teams: Cubs, Indians, Padres, Blue Jays, Orioles, Giants
Career Record: .259 Avg., .306 On-Base Pct., .464 Slug Pct., 2,184 Hits, 396 HR, 231 SB

So what happened? The voters saw past the RBI column. That's what. Carter may have had as many 100-RBI seasons as Willie Mays. But that *doesn't* inherently make him one of the great clutch forces in history. In all those 100-RBI seasons, he hit .300 with runners in scoring position in exactly *one* of them. And when those sharp analysts from Baseball Prospectus ranked the 50 "worst" 100-RBI seasons since 1972 in their *Baseball Between the Numbers* book, Carter made the list five times—including three of the worst eight. Now, Joe Carter was a terrific guy who played baseball hard, represented it well, and lived out a magical October moment. But his career on-base percentage (.306) and slugging percentage (.464) were lower than Dean Palmer's, Jesse Barfield's, and Leon Durham's. So we would like to thank him for serving as human proof that RBIs aren't everything your grandfather cracked them up to be.

3. VINCE COLEMAN

If we rated baseball players with a stopwatch, Babe Ruth would have nothing on Vince Coleman. The guy was a human track meet. In his last two minor league seasons, he stole 145 bases in one and 101 in the other. Then he got to the big leagues and topped 100 three years in a row. He was so unstoppable, Reds pitcher Chris Welsh once threw to first 19 times after Coleman reached base in a game in 1986—after which the man stole second, anyway. But baseball, as you may have noticed, is slightly more complicated than the 100-meter dash. And it was those complications that earned Coleman this exalted spot on

vince coleman

Played From: 1985–1997
(Also played 155 games in CF)
Teams: Cardinals, Mets, Royals,
Mariners, Reds, Tigers
Career Record: .264 Avg., .324
On-Base Pct., .345 Slug Pct., 1,425
Hits, 28 HR, 752 SB

the overrated list. He was a leadoff man who piled up twice as many strikeouts (960) as walks (477). He was also a leadoff man with a .324 career on-base percentage. (Worse then Jeff Reboulet!) He was a disappointing outfielder who led his league in errors four times. And his "coup de disgrace"—tossing a lit firecracker at autograph seekers who surrounded his car—didn't quite make him the number one model for fan friendliness. So add Coleman to the list of sprint champs whose big SB numbers hid their other flaws for years—until our Overrated-Undercover Unit finally tracked them down and splattered them all over these very pages.

4. LONNIE SMITH

No player in history has a funkier October claim to fame than Lonnie Smith. Who's the only guy to play in a World Series for four different teams? Here's

lonnie smith

Played From: 1978–1994
Teams: Phillies, Cardinals, Royals,
Braves, Pirates, Orioles
Career Record: .288 Avg., .371
On-Base Pct., .420 Slug Pct., 1,488
Hits, 98 HR, 370 SB

your man. But what does that mean, exactly? In his time, Smith was portrayed as a "winner." Here, though, is what he really was, according to one of our scouting buddies: "He's Phil Linz. He's got a lot of rings, but only because he happened to play on teams that won a lot." Great quip. But not an exact comparison. Linz was just a hanger-on with three Yankees World Series teams in the 1960s. Lonnie Smith was a big reason at least *one* of his teams won—the 1982 Cardinals. (Heck, he finished *second* in the MVP voting.) But most of the rest of Smith's career was a never-ending, he's-up, he's-down crash-fest between his strengths and his failings. He stole a ton of bases, but he often had issues just trying to *run* the bases. (See: 1991 World Series, Game 7.) He scored 120 runs once (1982) but never even scored 100 after that. He hit 21 homers once (1989), but never even hit 10 in any other season. And in the outfield, hoo boy. I'm willing to bet (in part because nobody keeps stats on this) Lonnie Smith fell down more than any guy who ever played the outfield. Best explanation ever for that: "He runs so fast," said his late, great general manager in Philadelphia, Paul Owens, "his feet can't catch up with the rest of him."

5. GEORGE FOSTER

As great baseball jobs in the 1970s go, batting cleanup for the Big Red Machine was way up there—right below Charles O. Finley's elephant trainer. Hitting in that very cleanup spot, George Foster led his league in RBIs three years in a row (1976–1978), won an MVP award (1977), and became the only man to pound 50 homers in any season between 1965 (Willie Mays) and 1990 (Cecil Fielder). Trouble was, Foster's career kept going—until, in 1982, the Mets decided to trade for him and construct a team around him. Which turned out to be not quite

george foster

Played From: 1969–1986
(Also played 267 games in CF, 178 games in RF)
Teams: Giants, Reds, Mets, White Sox
Career Record: .274 Avg., .338 On-Base Pct., .480 Slug Pct., 1,925 Hits, 348 HR

as brilliant an idea as drafting Dwight Gooden. Over the next four and a half seasons, Foster mustered a piddly .728 OPS (lower than Reid Nichols!) and .422 slugging percentage (lower than Oddibe McDowell!)—and wound up getting released. "He hit a lot of home runs in Cincinnati when he was protected in that lineup," said one scout. "But when he was supposed to be The Man in New York, he had one of the most precipitous dropoffs I've ever seen." Hey, there's nothing like a precipitous dropoff to land you on one of these Overrated lists.

The Most Underrated Left Fielder of All Time

STAN MUSIAL

Stan Musial ought to be a character on *Lost.* For that matter, he could easily have been the inspiration for *Lost.* I keep waiting, one of these weeks, for Locke and Sayid to stumble onto another secret hatch—and find Musial trapped inside, watching the 1946 World Series film over and over and over.

Can there really be any better explanation for how virtually our entire culture (not including the state of Missouri) has managed to lose track of one of the greatest players who ever played? Cultural amnesia is an inexplicable phenomenon. But it has happened to Stan Musial, the legend America forgot.

Oh, maybe people know his name. (Who, after all, is the *second*-most famous human being named Musial?) Most of them even know he was a slightly better player than Putsy Caballero. But I can't think of any all-time great in any sport who gets left out of more who's-the-greatest conversations than Stan Musial.

Let's start with the All-Century Team. Tell me Musial didn't really finish 11th in the outfield voting. Tell me he didn't really need an emergency act of the Boy Are These Voters Blockheads Committee to stampede to his rescue

One of life's great mysteries continues to be why people always seem to forget just how great Stan Musial was.

and add him to the team in order to avoid discrediting the whole process. Tell me this was simply due to some sort of hanging-chad-type mechanical glitch with the ballot itself. Please tell me this didn't really happen on the up-and-up. I'd sure feel a lot better.

Then there was Ken Burns's 914-part documentary on baseball in the mid-1990s. How much air time did Musial get in that otherwise remarkable epic? Twelve seconds? Possibly 18 if you count the credits? What's up with that? Apparently, it wasn't possible to work *all* the members of the 3,600-Hit Club (all four of them) into that opus. Maybe if it had been a 5,000-part series, the Man could have gotten his very own minute and a half.

And now our final beef—the never-ending Greatest Living Player debate. Look, I understand if, during the last four decades, people wanted to hand that crown to Joe DiMaggio or Ted Williams or Willie Mays. I'm not sure I can argue that Stan Musial ever deserved that GLP mantle more than those men. But how hard would it be to work him into the dialogue, at least? The spring after Williams died (2003), *Sports Illustrated* polled 550 active players and asked them to name the Greatest Living Player. It was terrifying enough that A-Rod got more votes than Mays and Nolan Ryan got more votes than Hank Aaron. But here's what really hurts: not only did Musial finish *eighth*, but he barely got more votes than Babe Ruth—whose "living player" credentials apparently weren't hurt by the minor technicality that he'd been dead for 55 years.

So when a man barely outpolls a dead guy in a poll where the only qualification for eligibility is "currently breathing," we Most Underrated authors know we've stumbled upon a truly superlative candidate. What we still don't get is how Stan the Man (also, by the way, the most underrated nickname ever) got so darned underappreciated.

"Part of it, in my opinion, is that Stan was a guy who never ran his mouth," said the universally respected *St. Louis Post-Dispatch* columnist Bernie Miklasz. "He's about as uncontroversial as you can be. A lot of old-timers keep their names prominent because they're always barking about stuff. Guys like Ted Williams, Bob Feller—they always had something to say. And don't get me wrong. I love it. But Stan was never a guy who went on talk shows and whined about how 'today's players couldn't even carry our bats.' He feels absolutely no need to protect his legacy or remind people how great he was. He may blow his harmonica, but he *doesn't* blow his horn."

Well, in that case, it's up to us to cue the bugles. Which is so easy, I almost feel guilty that I don't have to work harder to unearth Stan Musial's underratedness credentials. Just open a page of the ESPN Encyclopedia, and they'll bonk you over the head. Go ahead. Let's all try it.

Ooh. Sorry. I just regained consciousness. Now on with our show.

Only three men in history—Pete Rose, Ty Cobb, and Aaron—got more hits than Musial (3,630). Only three men—Aaron, Babe Ruth, and Lou Gehrig—drove in more runs (1,951). Just seven men scored more runs (1,949). Only Cobb, Tony Gwynn, and Honus Wagner won more batting titles (seven).

Just Aaron and Barry Bonds got more extra-base hits (1,377). Only Tris Speaker and Rose cranked out more doubles (725). Just Aaron accumulated more total bases (6,134). Only Aaron played in more All-Star Games (24). Only Cobb and Speaker had more seasons batting .300 (17). Pretty cool, huh? And we're just getting rolling.

Musial had such a good feel at the plate, he walked more than twice as many times (1,599) as he whiffed (696). That may not sound as incredible as it is—but only until you hear this: among all members of the 400-, 300-, or even 200-Homer Clubs, only he and Ted Williams can make that claim. And while Ted always thought *he* held the patent on Most Disciplined Hitter Ever, guess what? Musial struck out fewer times in 22 seasons than Williams did in his 19 seasons.

The Man can roll out a career batting average (.331), on-base percentage (.417), and slugging percentage (.559) so spectacular, he tops Willie Mays and Hank Aaron in *all three categories.* Musial also unfurled a .702 slugging percentage one year (1948)—a number no other National Leaguer matched between the 1930s and the 1990s.

And if you compare Musial's numbers to the other players of his own generation, they look even greater. His OBP was 84 points higher than the average hitter of his time. His slugging was 151 points higher. Add them together, then adjust for ballparks and generations, and Musial's "OPS-plus" figures out to 159—meaning it was 59 percent better than your typical player.

Over the last 65 years, just two retired players beat that: Ted Williams (190) and Mickey Mantle (172). So do the math on who *didn't* beat that. Yep, Mays, Aaron, DiMaggio— they're all in Musial's rearview mirror.

Some of Musial's foremost qualities, the numbers can't even capture. So let's go to the eyewitnesses. Tim McCarver, who played with the Man at the end of Musial's career, calls him "the greatest low-ball hitter in the history of the game." That's a big-time statement, but McCarver saw it with his own eyes. He saw it in August 1960, when Musial broke up a riveting pitchers' duel between the Cardinals' Ernie Broglio and the Pirates' Bob Friend by 7-ironing a Friend curveball deep into the seats of Forbes Field for a stunning, game-winning, twelfth-inning home run.

stan musial

Played From: 1941–1963
(Also played 750 games in RF, 325 games in CF, 1,016 games at 1B)
Team: Cardinals
Career Record: .331 Avg., .417 On-Base Pct., .559 Slug Pct., 3,630 Hits, 475 HR

"He won that game with a ball he hit off the *ground*," McCarver said, as incredulous now as he was then, as an 18-year-old rookie. "And the next day, around the batting cage, guys were still talking about it. It was the first time I ever heard anybody say, 'He hit it with a shovel.'"

Ted Williams, you know, probably wouldn't even have swung at a pitch he had to shovel. If it wasn't a strike, it wasn't his style. But Musial defined style in a very different way, on many different levels. Williams always had a thunder cloud following him. Musial just played baseball. He piled up astonishing numbers. But "everyone who ran into Stan," said McCarver, "was as affected by his grace, his humility, and his class as they were by his numbers."

As we look back on Musial now, our perceptions couldn't be more skewed. We think of him as having been overshadowed all his career—by Williams and DiMaggio in the '40s, by Mays, Aaron, and Mantle in the '50s. But back when Musial was playing, those shadows weren't anywhere near as wide or as dark.

If he was so overshadowed, how the heck did he make the All-Star team *20 seasons in a row* (not counting his year in the military), at four different positions? If he was so overshadowed, how did he become the first three-time MVP *in the history of the sport?* If he was so overshadowed, how did he finish in the top five *eight times in nine MVP elections* (1943–1952)—and keep accumulating top-10 finishes until age 42?

How? Because, like a few other men in this book, Musial was forgotten by folks in *our* time, not *his* time. He certainly wasn't forgotten by the people who played against him. After Williams's death, the *Rocky Mountain News* asked 35 Hall of Famers to name the Greatest Living Hitter. The man who got the most votes: Stan Musial.

So it's just the rest of civilization that stopped worshipping, or even Googling, this man. But why? Maybe, said Bernie Miklasz, it's because we're a highlight-driven generation, and Musial, great as he was, "didn't have that big signature moment."

DiMaggio had his hitting streak. Williams had .406. Mays had "the Catch." Aaron had 755. Mantle hit all those home runs that never came down. But Musial just had "a thousand little moments," Miklasz said. "He didn't have that signature moment that hangs up there in the sky."

Well, if it means anything to him, he can hang up there in our sky any time—golfing game-winning home runs deep into the section of the ballpark where the fans of the most underrated players of all time hang out. And by the way, have I mentioned lately how much I love all players from St. Louis? Sure do. But none more than Stan Musial.

The Rest of the Top Five

2. TIM RAINES

To sum up the brilliance of Tim Raines in his prime, let's point you back to spring training 1987. Why? Because Raines didn't take part in it. Not for one inning. Thanks to the owners' most overrated brainstorm of all time (a chapter in itself)—collusion—Raines spent the entire off-season as an unsigned free agent, even though he was the defending National League batting champ. So he spent the spring working out with a girls' high school track team, featuring, he said, "a couple of girls who were faster than me." He didn't get to rejoin the Expos until May. Whereupon he tripled on the first pitch he saw, hit a game-winning grand slam the same afternoon, and went on to lead the major leagues in runs scored—even though he wasn't allowed to play for a month. But hardly anybody remembers that, probably because hardly anybody remembers much of anything about what a tremendous player Raines was. He owns the best stolen-base success rate (84.7 percent) of all time. And he was the only player in history to steal 70 bases or more six seasons in a row (1981–1986). But Tim Raines was more than a base-burgling machine. He was such a versatile offensive force, he had a seven-year stretch (1982–1988) where he led the NL in walks, singles, doubles, *and* triples. And he's one of only four left fielders in the expansion era (1961–present) whose career on-base percentage (.385) was at least 50 points better than the average hitter of their eras. The others: Barry Bonds, Rickey Henderson, and Carl Yastrzemski. Had Henderson found another line of work, the world would recognize Raines as the greatest leadoff hitter of his era. Instead, Rickey is heading for the Hall of Fame, while poor Tim Raines is stuck hanging out with the other guys on this page. That's a bigger injustice than collusion.

tim raines
Played From: 1979–2002
(Also played 165 games in CF, 131 games at DH)
Teams: Expos, White Sox, Yankees, A's, Orioles, Marlins
Career Record: .294 Avg., .385 On-Base Pct., .425 Slug Pct., 2,605 Hits, 170 HR, 808 SB

3. MANNY RAMIREZ

Life is different on Planet Manny than it is on our planet. The season there definitely isn't 162 games long. Spring training starts whenever it feels right. And running to first base is always optional. But let's forget all that for a few sentences. The residents of Planet Earth are so fascinated with the resident of Planet Manny being Manny, they've overlooked something: Manny Ramirez is arguably one of the five greatest right-handed hitters who ever lived. The .300-.400-.600 Club isn't a group you'll ever find signing autographs at the mall. But the only right-handed members of that club—men with a career batting average over .300, on-base percentage over .400, and slugging percentage over .600—are Jimmie Foxx, Hank Greenberg, Albert Pujols, and Manny. And if we count just players who have

manny ramirez
Played From: 1993–2006 (active)
(Also played 900 games in RF, 256 games at DH)
Teams: Indians, Red Sox
Career Record: .314 Avg., .411 On-Base Pct., .600 Slug Pct., 2,066 Hits, 470 HR

been to home plate as many times as Ramirez, we're down to only Foxx and Manny. But there's more. Manny also owns a batting title, a home-run title, an RBI title, and a World Series MVP award. He's done something Ted Williams, Joe DiMaggio, and Barry Bonds never did—finish in the top 10 in *eight* straight MVP elections (1998–2005). And through 2006, Ramirez's career OPS (1.011) was 238 points higher than the average hitter of his time. Which means he ranks ahead of Willie Mays, Hank Aaron, Joe DiMaggio, and a cast of billions in that revealing department. Of course, those guys were slightly more interested in the other parts of the game than our man Manny. But there's a word we use to describe an all-time great whose off-the-field exploits dominate 98 percent of all conversations about him. And that word, naturally, is "underrated." You were expecting maybe: "discombobulated?"

4. RALPH KINER

Back in the days when I wrote a humor-tilted baseball-notes column for *The Philadelphia Inquirer,* I somehow became the world's foremost authority on Ralph Kiner. Not on any of the spectacular things he used to do at home plate, however. Just on the creative sentences that used to come out of his mouth when he was way too close to an open microphone. As a fabled Mets broadcaster, Kiner is a man who once got his *own name* wrong ("Ralph Korner"). He's a man who once told viewers that pitcher Keith Comstock had been "released by four different countries." And he's a man who once went to a pregame commercial by announcing: "We'll be back with Mets baseball right after this season is over." I once figured out I published 200 wacky quotes just like those over the years. But amazingly, Ralph never got mad at me. He even told the author of his biography to call me, just so they could get his *best* malapropping moments in there. So this is my way of making it up to him. Bet you didn't know Ralph Kiner, not Babe Ruth, was the only player to lead his league in homers (or tie for the lead) seven straight years. Bet you didn't know that between the demise of Ruth and the arrival of Mickey Mantle, Kiner and Jimmie Foxx were the only men who hit 50 homers more than once. Bet you didn't know that until

ralph kiner

Played From: 1946–1955
Teams: Pirates, Cubs, Indians
Career Record: .279 Avg., .398 On-Base Pct., .548 Slug Pct., 1,451 Hits, 369 HR

the 1990s wrecked *all* the good numbers, Kiner had the best home-run ratio (one every 14.1 at-bats) in National League history. Well, you know now that just because Ralph Kiner was overrated as a linguist doesn't mean he couldn't be underrated in this book.

5. MINNIE MINOSO

The question: which player got a hit in the 1970s, even though he'd already appeared on a Hall of Fame ballot in the 1960s? The answer: Minnie Minoso. Feel free to try that one out on your beer buddies some time. But after you do, please join me in wondering why nobody in Hollywood has made a motion picture on this guy's life. After all, how many players have played in the Cuban League in their teens, in the Negro League in their twenties, in the big leagues in their fifties, and in the Northern League in their seventies? There's only one. And it's the astounding Minoso. Evaluating just how good a career he had (or would have had) isn't easy, since he didn't reach the big leagues until age 28. But this man could *play*. He led the American League in stolen bases three times, in triples three times, in hits once (at age 37), in doubles once, in outfield assists three times, and in his specialty, getting hit by a pitch, 10 times. He won three Gold Gloves, had a .389 career on-base percentage, and made seven All-Star teams. Yet he's most remembered for coming out of retirement *three* different times (1976, 1980, and 1993) to get a few more swings in. Well, all those comebacks may have been publicity stunts. But his Most Underrated award here is anything but.

minnie minoso

Played From: 1949–1964
(Also played three games in 1976, two games in 1980)
Teams: Indians, White Sox, Cardinals, Senators
Career Record: .298 Avg., .389 On-Base Pct., .459 Slug Pct., 1,963 Hits, 186 HR, 205 SB

CHAPTER 11

Center Fielders

The Most Overrated Center Fielder of All Time

ANDRUW JONES

I was sitting in a makeshift press box in the grandstand of Yankee Stadium on October 20, 1996, the night the Legend of Andruw Jones erupted on America's stage.

I'll never forget it. In the first at-bat of the first World Series game this 19-year-old kid from Curaçao had ever seen, let alone played in, the phenom pounded a home run halfway to White Plains. One inning after that, he creamed World Series home run number two. That one landed in Monument Park, right in front of Mickey Mantle's No. 7.

Did Andruw Jones know how to make an entrance, or what?

There is a feeling we get when we watch an exhibition like this that defines why sports have such a magnetic pull on our souls. So many exhilarating thoughts explode inside our brains. Where did this guy come from? How do you spell C-U-R-A-Ç-A-O? Had anyone else ever done anything like this?

And then you contemplate the most exciting question of all:

Could something even *better* possibly be yet to come?

Was there any doubt that night that Andruw Jones was destined to be anything other than one of those special, charismatic, must-watch athletes who

Andruw Jones was baseball's best defensive center fielder for several years, but his focus has since changed to offense, causing his defense to slip dramatically.

would tug us in his direction for however many more years we were lucky to have him around?

He had just become the youngest player in history to hit a World Series home run, wiping someone named Mickey Mantle out of the record book. Counting his final swing of the National League Championship Series, Jones had just joined Reggie Jackson as the only men to hit October home runs in three consecutive at-bats. He was still a teenager. And this part of his game—offense—wasn't even the part he was best at. Phew.

His general manager, John Schuerholz, dropped his name into the same sentence as Hank Aaron that night. Was *that* where Andruw Jones was heading? Whoa.

Well, here it is, more than a decade later. And this guy owns nine Gold Gloves, more than any center fielder in history except Willie Mays (12) and Ken Griffey Jr. (10). There is also a 51-homer season on Andruw Jones's page in the *Baseball Register*. And five All-Star teams. And five 100-RBI seasons. All before he'd even turned 30.

So it's probably right about now that you're checking the beginning of this chapter to make sure that this fellow was really listed under the heading "Most Overrated Center Fielder of All Time." Yep. Sure was.

Which means you very well could be thinking next that anyone who would put something that debatable in an actual book must be the Biggest Mush Brain of All Time. Yep. Could be. But there *is* an explanation for this. I promise.

We'll start with a major confession: of all the chapters in this book, none came tougher than this one. That's because of what center field represents within the fabric of baseball. It's the position of Mays, Mantle, and DiMaggio. Of Cobb, Puckett, and Griffey. Those aren't just names on a lineup card. Those are names that conjure up magic. This is *the* glamour position in baseball. Nothing else is close.

So when it came time to pick the most overrated center fielder of all time, I found myself sifting through some truly spectacular names. You wouldn't believe some of the center fielders I considered, who were nominated by people all over the sport. The most astonishing name was this one: Joe DiMaggio. And I'll admit this now. I thought about it.

My first instinct undoubtedly matched your first instinct: what dope could make a coherent argument that Joe DiMaggio was overrated? Then I stopped. And mulled it over. If the essence of this book is its continuing quest to draw a big black line between myth and reality, then all the myths surrounding DiMaggio made him a player who could conceivably fit this debate.

Then, luckily for me, sanity kicked in. And not a paragraph too soon. Nine World Series won. The Hitting Streak. The highest slugging percentage (.579) of any retired right-handed hitter in history. Marilyn....What the heck. Was I nuts or something?

Then an old scout friend said the words that led me here: "I'll tell you the guy who isn't the player people think he is anymore—Andruw Jones."

Again, my first instinct was: no way. Then I took a closer look. And couldn't believe what I learned.

Andruw is a man who has built his reputation around his Gold Glove parade, his exceptional ability to glide around center field and suck sure-thing doubles out of the sky without overheating a single sweat gland. But while most of us weren't paying attention, Andruw was slowly, apparently impercep- tibly, losing the part of that gift that made him special.

From 1998 through 2002, he was still That Guy. He topped 400 putouts five years in a row. No outfielder had done that since Mays (1954–1958). He was The Best. Clearly. But since then? Not the same player.

He peaked at 493 putouts in 1999. He was still slurping up 461 in 2001. But by 2005 he was down to 365. In 2006 he was at 377. I tried looking at his total chances per game. Still way down. We're talking about 100 or so balls a year he wasn't getting to that he used to. *A hundred.*

I thought: that can't be right. A friend suggested maybe it was a function of the Braves' pitching staff. Maybe they were just throwing fewer fly balls than they used to. Great point. So I checked. Fortunately, there's a stat that measures that, too—zone rating (the percentage of balls fielded by a player in his typical zone).

So I called up the 2006 zone rating of all qualifying major league center fielders on ESPN.com. Guess who was *last* on the list? Yessir, Andruw. He also finished last in 2004. And fifth from the bottom in 2005. I kept check- ing. As recently as 2001, he *led* his league in zone rating. So obviously, we had a definitive trend on our hands. I then went back to the scout who started all this to report my findings.

"I first noticed it two or three years ago," he said. "Just from sitting there, scouting, watching balls dropping in that should have been caught. I'm not talking about balls that needed to be dived for. I'm talking about balls that should be caught."

I surveyed other scouts. They'd begun to see the same things. Not getting the same jumps. Not reacting. Not putting in the defensive effort he used to. His body getting thicker. A sudden obsession with home-run hitting over everything else.

"He *was* a great defender," said one scout. "He's slipped. People used to compare him to Mays and Mantle. I wouldn't put Andruw anywhere near those guys. Now he's become an offensive player, and his defense has suffered ever since."

But even Jones's big offensive surge has been misleading. Amazingly, one scout called him "not a very good offensive player...If he wants to hit a home run, he'll try to hit a home run at the expense of everything else."

andruw jones

Played From: 1996–2006 (active)
Team: Braves
Career Record: .267 Avg., .345 On-Base Pct., .505 Slug Pct., 1,556 Hits, 342 HR, 133 SB

He smoked 51 home runs in 2005, a very seductive number. But I checked every 50-homer season in baseball history. Again, I had a tough time digesting what I found.

Jones had the lowest batting average, slugging percentage, OPS, and park-adjusted OPS-plus that *any* player has ever had in a 50-homer season. He reached base fewer times than any 50-homer man ever. And if you take in the bigger picture, with Bill James's incisive runs-created stat, Andruw "created" fewer runs than any 50-homer man ever had. In fact, he created fewer runs that year with his 51-homer season than three hitters who didn't even have a *20-homer* season—Brian Roberts, Derek Jeter, and Brian Giles.

Yet Jones almost stole the MVP award from Albert Pujols. And, of course, he keeps raking in Gold Gloves. As if nothing had changed. As if he'd only been getting *better.*

"It's all perception," said one player who has played against Jones for years. "Perception is like muscle memory. People have a memory of you doing something. So you have to do something dramatically different to undo that memory."

Willie Mays basically announced he wasn't the same player anymore when he literally began falling down in the outfield. But Andruw Jones still *looks* the same. There's nothing "dramatically different" about those three extra fly balls a week he now just misses tracking down. It's only when we study the numbers and chart the trends that us folks who don't watch him closely—every day, every inning—start to catch on.

So how did he get to be overrated? This is precisely how. Look, there are worse commodities to have on your team than 50-home-run center fielders who have won nine Gold Gloves. And when Jones gets his shot at free agency after the 2007 season, I'm sure he'll find he's highly employable. Even a declining Andruw Jones in center still beats Brian Asselstine in center at his prime. But that isn't what this book is all about.

Overrated-underrated isn't a study in talent. It's a study of how what we perceive differs from what's actually going on out there. And Jones was good enough to turn himself into a fabulous poster boy for that study.

"I'm not detracting from what he *was*," said the scout who first nominated Andruw. "I'm just saying his reputation carried over when he started losing that range. The myth continued. And that's really what you're writing about, isn't it? The myths of baseball?"

It almost sounds like a National Geographic special—*The Myths of Baseball*. But don't consult your local listings. Consult *this* list, as Andruw Jones helps us Overrated-Underrated detectives apprehend yet one more mythmaker who was running around right before our eyeballs—and we'd never even noticed.

The Rest of the Top Five

2. HACK WILSON

If Hack Wilson had driven in 151 runs in 1930 instead of 191, he sure as heck wouldn't have a Hall of Fame plaque. He would be more like the Dante Bichette of his generation—a guy who had a five-year run of photogenic numbers in an age in which *everybody* had photogenic numbers (unless they had two broken arms or something). But 191 RBIs changed everything for old Hack. Now that almost all our treasured home-run records have been de-romanticized, 191 RBIs might stand as the coolest single-season record left—a record nobody has even taken a decent run at since the 1930s. But there's nothing like

hack wilson

Played From: 1923–1934
(Also played 190 games in LF, 148 games in RF)
Teams: Giants, Cubs, Dodgers, Phillies
Career Record: .307 Avg., .395 On-Base Pct., .545 Slug Pct., 1,461 Hits, 244 HR

one storied season (.356, 56 HR, 191 RBIs) to overinflate a guy's reputation. So one powerful record, a half dozen 100-RBI seasons, and even a .545 career slugging percentage don't make Hack Wilson a legitimate Hall of Famer. In the good half of his career, he hit .326, with 200 homers and 831 RBIs (nearly 140 *a year*). But in the awful half of his career (The Other Six Seasons), he was a .266 hitter, with only 44 homers and 232 RBIs. Yep, he knocked in just 41 more runs in all those seasons combined than he did in *one* season, in 1930. That's why it took him until his fifth time on the Hall of Fame ballot to get more than *two* votes. The Veterans Committee may have elected him anyway (45 years after his career ended). But little did those veterans know they were also guaranteeing him a prestigious spot on this Most Overrated list.

3. JUAN PIERRE

There's a side of me that doesn't want Juan Pierre to appear on this list. That's the side that roots for guys who love baseball so much, they show up at the ballpark before the grounds crew. *That's* not overrated. I've also seen what can happen when Pierre gets on base to lead off an inning late in a game, and pitchers start having nervous breakdowns. *That's* not overrated, either. But here's why Pierre made it into the overrated half of this chapter, anyway: Because he was the *first* player nominated. It happened way back when I

juan pierre

Played From: 2000–2006 (active)
Teams: Rockies, Marlins, Cubs, Dodgers
Career Record: .303 Avg., .350 On-Base Pct., .377 Slug Pct., 1,244 Hits, 12 HR, 325 SB

was just trying to come up with some standards for what makes a player over-rated or underrated. "I'll tell you who's overrated," said an American League general manager. "Speed guys are overrated. Juan Pierre is probably the number one overrated player in baseball." Hmm. Number one, huh? Now, obviously, not everybody agrees with that. In fact, GMs probably debate the overratedness or underratedness of Pierre (often depending on which league they come from) more than they do any other leadoff man alive. But it was easier to refute the *he's-overrated* crowd in 2003, the year Pierre and the Marlins won the World Series. That year, Pierre walked 55 times, struck out only 35 times, got 204 hits, reached base more than any leadoff man in baseball, and led the league in stolen bases. But leadoff hitters with .330 on-base percentages, who walk 32 times in 750 trips to the plate, who score just 87 runs—i.e., the Juan Pierre employed by the 2006 Cubs—*they're* overrated. And that's how Pierre is trending—fewer walks, too many times caught stealing, still no power, and one of the shakiest outfield throwing arms around. On any given trip around the bases, this guy could make me want to rewrite this chapter. But the fact he's still in here tells you there haven't been enough of those trips lately to make me edit any of this.

4. MICKEY RIVERS

Speaking of speed guys, Mick the Quick was Juan Pierre before Juan Pierre was. Back in the 1970s and early 1980s, Rivers was the fastest man in base-

mickey rivers

Played From: 1970–1984
(Also played 124 games at DH)
Teams: Angels, Yankees, Rangers
Career Record: .295 Avg., .327 On-Base Pct., .397 Slug Pct., 1,660 Hits, 61 HR, 267 SB

ball. And it's a good thing, because he once had a year (1976) when he walked 13 times in 613 trips to the plate. That allergy to count-working led the Mick to a frightening .327 career on-base percentage. Which helps explain how he managed to go through a 15-year career—hitting at the top of the order, stealing a bunch of bases, often hitting around .300—and *never* score 100

runs. In any season. But I'll admit that's not really why he sneaked into this book. He sneaked in mostly as an excuse to roll out my favorite Mickey Rivers quotes. Since there are so many to choose from, I'm going with his Weather Department Greatest Hits. Third prize: "The wind was blowing a hundred degrees." Second prize (on a day where the temperature hit 110°): "We're always going to lead the league in degrees." First prize: "The first thing you do when you get out to center field is put up your finger and check the wind-chill factor." Hey kids, please don't try that at home.

5. OMAR MORENO

Finally, let's complete our all-overrated track team with a man whose unofficial nickname said it all: "Omar the Out-Maker." There was a time, back in the Pirates' late-'70s, early-'80s glory days, when Moreno was a perfect anchor on Chuck Tanner's sprint-medley relay team. It was just the non-running portion of the program that gave him trouble. In a six-year stretch, from 1977 to 1982, Moreno cranked out seasons of 53, 71, 77, 96, 39, and 60 stolen bases. But that about does it for the positive offensive contributions

omar moreno

Played From: 1975–1986
Teams: Pirates, Astros, Yankees, Royals, Braves
Career Record: .252 Avg., .306 On-Base Pct., .343 Slug Pct., 1,257 Hits, 37 HR, 487 SB

he made. He would have struck out 100 times in all of those seasons if it weren't for the 1981 players' strike. He piled up more career caught-stealings (182) than doubles (171). And he finished his career by becoming the only outfielder in the live-ball era to rack up five straight seasons with an on-base percentage below .300. So about the only area where he was underrated was living up to his nickname. He led the league in outs made twice—and just missed two other years.

The Most Underrated Center Fielder of All Time

DUKE SNIDER

When a friend of mine found out I'd selected Duke Snider for this latest, greatest Underrated Academy Award, he reacted almost as if he'd just heard that Paris Hilton had been chosen Most Underpublicized Famous Person of the Millennium.

"It's impossible," he said, "for a Brooklyn Dodger to be underrated."

Nope. Not anymore. Doesn't matter that approximately 788,452 books, poems, odes, and major motion pictures have been devoted to the Brooklyn

Dodgers. Doesn't matter that about two-thirds of parts 1 through 644 of Ken Burns's *Baseball* documentary were devoted to the Brooklyn Dodgers. Doesn't matter that 93.1 percent of all residents of New York City still believe the departure of the Dodgers for California represents The Moment Modern American Society Officially Gurgled into the Septic Tank.

Duke Snider is *still* underrated. It says so right here in this book. So it must be true.

The Duke, in fact, is a thoroughly unique case in our underrated files. You think it's hard to be underrated when you've been deified in 788,452 books, poems, odes, and major motion pictures? That's nothing. It's way tougher to be underrated when you've appeared in the chorus (and unofficial title) of a baseball song that all living Americans have listened to, on average, 788,452 times apiece—and can't evict from the iTunes playlist in their heads despite numerous attempts and several court orders.

I almost hesitate even to type the name of that song, because I know the mere mention of it will trigger an automatic reaction in your subconscious. A little man up there will begin singing, "Willllll-ie, Mickey, and the Duke." And he'll refuse to stop. For the next month and a half. Watch, you'll be flossing your teeth in a couple of weeks, and you'll realize he's still singing that frigging chorus. And he won't quit, even if you then cut your gums so severely you wind up in the emergency room.

So I'm sorry. Really. But since I suspect it's already too late, and the little man is already warbling, I need to thank Terry Cashman for writing and crooning "Talkin' Baseball." He has created a category I never even contemplated when I started this book: Most Underrated Player of All Time to Be Featured in a Never-Ending Chorus that Will Hijack Your Brain and (Occasionally) Cause Severe Gum Damage. (*Important Disclaimer:* Author assumes no liability for said damage, or even unsaid damage.)

Technically, I realize, it wasn't Cashman who lumped Willie Mays, Mickey Mantle, and Duke Snider into the giant center fielders' Crock-Pot they've been simmering in for more than 50 years. That celebrated lumpage commenced as soon as New Yorkers realized they just might have three Hall of Fame center fielders in their midst, playing ball in the same metropolis at the same time. But for those of us who weren't riding the E train back then, it was

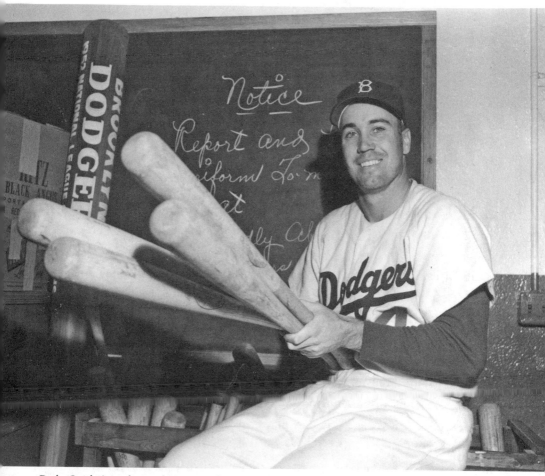

Duke Snider's underratedness stems from spending his career in the shadows of his fellow Hall of Fame center fielders in New York: Mays and Mantle.

"Talkin' Baseball" that forever burned that trio into our insides, like a cranium tattoo.

So given that their linkage is now so deeply imbedded, we're left to ponder the question that makes this chapter possible: how come Willie and Mickey remained such transcendent figures long after their retirement, while the Duke turned into sort of the Jay Buhner of his era—not exactly forgotten, but barely denting our radar?

The Duke's Buhner-ization is reflected by his low-wattage showing in— yeah, here it comes again—the 1999 All-Century Team voting. Not that

anybody expected him to outpoll Babe Ruth or anything. But when the votes
were counted, it sure didn't take as long to count Snider's votes as almost
anyone else's.

He finished 24th just among the outfielders on the ballot. If it's any conso-
lation, he did cream Goose Goslin and a few other guys. But otherwise, Duke
didn't do so hot. Check the vote totals for our three New York Song Chorus
Icons (cue the little man):

Willie Mays—1,115,896 votes (fourth among outfielders)
Mickey Mantle—988,168 votes (sixth among outfielders)
Duke Snider—63,410 votes (hey, at least he out-polled Harry Heilmann)

In other words, Mays got nearly 18 votes for every vote the Duke got.
Mantle got almost 16 votes for every vote the Duke got. Even Pete Rose, the
last outfielder elected, sucked in about 10 votes for every vote the Duke col-
lected. And while a few state's witnesses may have sung about Rose for Plea
Bargain Records somewhere along the line, when was the last time Terry
Cashman sang about him, huh?

I'm not going to pretend that Snider was quite as good a baseball player,
or quite as charismatic a baseball player, as either Mays or Mantle. I'm not
going to claim he sustained his greatness as long as either of those guys. I'm
not even going to stack up his career totals next to theirs, because they win
every battle. Snider himself acknowledges that.

But were those other two men really 900,000 or a million stinking All-
Century votes greater than the Duke was? Sheez, c'mon. That's where our
underratedness rescue squad comes sprinting into your picture, blowing the
whistle on this crazy injustice. How did this happen, anyway?

"Because he's The Third Center Fielder," said Phil Pepe, a terrific longtime
New York baseball writer and author. "That's all it is. And the other two were
so great."

Then again, Pepe said, "Sometimes there's no real explanation for: why
does one guy capture the public's imagination and another guy doesn't? It's
really interesting. Now Mantle, I understand. Mantle, in my experience, was
the most famous, most popular, most beloved figure who ever played in New

York.… And Willie, of course, had such great charisma. And he may have been the best all-around player of all time. A lot of people think so."

But we all concede that. That's not our issue. The issue is whether Snider at least deserves to float along in their general orbit.

"Oh, I think he does," Pepe said. "But the other two are so revered and so great, maybe *anybody* would suffer by comparison."

And that, friends, sums up precisely what happened here. Mays and Mantle have grown, over the years, more immense than life itself, for reasons having as much to do with our need to mythify our heroes as with their brilliance on a ballfield. How could Snider—how could anyone—compete with that?

Yet, back in their heyday, it was Snider—not the other two—who became the third player in history to deliver *five* 40-homer seasons in a row (1953–1957). (Babe Ruth and Ralph Kiner were the others.) It was Snider—not the other two—who hit more home runs (326) and drove in more runs (1,031) than any player in baseball in the 1950s. So in their primes, the separation wasn't as pronounced as many folks now perceive it to be.

duke snider

Played From: 1947–1964
(Also played 293 games in RF)
Teams: Dodgers, Mets, Giants
Career Record: .295 Avg., .380 On-Base Pct., .540 Slug Pct., 2,116 Hits, 407 HR

Oh, Snider did have certain advantages. He was the only left-handed hitter in the most thunderous lineup in baseball, so he faced fewer left-handers than he would have otherwise. And the right-field fence of his home park, Ebbets Field, conveniently stood 297 feet from home plate. So it was no accident that the Duke's career slugging percentage in Flatbush was 100 points higher than it was everywhere else.

But wait. There's a mitigating-circumstance alert coming. That right-field fence was also nearly 40 feet high. So many people think it *cost* Snider some home runs. Plus, the Dodgers' move to L.A. sentenced him to life in a horrible hitter's park (The Coliseum)—and no doubt obliterated his shot at 500 homers. So on balance, it's not as easy to devalue his stats as the Willie-and-Mickey fans think.

All right, now that we've got all that in perspective, suppose we do something *really* shifty. Suppose we pretend that Mays and Mantle had taken up, say, plumbing and never played baseball at all. Pretend along with us, and *now* look at all the center fielders in history. Here's what you'll find:

Duke Snider out-homered all the other center fielders who ever lived—until Ken Griffey Jr. roared into this scene. Only Joe DiMaggio had a better slugging percentage in the pre-Griffey era. And *nobody* can match Snider's numbers across the board—a .540 career slugging percentage *and* a .380 on-base percentage *and* a .295 lifetime batting average *and* 407 homers.

Nobody except those two legends we're trying not to mention, that is.

"I don't think Duke feels slighted [in comparison to Mays and Mantle]," said Pepe, who coauthored a book (*Few and Chosen*) with Snider. "He recognizes that the other two have greater numbers than he does, and they deserve all the recognition they got. But I suspect that if he had his druthers, he'd rather have played in a different era, because if he'd played in a different era, *he'd* have gotten the recognition *they* got."

Ironic, don't you think? On one hand, playing in the same town and the same era as Willie and Mickey elevated Snider into the realm of American folklore. (Uh-oh, anybody else hear that singing again?) But there is another side to that story: sharing the stage with those two Goliaths actually *denied* the Duke his due as one of the half dozen greatest center fielders ever. And that's a shame.

Well, it's a shame for him, that is. But for authors combing the universe in search of The Most Underrated Center Fielder of All Time, eh, not so shame-inducing. It's clear now Duke Snider deserves *that* honor, even more than he deserved another million All-Century votes. For that matter, he even deserves his very own song. And at this point, I'm even thinking about writing one—just to make that little man stop singing.

The Rest of the Top Five

2. RICHIE ASHBURN

If Duke Snider thinks *he* was overshadowed by Mays and Mantle, he's Babe Ruth compared to Richie Ashburn. You think it took the Duke a long time (11 elections) to make the Hall of Fame? It took the Phillies' lovable center fielder *33 years,* until the Veterans Committee finally got one right in 1995. What Omar Vizquel is to modern shortstops, Ashburn was to center fielders of the '50s. Because he was great in a different way than his peers were great, he could never nudge the spotlight far enough down the Jersey Turnpike to find him.

richie ashburn

Played From: 1948–1962
Teams: Phillies, Cubs, Mets
Career Record: .308 Avg., .396 On-Base Pct., .382 Slug Pct., 2,574 Hits, 29 HR, 234 SB

But Ashburn was such a phenomenal defensive center fielder, he owns as many 500-putout seasons (four) as all the other outfielders in history *combined.* And offensively, he led his league in hitting twice, in on-base percentage four times, in triples twice, and in walks four times. In fact, he's the only player besides Rogers Hornsby to lead his league in hits, walks, and batting average in the same year (1958). Ashburn also got more hits than any other player in the '50s, and reached base more than 100 more times than any other hitter in the '50s. And no matter how good Mays and Mantle may have been, they never had a day like Ashburn had on August 17, 1957—when he managed to plunk a fan named Alice Roth with two foul balls in the *same at-bat.* Philadelphia is a town that chews up almost all of its sports heroes, spits them out, and drives them out of town. But I never met any Philadelphian who didn't love Richie Ashburn. And that may be his greatest feat of all.

3. JIMMY WYNN

We live in a what-if world, and there are no sure answers to the what-if questions in that world. But it's still fair to ask what kind of career Wynn would have had if he hadn't spent nine of his 15 seasons playing in Houston's canyonesque Astrodome. My ESPN.com colleague Rob Neyer has called Wynn one of the dozen best center fielders of all time. Bill James ranked him as the 10th-greatest center fielder in history. And they're talking about a man who *never got a Hall of Fame vote.* So if nothing else, that makes Wynn one of the most intriguing players in history. Nobody debates that he was an outstanding defender. And because of the

jimmy wynn

Played From: 1963–1977
(Also played 355 games in RF, 298 games in LF)
Teams: Astros, Dodgers, Braves, Yankees, Brewers
Career Record: .250 Avg., .366 On-Base Pct., .436 Slug Pct., 1,665 Hits, 291 HR, 225 SB

patience-power combo that made him unique in his era, his career on-base percentage (.366) is more than 100 points higher than his batting average (.250), and his career OPS (.802) is the second-highest of all time (behind Greg Vaughn) among players who hit .250 or lower. But is Jimmy Wynn a Hall of Famer? You need to make a major what-if leap of faith to jump to that conclusion. For what it's worth, the amazing "stat neutralizer" at baseball-reference.com estimates that all those years in the Dome cost Wynn nearly 30 home runs and almost 40 points off his slugging percentage. But that would still leave him well short of 400 homers or a .500 career slugging percentage. So is he a Cooperstowner? Not quite. But did the Astrodome turn him into one of the most underrated center fielders ever? I'll vote for that.

4. TRIS SPEAKER

If I ever write a *Most Underrated Players Before 1930* book (a guaranteed AARP best seller), Speaker might be the guy on the cover. Bet you didn't

tris speaker

Played From: 1907–1927
Teams: Red Sox, Indians, Senators, A's
Career Record: .345 Avg., .428 On-Base Pct., .500 Slug Pct., 3,514 Hits, 117 HR, 434 SB

know that he and Ty Cobb are the only men before 1930 to slug .500 in more seasons (11) than Babe Ruth (10). Bet you didn't know Speaker hit more doubles (792) than any player in history. Bet you didn't know he's That Other Guy in the 3,500-Hit Club (the one whose name isn't Pete Rose, Cobb, Hank Aaron, or Stan Musial). Bet you didn't know he batted .345 lifetime (number five all time). And now that you know all that, it's a good time to mention he was probably an even better *defensive* player than offensive player. Yet Speaker has drifted so far off our main menu, it took a special Committee to Save MLB from a Massive Historical Travesty to get Speaker added to the Indians' Hometown Heroes ballot in 2006. But clearly, he can appear on our Most Underrated ballot without any help whatsoever.

5. ANDY VAN SLYKE

There are a bunch of great players I could have included on this list instead of my buddy Andy Van Slyke. So to Wally Berger, Reggie Smith, Larry Doby, Lenny Dykstra, and Dale Murphy, I can only say: sorry, men. I owe you one.

But this is my book. So *my* favorite players get to nudge their way in here. And I always felt Van Slyke never got his due. The guy won five straight Gold Gloves and had the best center-field throwing arm of his time. He had years where he led the league in hits, doubles, triples, and sacrifice flies. He nearly won a batting title in 1992. He could steal a base (swiped 20-plus

andy van slyke

Played From: 1983–1995
(Also played 339 games in RF)
Teams: Cardinals, Pirates, Orioles, Phillies
Career Record: .274 Avg., .349 On-Base Pct., .443 Slug Pct., 1,562 Hits, 164 HR, 245 SB

six years in a row and had an 81 percent career success rate). And he had a couple of top-five MVP finishes. But I'll be honest. The big reason Van Slyke is in this book is that he ranks among my own personal all-time leaders in Most Career Quips. He once watched the Phillie Phanatic make a diving catch of a foul ball and joked: "He caught the ball better than we did tonight." He once said that if a tourist from Germany ever laid eyes on John ("I'm No Athlete") Kruk, "he'd wonder why the beer-truck driver was playing first base." And Van Slyke once summed up a nutty game in which Gregg Jefferies's wife went into labor—while her husband was hitting for the cycle—with this gem: "His cycle was 20 minutes apart. His wife's were seven." No player of his generation had more fun than Andy Van Slyke. And even in baseball, fun is a commodity that will *never* be overrated.

CHAPTER 12

Right Fielders

The Most Overrated Right Fielder of All Time

DAVE WINFIELD

There should be a whole separate chapter in this book for The Super Athletes. You know the type. Back in high school, they were better than you in, well, *everything*—baseball, football, basketball, volleyball, golf, poker, video games, cheerleader-dating, avoiding homework, and, 99 times out of 100, good hair days.

"When I was growing up," said Dodgers coach Rich Donnelly, "I used to play ball with a kid named Oats DiBacco. Oats was 6'1" when he was 12, so he immediately went in the overrated category because he struck out everybody. And he was overrated his whole life, because people in Steubenville [Ohio] kept waiting for him to do something since Little League. For us, he was like Nolan Ryan was to the rest of the human race. Nolan was always the hardest thrower on earth. So he went in the overrated category at birth. And once you're there, you stay there. You don't jump around."

If that's true—and hey, it works for me—then Oats DiBacco should be able to totally relate to Dave Winfield. Of all the great multi-sport Super Athletes to pass through the major leagues, Winfield was our modern-day Jim Thorpe. Not that guys like Bo Jackson, Deion Sanders, and Danny Ainge weren't fun to have around. And, just for his niche in trivia history, you can't

Unfortunately for Dave Winfield, a player is almost destined for overratedness when people assume that he was born with superpowers.

beat Gene Conley (played for the World Series champs *and* the NBA champs in the 1950s). But sorry, they were no Dave Winfield.

When Winfield was in college, at the University of Minnesota, he was the best hitter on his team, the best *pitcher* on his team, and the starting power forward on the Big Ten basketball champions. The only reason he wasn't a stud on the football team was that he couldn't clone himself. And when he got out of college, he was drafted by one baseball team (the Padres), two basketball teams (Atlanta Hawks in the NBA, Utah Stars in the ABA), and one NFL team (Minnesota Vikings). So you almost expected him to wander accidentally into the Olympics and win gold medals in the 100 meters, decathlon, pole vault, platform diving, parallel bars, and Greco-Roman wrestling.

Dave Winfield just *looked* like a man who could wake up in the morning and do anything he willed himself to do. At 6'6", 220 pounds, he was a baseball player who had physique-napped a tight end's body. He ran like a superstar. He threw like a superstar. He hit like a superstar. He smiled like a superstar. He walked like a superstar. And he definitely talked like a superstar.

So he breezed directly from his college locker room to right field in San Diego, skipping the minor leagues entirely. And if you listened closely, you could probably hear folks in upstate New York start chiseling his Hall of Fame plaque right then. From the moment he showed up, Dave Winfield felt more like a Hollywood creation than he did a real member of the species the rest of us belong to. They'd written him an All-American script, so darned if he wasn't going to live it out.

But back here on the overratedness judges' stand, it's our job to do with Winfield what we've done with just about everyone who has rollicked through these pages—separate reality from the myths that billowed all around this man. So make sure you understand that mission before you read another word.

This isn't about whether David M. Winfield belongs in the Hall of Fame. You'd have to be a genuine lunkhead to think he doesn't. The question before this jury, however, is whether he was, like Oats DiBacco, destined to be overrated from the minute he journeyed out of the womb.

About his only hope to avoid that fate was to live up to the superhuman expectations that were overstuffed in his duffel bag the day he arrived in San

Diego in June 1973. And that might not have been possible, even if George Steinbrenner *hadn't* hired a low-rent weasel to help debunk Winfield's super-humanity in the glorious 1980s.

"You looked at him the first time you saw him and you said, 'This guy might hit 60 homers,'" said one scout. "He had all the components you'd want in a player—power, speed, great arm. A guy like that, no matter what he would have done, it might not have been enough. With the type of tools he had, the expectations start out so high. Then you put him in New York, and the expectations just get higher."

The great stuff Winfield did isn't real complicated to explain. He made 12 All-Star teams in a row. He drove in 100 runs eight times. He won seven Gold Gloves. And he kept on playing, well into his forties, until he'd blown past 3,100 hits and hit 465 homers. The only players in history with that many hits *and* home runs are Hank Aaron, Willie Mays, Stan Musial, Carl Yastrzemski, and Eddie Murray. No schlubs in that group.

But there's a subtle difference between Winfield and the other Hall of Famers on that list. Those other men had multiple years where they led their league in all kinds of categories and/or won baseball's biggest awards. I bet you'll be shocked to learn that Winfield, on the other hand, never won *any* major award. And he had just *one* season in which he led his league in any significant offensive department. That was 1979, when he was tops in the National League in RBIs, total bases, and intentional walks.

If you peruse the rest of his page in the encyclopedia, however, you'll find none of that **all-important boldfaced type**—the official typeface of league leaders—not even if you take out your best reading glasses. Bill James actually devised a stat once that accounts for that league-leader factor. It's called Black Ink. Incredibly, in 22 seasons—on the way to all those hits and home runs—Dave Winfield somehow racked up only four Black Ink points (for his RBI title in 1979).

I'll be honest. I pride myself on how closely I try to pay attention to just about everything in this sport. And even I was stunned by that. The indispensable baseball-reference.com lists the all-time top 200 in Black Ink points. Winfield isn't even close to appearing on it. The average Hall of Famer settles in at 27 points. You'll find guys like Dante Bichette, Juan Pierre, and Topsy

Hartsel in double figures. And Babe Ruth, who is number one, is way, way up there at 162. But Dave Winfield? He has as many Black Ink points as Neifi Perez. Seriously, Neifi Perez. I typed that sentence five minutes ago, and my mind hasn't unboggled yet.

To be fair—and fairness matters here—Winfield did go down to the last day of the season before getting edged by Don Mattingly

dave winfield

Played From: 1973–1995
(Also played 219 games in CF, 419 games at DH)
Teams: Padres, Yankees, Angels, Blue Jays, Twins, Indians
Career Record: .283 Avg., .353 On-Base Pct., .475 Slug Pct., 3,110 Hits, 465 HR, 223 SB

for the 1984 AL batting title. And he did finish third in his league in homers a couple of times. But here's the point (and I'm sure you knew I'd stumble upon a point eventually):

This man never really had that King Kong year where he towered over his sport—devouring pitchers, fielders, broadcasters, award voters, gravity, Einstein's theory of relativity, and everything else that made the mistake of landing in his path.

Humongous as he always appeared stalking toward that plate, he never had a 40-homer season—and he passed 35 just once. True, his home parks in San Diego and the Bronx weren't especially right-handed-hitter-friendly. But Nate Colbert had two 35-homer seasons as a Padre. Winfield beat 25 only once (when he hit 34, in 1979).

As for New York, Joe DiMaggio had a 46-homer season when the left-center-field alley in Yankee Stadium was 457 feet deep. In Winfield's time, that alley was moved in twice—from 430 feet in his early years to 399 by the time he departed. But Winfield peaked at 37 in his first full season as a Yankee (1982) and hit 30 only one other time in his decade in New York.

None of that is intended as some kind of rip job. It's merely an attempt to distinguish image from reality. Has anyone ever mentioned that's what this book is all about?

Okay, here come more surprises: of the 32 hitters in the 450-Homer Club, Winfield ranks *last* in career OPS (.828). And he is 31st (next to last) in both slugging (.475) and home-run ratio (one every 23.7 at-bats). Now, if we shift on over to the 3,000-Hit Club, he's 23rd out of 25 in career batting average (.283). And if you calculate the runs he "created" compared to the average outfielder of his era (with a stat called "runs created above position"), he's 24th out of 25.

Look, I recognize that those rankings measure him against the greatest hitters of all time. So if a guy is the worst offensive player in the whole group, he could still be considered the best player in the history of about eight franchises. But what if I expanded the pool? What if I looked at all the men, from the beginning of baseball time, who came to the plate 5,000 times? Where would you figure a Hall of Fame Super Athlete like Winfield would rank in career slugging? Uh, would you believe 150th? (Behind Roy Sievers and Jack Fournier!) Staggering, isn't it?

To tell you the truth, it staggered *me*. The Dave Winfield I remember seemed way more formidable than Roy Sievers. The Dave Winfield I remember felt like some kind of superhero. He was a gigantic human being with a quick bat. Who hustled. And played his sweatsocks off in the outfield, climbing walls and gunning down base runners. And dragged himself out there 150 games a year unless he was in traction. Even drove in 108 runs when he was 40 years old.

So this half of this chapter is *not* some misguided attempt to prove this man would have been better off dunking red-white-and-blue basketballs in the ABA. And it's definitely not a campaign to establish that his career was indistinguishable from Neifi Perez's. If you even *thought* that, you're taking these factoids I toss out there way too literally. Don't let that happen again.

If I wanted to paint Winfield as a bum, I'd be dragging his Mr. May-ish career World Series numbers (6 for 44) into this debate. (Whoops!) And I'm not even going to dignify Steinbrenner's insane, obsessive smear campaign against a man who didn't deserve that, either. Not necessary. That's not why Dave Winfield made this list.

He's here, in truth, through very little fault of his own. He's here because we trapped him into helping us demonstrate one more fascinating subtlety of the entire overrated-underrated concept—a concept that is all about perception, not talent. Dave Winfield is the best position player in the whole overrated hemisphere of this book. That's a fact. So he doesn't fit the typical profile of an overrated *anything*.

But overratedness isn't as simple a notion as people often think it is. That's what we're getting at. In reality, it has nearly as many levels as the Empire State Building. And one of those levels is the Oats DiBacco Principle—the guys who are so freaking good so young, they can't possibly be as great as their own first impressions make them out to be. Alex Rodriguez could tell you all about it. But before there was A-Rod, there was Dave Winfield—Super Athlete. He, too, went in the overrated category at birth. And I guess he knows, now that he's in this book, that there probably wasn't much he could have done to launch himself out of that category, even if he'd bought his own space shuttle.

The Rest of the Top Five

2. J.D. DREW

Since the day he got drafted by the Phillies in 1997 and volunteered as a conscientious draft objector, I've astutely detected two themes running through the overhyped J.D.'s career: 1) he has kept aspiring to get paid for his reputation instead of his production and 2) he's always about 15 minutes away from some kind of injury—probably one that wouldn't have caused Cal Ripken to miss two-thirds of an inning. Not that Drew doesn't have talent. When the 2006 season ended, he was one of only 13 active players with a career slugging percentage over .500 and an on-base percentage over .390. So what's the difference between J.D. and the rest of that group? Those other dozen guys have made a combined 70 All-Star teams (and all 12 have made at least two apiece). Through 2006, Drew had made zero. So he's now a $14 million-a-year player with no All-Star at-bats, no energizer intangibles, one 30-homer season, one 100-RBI season, a .233 lifetime average in seven postseason series, and 390 games missed in his first eight seasons for one reason or another. The people who run the Red Sox are smart men. But their computer printouts might have misled them a tad about this guy.

j.d. drew

Played From: 1998–2006 (active)
(Also played 215 games in CF)
Teams: Cardinals, Braves, Dodgers, Red Sox
Career Record: .286 Avg., .393 On-Base Pct., .512 Slug Pct., 905 Hits, 162 HR

3. DARRYL STRAWBERRY

The day Strawberry got his first career hit in 1983, Mets broadcaster Ralph Kiner low-keyed the occasion by gushing: "That could be the first of 3,000 or more."

darryl strawberry

Played From: 1983–1999
(Also played 143 games at DH)
Teams: Mets, Dodgers, Giants, Yankees
Career Record: .259 Avg., .357 On-Base Pct., .505 Slug Pct., 1,401 Hits, 335 HR, 221 SB

Yeah, well, the Straw Man only missed by a mere 1,599 hits. Then again, Darryl Strawberry caused 7 million New Yorkers—and every baseball scout on earth—to miss on all kinds of predictions during his sad, frustrating, turbulent, 17-year career. On the good side of his column, Strawberry was the first player picked in the entire 1980 draft. He was elected to start seven All-Star Games in eight years. He got more All-Star votes in 1986 than any player in baseball. And eight seasons into his career, he'd already slugged over .500 more times (six) than Don Mattingly or Andre Dawson totaled in their whole careers. But you know the other side of his story. Drugs. Alcohol. Three substance-abuse suspensions. Arrests. Jail. A tax-evasion conviction. And plenty more trouble where that came from. Such a sweet swing. Such a likeable personality. All undone by a series of awful, self-destructive decisions. There's nothing more tragic in sports, or life, than wasted talent. And no player of his generation wasted more of it than Darryl Strawberry.

4. CHUCK KLEIN

It's never a good feeling calling a Hall of Famer overrated. But Chuck Klein is overrated in almost the same way that Sandy Koufax is overrated. Just as Koufax

chuck klein

Played From: 1928–1944
(Also played 261 games in LF)
Teams: Phillies, Cubs, Pirates
Career Record: .320 Avg., .379 On-Base Pct., .543 Slug Pct., 2,076 Hits, 300 HR

was the Greatest Pitcher Alive over the last six years of his career, Klein was in the middle of the argument for Greatest Hitter Alive Not Named Ruth or Gehrig during his *first* five full seasons. Those five years (1929–1933) are flat-out unbelievable: .359 average, .414 on-base percentage, .636 slugging, 180 homers, 458 extra-base hits, 693 RBIs (an *average* of 139 a year), 658 runs scored, and (get this) 1,118 hits (an *average* of 224 a year). Not to mention he won a Triple Crown (1933), led his league in homers *and* steals in 1932, and racked up 44 outfield assists in 1930 (still an NL record). Trouble was, Klein didn't play just five seasons. He played 17. And he had more hits, homers, extra-base hits, RBIs, and runs scored in those first five than he had in the other 12 seasons put together. Plus, all those early stats come attached to a gigantic asterisk: *got to play in Baker Bowl.* How awesome a hitter's paradise was *that* place? The right-field fence was 280½ feet from the plate. So in 1929, according to Philadelphia baseball historian Rich Westcott, the Phillies' *team* batting average at home was .340. (Of course, their opponents' average was .339.) It isn't Chuck Klein's fault that his ballpark helped propel him into the Hall of Fame. But it isn't the kind of thing our Overratedness Watchdog Force can ignore, either.

5. BOBBY ABREU

If your reaction, when you read this name, went something like, "What the xpf#&zxb#k?" I'm guessing you've seen Bobby Abreu play about a thousand fewer games than I have. But those of us who watched him all those years in Philadelphia know exactly why he made this list. Over-ratedness, you see, is a complicated concept. And Abreu falls into that group of men who sometimes manage to be less than the sum of their photogenic numbers. Now I'll respectfully

bobby abreu

Played From: 1996–2006 (active)
Teams: Astros, Phillies, Yankees
Career Record: .302 Avg., .412 On-Base Pct., .507 Slug Pct., 1,595 Hits, 205 HR, 271 SB

admit those numbers tell you there isn't much this guy can't do. Through 2006, Abreu was the only active player with a .300 career batting average, a .400 on-base percentage, 200 homers, and 250 stolen bases. But while the Yankees were busy congratulating themselves at the 2006 trade deadline for stealing a player this multitalented for four minor leaguers they've already forgotten they had, how come more people weren't psychoanalyzing the Phillies' motivations? Weren't the Phillies essentially telling the world this guy was overrated, simply by their willingness to unload him for the joy of saving $21 million on their car insurance? Of course they were, on at least some subtle level. Bobby Abreu might have only one fault—and it's one that doesn't turn up on any stat sheets. But it's still a killer. What this man seems to lack is that all-important Derek Jeter Gene. There is no voice in his head, shouting: "This ball *has* to be caught." Or: "This is one at-bat where I *can't* take a walk." And on a team like the Phillies, where he was the centerpiece of the roster, that failing showed up a little too often. Blend him into the Yankees' star-studded ensemble, and maybe it won't. But until he causes me to change my mind, he's the number three hitter on my All-Gifted-Accumulator team. And players like that are almost always overrated.

The Most Underrated Right Fielder of All Time

FRANK ROBINSON

When you write a book like this—and that's probably not a good idea anymore, since *I've already written one*—there's nothing more fun, more challenging, or more likely to cause major insomnia than choosing the players who appear in it.

I warned you way back in the opening pages that I'd be using no ironclad statistical formulas to make these picks. No multiplying OBP times GP, minus outs made, divided by the square root of a guy's uniform number. Or anything like that.

But if you look over the players I selected, I bet you've noticed some common threads that wove their way through these choices. And if you didn't notice, it's time to locate your nearest Starbucks—because you obviously nodded off somewhere around chapter 3.

One player, however, doesn't fit any of those threads. And he's this man— the great Frank Robinson. How the heck did he ever wind up on the All-Underrated Team? There's no sane reason he should be hanging out with this group. Not one.

It's not as if he played in the 1890s. He doesn't have a name that would stump anybody in a spelling bee. He didn't switch positions seven times. He sure wasn't one of those low-key, low-energy players nobody ever noticed was out there. And you definitely can't say he disappeared after he quit playing— unless you count his three seasons managing in front of 73 spectators a night in Montreal.

So Frank Robinson? Underrated? How'd *that* happen?

"It really makes no sense, because he's been around forever," said Jim Henneman, the esteemed, longtime Baltimore baseball writer who covered Robinson as a player and manager. "He's been so visible. He worked in the commissioner's office. He's been managing, playing, coaching. He's always been there. I just think Frank is one of those guys you take for granted."

Could be. But if that's true, you're taking an awful lot of greatness for granted.

You're taking a Triple Crown winner (1966) for granted. You're taking the only man to win MVP awards in both leagues for granted. You're taking for granted a man who was just 57 hits and 14 homers from joining Hank Aaron and Willie Mays in the Royal 3,000-Hit, 600-Homer Society. You're taking the only man ever to win the Grand Slam of Baseball Trophies—MVP, Rookie of the Year, World Series MVP, and All-Star Game MVP—for granted. And that just doesn't compute. Does it?

Correct answer: *nooooo.* But Frank Robinson's underratedness isn't something I fabricated, exaggerated, or exacerbated just to stagger through another chapter. To prove that, I'm going back to a card I've already played a bunch of times in this book when I needed a barometric reading on how underrated or overrated somebody was. Sorry about doing this yet one more time, but I have no choice.

(*Anguished reader cries:* Oh, no. Not *this* again.)

Yes, friends. This again. Let's all look back on the 1999 fan voting for...(what else?)...the All-Century Team.

Where do you suppose Robinson finished among the outfielders in that All-Century voting? Sixth? Eighth? Tenth? Nope. Wrong, wrong, and wrong. Those guesses are *way* too high. How about 16th? Right, 16th.

This man got fewer votes than Shoeless Joe Jackson, Pete Rose, and Reginald Martinez Jackson. He got *one-third* as many votes as Junior Griffey.

Whew, no disrespect to any of those fellows—but how crazy was that? At the time, only Aaron, Babe Ruth, and Mays were ahead of Robinson on the all-time homer list. Only five players led him in extra-base hits. Just 10 players could say they'd scored more runs. It wouldn't be totally knuckleheaded to say that Frank Robinson was among the dozen most productive hitters of all

Frank Robinson, for whatever reason, falls into the Stan Musial category as truly one of the game's best players ever who seldom gets a mention in that debate.

time—but he couldn't even crack the top dozen *at his position.* So the All-Century Team was rolled out without him. That's a disgrace so abominable, they should have just disbanded the whole darned production.

It's possible, though not acceptable, to excuse the voters who weren't born when Robinson was in his prime. (Then again, that means they weren't born when Ernie Banks or Brooks Robinson were playing, either, and those guys still got elected.) But for you voters who *were* alive, and out of diapers, in the 1960s, if you left Frank Robinson off your ballot, what's up with that? You'd better send a note from your doctor saying you were in a lonnnggg coma. Or at least experiencing coma-like symptoms.

In fact, this man should have ranked right behind Aaron (number two in the voting) and Mays (number four). For evidence of that, we turn to Ken Shouler—who wrote a terrific book on *The Real 100 Best Baseball Players of All Time* and provided invaluable research for this book. He worked up a chart comparing Mays, Aaron, and Robinson during the 10 seasons (1956–1965) they were together in the National League. Take a look:

Player	Home Runs	No. Times Led League in Home Runs	No. Times Led League in Slugging Pct.	No. Times Led League in OPS-Plus	Career OPS
Aaron	358	2	2	2	155
Mays	389	3	3	5	156
Robinson	324	0	3	3	154

This chart doesn't even count the *next* season (1966), when Robinson got traded to Baltimore and immediately went out and won the Triple Crown in his first year in the American League. He also led the AL that year in slugging and OPS-plus (which adds a player's on-base and slugging percentage, then adjusts them to his ballpark and compares them to his peers). So over those 11 years, Frank Robinson had strikingly similar numbers to those of the two greatest players of his generation—and actually led his league in slugging more times than either of them. In fact, he led the NL in slugging three years *in a row* (1960–1962)—at a time when Mays, Aaron, Banks, Willie McCovey, Orlando Cepeda, Eddie Mathews, Frank Howard, Roberto Clemente, and Stan Musial were all in that league. Mull the magnitude of that for a minute.

But it's impossible to paint a full portrait of Frank Robinson with numbers alone. He played the game with such ferocity, middle infielders were terrified of turning a double play when he was rampaging in their direction. He hulked over home plate, a five-alarm fire raging out of his eyeballs, and challenged pitchers to drill him. And he projected a single-minded, almost

Vince Lombardi–like intensity every inning, every at-bat, every day. Baseball was no trip to the Fun House for this guy. Losing was just about intolerable.

"Brooks Robinson will tell you, 'We learned how to win when Frank Robinson showed up,'" said the amazing Tim Kurkjian, my ESPN buddy and colleague who covered Robinson's managerial tenure in Baltimore. "I've heard him say that: 'We learned how to win from Frank Robinson.' And that's *Brooks Robinson* talking."

frank robinson

Played From: 1956–1976
(Also played 820 games in LF,
305 games at 1B, 321 games at DH)
Teams: Reds, Orioles, Dodgers,
Angels, Indians
Career Record: .294 Avg., .389
On-Base Pct., .537 Slug Pct., 2,943
Hits, 586 HR, 204 SB

Yet Brooks is just one of the many players who somehow left a bigger mark on our new-millennium brains than Frank Robinson did. And why? How? I've asked those questions more about Frank and about Stan Musial than just about anyone else in this book. But even the theory we settled on for Musial's underratedness—no signature moment—doesn't apply to Robinson.

He left his signatures all over our history books. Triple Crown. Dazzling stardom in the 1966 World Series. A daring, game-winning, base-running exhibition that carried the Orioles to a seventh game in the 1971 Series. The only home run ever to fly completely out of Baltimore's late, great Memorial Stadium. And, of course, his biggest mark on history—as the first African American to manage a major league team (the 1974–1977 Indians).

True, his best years came in Cincinnati and Baltimore, which are both a hefty commute from Broadway and the Sunset Strip. But if that's a problem, how come it wasn't a problem for Rose, Joe Morgan, Johnny Bench, Jim Palmer, or Brooks Robinson?

Tim Kurkjian's theory is: "I think it's possible Frank's personality was such that some people just chose not to like him, and they didn't give him the benefit of the doubt. To me, that's ridiculous, because I've seen him be as charming and fascinating and funny as anybody you'd ever meet. But he can also be abrasive. And it's possible that side of him just put people off."

An excellent premise. Except couldn't we utter the same four sentences about Ted Williams? So that leaves us with the dreaded it's-gotta-be-racial theory. And that's one none of us can completely discount.

But you know what? In the end, it doesn't matter. The famed *Boston Globe* columnist Dan Shaughnessy once called Frank Robinson "quite possibly the most underrated player in the history of baseball." And if you're a player who can inspire a quote like that, you're just about destined to end up in this book—no matter what you did to deserve it.

The Rest of the Top Five

2. DWIGHT EVANS

Jim Rice emerged as the official Top Red Sox Hall of Fame Candidate from the 1970s and 1980s. But there are thousands of Red Sox fans roaming the planet, arguing that Evans had the better career—even though he got lopped off the Hall ballot after three years and never got within 300 votes of being elected. Well, keep in mind that there are also thousands of Red Sox fans who believe their team's 86-year title drought had something to do with the submerging of Babe Ruth's piano—but they're still right about this guy. Evans actually wound up with more career homers than Rice (385–382)

dwight evans

Played From: 1972–1991
(Also played 282 games at DH)
Teams: Red Sox, Orioles
Career Record: .272 Avg., .370 On-Base Pct., .470 Slug Pct., 2,446 Hits, 385 HR

and annihilated him in on-base percentage (.370–.352) and Lee Sinins's "runs created above average" stat (378–270). Some of that is because of longevity. (Evans played 20 seasons, Rice only 16.) And even more of it is because Evans was the greatest base on balls machine of his (pre-moneyball) generation. But from 1978 to 1988, Evans still ranked number three among all American Leaguers in homers (behind just Eddie Murray and Rice), number seven in slugging, and number four in OPS (behind only Wade Boggs, George Brett, and Murray). And don't forget that the only right fielders in history with more Gold Gloves than Dwight Evans (eight) are Roberto Clemente (12) and Al Kaline (10). So does that make this man a Hall of Famer? Not quite. Does it make him really, really underrated? Of course. He's in this book, isn't he?

3. BOBBY BONDS

Here at World Underratedness Headquarters, we love guys who aren't even the greatest players in their own family. If they're any good, they're can't-miss entries in this book. And of all the baseball dads who ever got overshadowed by their sons, Bobby Bonds might be the best player in the Father Didn't Know Best Club. (At the very least, he's in a dead heat with Ken Griffey Sr.) Papa Bonds had his flaws, on and off the diamond. But he was one of the great power-speed combo packages in history. His five 30-homer, 30-steal seasons tie his kid for most ever. He and Barry are also the only members of the 300-Homer, 400-SB Association. And the only players who rank ahead of him on the all-time career list for most Bill James Power/Speed points are the other Bonds, Rickey Henderson, and Willie Mays. There was a little too much swinging and missing (nine seasons of 130 strikeouts or more, including a then-record 189 in 1970) for a leadoff man. But Bobby Bonds was still a spectacular talent. So the only real reason he landed in a book like this is that his DNA helped produce an even more talented offspring.

bobby bonds

Played From: 1968–1981
(Also played 285 games in CF)
Teams: Giants, Yankees, Angels, White Sox, Rangers, Indians, Cardinals, Cubs
Career Record: .268 Avg., .353 On-Base Pct., .471 Slug Pct., 332 HR, 461 SB

4. PETE ROSE

I bet you think I only tossed Rose into this list as a desperate gimmick to attract attention to this book. But you're wrong. I'm not desperate, just sneaky. I covered Rose in Philadelphia for a few years. And he's the most mesmerizing baseball figure I ever chronicled. The energy emanating from Pete Rose, the baseball player, was so overpowering, you could have plugged every TV in America into his uniform. His numbers probably suggest he was overrated by the time he got to Philadelphia. But I saw, with my personal ocular lenses, that this man had a quality underestimated by any numbers. Anyone who thinks it's a coincidence that the 1980 Phillies won the only World Series in franchise history after Rose showed up must also think it's a coincidence that cars always stop when the light turns red. Pete Rose lifted that team to a different level—in the standings, in October, and in their heads. Don't tell me I hallucinated that. I saw it. On the big scale, Rose was probably an overrated second baseman, first baseman, and bet-placer. But he was underrated in the outfield. During his eight seasons out there, he led all big-league outfielders in hits, doubles, singles, on-base percentage, most times on base, and even one of the sabermetricians'

pete rose

Played From: 1963–1986
(Also played 939 games at 1B,
634 games at 3B, 628 games at 2B,
671 games in LF)
Teams: Reds, Phillies, Expos
Career Record: .303 Avg., .375
On-Base Pct., .409 Slug Pct., 4,256
Hits, 160 HR, 198 SB

favorite stats, runs created. *And* he won two Gold Gloves. So, sorry, I'll never believe this guy was just an over-ballyhooed singles hitter who ran harder to first base after ball four than Barry Bonds does on a gapper. The ability to elevate men around you is a quality that is way too underrated.

5. JOHNNY CALLISON

Our boyhood heroes will always be underrated. So this is my way of thanking the late, great Johnny Callison for the thrills he provided me as a kid and the laughs he delivered after I got to know him in adulthood. I recognize this guy was no Cooperstown candidate. But for three years (1963–1965), there weren't many better right fielders anywhere. He out-homered Frank Robinson (89–83) in that period, got more extra-base hits than Hank Aaron (217–206), outslugged Willie Stargell (.501–.483), and unleashed his awesome throwing arm to record

johnny callison

Played From: 1958–1973
(Also played 189 games in LF)
Teams: White Sox, Phillies, Cubs,
Yankees
Career Record: .264 Avg., .331
On-Base Pct., .441 Slug Pct., 1,757
Hits, 226 HR

18 more assists than any outfielder in baseball. There were a couple of three-homer games in there and a cycle. And there was one of the coolest All-Star Game moments in *anybody's* career—his storied 1964 game-winning three-run homer with two outs in the ninth off the theoretically untouchable Dick Radatz. But unfortunately for Johnny Callison, what people seemed to connect him with most was the collapse of the 1964 Phillies (up six and a half games with 12 to play) and the 23-game losing

streak by his 1961 Phillies, still the longest ever. When the 1988 Orioles lost 21 in a row, Callison unabashedly rooted for them to keep losing and extricate him from the record book. "I've been hoping they lose 30 [in a row]," he told me. "Get me out of there." Sorry, John. Never happened. So for the rest of his life, any time a team got on one of those streaks, his phone rang, bringing it all back from the dead. "And here," he once laughed, "I thought I was *good*." Well, you know what? He was. Good player. Great guy. So the replay machine in my head is stuck on that Dick Radatz homer. Always.

APPENDIX

Overrated/Underrated by Franchise

Every town has a guy it thinks is The Greatest Player the Entire Remainder of the Planet Never Seems to Notice.

Every town also has a guy it thinks is The Most Overpaid, Overrated, Overhyped Player in History But Only Those of Us Who Have Watched Him Get That.

In fact, come to think of it, every town has *lots* of those guys.

Which is why I'm about to do something that could really get me in trouble: I'm about to list the three most underrated and overrated players for all 30 franchises.

Theoretically, this is supposed to be the most underrated and overrated players in those teams' "history." But I'm using that term even more loosely than usual. Mind-sets have evolved slightly since 1876. And quite a few of these franchises have changed cities, team names, or both. So I'm letting you know now this is mostly a "modern" list.

Not in all cases, though. Some players were so underrated or overrated, I couldn't help but include them, even if they hadn't played for one of these teams since, say, 1919. In other cases, just to find a legitimate number one name on these lists, I had no choice but to hitch a ride on that time machine.

195

So I confess. I broke my own rules—many times. There were times I plucked these names right out of the chapters that preceded this appendix. There were times I ignored those names, for the sake of getting other deserving candidates into this mix.

Some of these players were *not* underrated or overrated in their own cities—but they sure were everywhere else. Other names on these lists were way more underrated or overrated in their own cities than they were in those other area codes.

With so many different teams, from so many different places, with so many different franchise histories, I had no choice but to change criteria on the fly—team-by-team, even player-by-player. Oh, all right, I *had* a choice. But I did it that way, anyhow.

After all, it's my book. So I get to vote on my own rules. And what the heck. I knew you were going to disagree with at least half of these names no matter which guys I picked. But I'll let you in on a little secret, now that we've reached the finish line:

That's the whole idea.

If we didn't disagree—about pretty much everything—we wouldn't care who's underrated or overrated in the first place.

ANGELS

OVERRATED

1. Mo (What Were We Thinking) Vaughn
2. Mark (Hey, At Least I Won Some Gold Gloves) Langston
3. Danny (First Player Picked in *Two* Drafts) Goodwin

UNDERRATED

1. Bobby (I Wish I'd Hired an AC Delivery Man) Grich
2. Jim Fregosi—and not just because of that guy they traded him for
3. Tim (Face of the Franchise) Salmon

ASTROS
OVERRATED
1. Nolan (Really Great But *Not* the Greatest Pitcher of All Time) Ryan
2. Richard (Maybe They Should Have Kept Bobby Abreu) Hidalgo
3. Jose (Should Have Refused to Leave the Astrodome) Lima

UNDERRATED
1. Craig Biggio—underrated in the other 49 states, anyway
2. Roy Oswalt—ditto
3. Jimmy (The Astrodome Ate My Hall of Fame Résumé) Wynn

ATHLETICS
OVERRATED
1. Mike (The *SI* Cover Boy) Norris
2. Eric (Possibly Not the Next Mike Schmidt) Chavez
3. Todd (Definitely Not the Next Nolan Ryan) Van Poppel

UNDERRATED
1. Lefty (Never Left His Heart in Oakland) Grove
2. Dave Stewart—circa 1987–1990
3. Bert (I Should Never Have Thrown That Bat) Campaneris

BLUE JAYS
OVERRATED
1. Joe Carter—except for That Swing
2. Kelly (Highest Paid Third Baseman in Baseball) Gruber
3. David Wells—the Toronto portion of the festivities

UNDERRATED
1. (The Bespectacled, Vastly Underappreciated) Tom Henke
2. Dave (Mind If I Throw Another One-Hitter?) Stieb
3. (The Young, Mashing) Fred McGriff

BRAVES
OVERRATED
1. Andruw (Anybody Seen My Range Factor?) Jones
2. Bob (Who Needs the Minor Leagues?) Horner
3. Javy (There Was a Reason Maddux Wouldn't Pitch to Him) Lopez

UNDERRATED
1. Warren (No Wonder They Prayed for Rain) Spahn
2. Eddie (Not Just Hank's Understudy) Mathews
3. (The Relentlessly Classy) Tom Glavine

BREWERS
OVERRATED
1. Dave Nilsson—especially in Sydney
2. Marquis Grissom—the Brew Crew years
3. Pat (Rookie of the Year) Listach

UNDERRATED
1. Paul Molitor—but not underrated in Bud Selig's household
2. Cecil (Seven Straight .300 Seasons) Cooper
3. Dan (A Quote for All Occasions) Plesac

CARDINALS
OVERRATED
1. Lou Brock—aw, just read that left fielders chapter
2. Dizzy (If I'd Only Made It Through that All-Star Game) Dean
3. Vince (Watch Out for that Tarp Machine) Coleman

UNDERRATED
1. Stan Musial—anywhere but St. Louis
2. Ken Boyer—anywhere but St. Louis
3. Ted (Why Isn't This Man a Hall of Famer?) Simmons

CUBS
OVERRATED
1. Steve Bartman—now, officially, pardoned
2. Kerry (You Can't Whiff 20 *Every* Day) Wood
3. Ernie Banks—the first-base years

UNDERRATED
1. Ron Santo—definitely not underrated at Clark and Addison
2. Ernie Banks—the shortstop years
3. Mordecai (Three Finger) Brown—even greater than his nickname

DEVIL RAYS
OVERRATED
1. Ben (Seemed Like a Good Idea at the Time) Grieve
2. Wilson (What Do You Want for $35 Million?) Alvarez
3. Toe Nash—a star in the cane fields, a real-life tragedy

UNDERRATED
1. Carl (Best Athlete in Baseball) Crawford
2. Julio (I Even Made Them Forget Kevin Stocker) Lugo
3. (Public Relations Genius) Rick Vaughn—hey, you find three underrated D-Rays!

DIAMONDBACKS
OVERRATED
1. Travis (Why'd We Give Him $10 Million Again?) Lee
2. Todd Stottlemyre—$32 million, 15 wins
3. Russ Ortiz—$25 million, five wins

UNDERRATED
1. Steve (Best D'backs Free Agent Not Named Randy Johnson) Finley
2. Matt Williams—might have hit 60 in 1994 if it weren't for that darned strike
3. Greg Colbrunn—yeah, Greg Colbrunn

DODGERS
OVERRATED
1. Sandy Koufax—this just in: the first half of his career counted, too
2. Steve (He Really *Was* Too Good to Be True) Garvey
3. Darren Dreifort—$55 million, nine wins

UNDERRATED
1. Duke Snider—doomed to underratedness by a frigging *song*
2. Reggie Smith—more underrated in Boston, but we had to get him in here someplace
3. Ron (March of the Penguin) Cey

GIANTS
OVERRATED
1. Rube (How'd *He* Make the Hall of Fame?) Marquard
2. Jeffrey (Only My Trot Was Underrated) Leonard
3. Jim Ray (44 Home Runs After Age 26) Hart

UNDERRATED
1. Juan Marichal—but Not in San Francisco or Santo Domingo
2. Willie McCovey—but not in the Cove
3. Bobby (Almost as Good as My Kid) Bonds

INDIANS
OVERRATED
1. Cory (Don't Call Me "Can't-Miss") Snyder
2. Charles (Run Support Is a Beautiful Thing) Nagy
3. Carlos (It Was Fun While It Lasted) Baerga

UNDERRATED
1. Bob (Where's That Electric Cell Device When I Need It?) Feller
2. Omar (Surest Hands in the West—or Midwest) Vizquel
3. Andre (Bet You Didn't Know I Out-Homered Rocky Colavito with This Team) Thornton

MARINERS
OVERRATED
1. Jim (Okay, So I *Wasn't* Better than Edgar) Presley
2. Gil (You Too Can Be Worth $55 Million) Meche
3. Phil (Never Drove in 90 Runs) Bradley

UNDERRATED
1. Edgar (Greatest DH of All Time) Martinez
2. Jamie (Life Begins at 33) Moyer
3. Ken (Don't Believe What You Heard on *Seinfeld*) Phelps

MARLINS
OVERRATED
1. A.J. (King of the Nine-Walk No-Hitter) Burnett
2. Preston (I'd Have Whiffed 200 Times That Year if They'd Have Let Me) Wilson
3. Antonio (Six of One, Half Dozen of the Other) Alfonseca

UNDERRATED
1. Derrek (In Case You're Not Familiar with My Pre-Cubs Career) Lee
2. Cliff Floyd—did *anybody* notice he slugged .523 as a Marlin?
3. Mike (The Best Backup Catcher You Never Heard Of) Redmond

METS
OVERRATED
1. Darryl (Ah, What Might Have Been) Strawberry
2. Howard (Founder of the 30-30-30 Club) Johnson
3. Ron (Well, At Least I Made One Great Catch) Swoboda

UNDERRATED
1. Jerry (Seaver Didn't Pitch *Every* Day) Koosman
2. Keith (No Longer Helping Seinfeld Move) Hernandez
3. Jon (Seaver and Koosman Didn't Pitch Every Day) Matlack

NATIONALS/EXPOS
OVERRATED
1. Jeff (Didn't I Used to Be the "All-Time" Saves Leader?) Reardon
2. Ellis (Tools Alone Are Always Overrated) Valentine
3. Floyd (Guilt by Boyhood Association with Dwight Gooden) Youmans

UNDERRATED
1. Tim (Best Stolen-Base Percentage of All Time) Raines
2. Dennis Martinez—made a better escape from Baltimore than Bob Irsay
3. Steve Rogers—second-leading north-of-the-border winner ever (behind Dave Stieb)

ORIOLES
OVERRATED
1. Rick (.233 Lifetime) Dempsey
2. Ben (Should Have Stayed on the Bayou) McDonald
3. Glenn (They Traded All *Those* Guys For Me?) Davis

UNDERRATED
1. Frank (How'd I Finish 16th in the All-Century Outfield Voting Anyhow?) Robinson
2. Boog Powell—except at the barbecue stand
3. Ken Singleton—greatest Orioles hitter of the 1970s, bar none

PADRES
OVERRATED
1. Benito (It's All Downhill Once Your Rookie of the Year Trophy Arrives) Santiago
2. Kevin (They *Did* Get Kevin Mitchell for Me) McReynolds
3. Andy (Gave Up Four Runs in My Own No-Hitter) Hawkins

UNDERRATED
1. Trevor (Compare My Stats to Mariano's Sometime) Hoffman
2. Nate (Drove in 13 in One Doubleheader) Colbert

3. Fred McGriff—won two home-run titles in San Diego, then (to quote the immortal Lisa Stark) "headed out of the fire sale, into the fire"

PHILLIES
OVERRATED
1. Chuck (Prez of the Baker Bowl Fan Club) Klein
2. Von (5-for-1) Hayes
3. Lance (Toto, We're Not in Tiger Stadium Anymore) Parrish

UNDERRATED
1. Dick (Okay, You Can Stop Booing Now) Allen
2. Steve (He Won 27 for *That* Team?) Carlton
3. Robin Roberts—only pitcher in the 1950s with 20 wins six years in a row

PIRATES
OVERRATED
1. Pie Traynor—would have been the perfect teammate for Bake McBride
2. Manny (This Hack's for You) Sanguillen
3. Lloyd (The Other Brother) Waner

UNDERRATED
1. Arky (So I Wasn't Honus Wagner—So What?) Vaughan
2. Ralph Kiner—big malapropper, bigger bopper
3. Jason Bay—name any other current Pirate, we dare you

RANGERS
OVERRATED
1. Ruben (Not So High) Sierra
2. Chan Ho Park—$55 million, 22 wins
3. David (Peaked in High School) Clyde

UNDERRATED
1. Michael Young—as many 200-hit seasons (four) as A-Rod and Nomar combined

2. Charlie (An Honorary Niekro Brother) Hough
3. John (There *Was* Life After the Bronx) Wetteland

REDS
OVERRATED
1. Tony (With a Little Help from His Friends) Perez
2. Ray (A Really Hard Day's) Knight
3. Johnny (If Only Every Week Could Have Been Like *That* Week) Vander Meer

UNDERRATED
1. Frank (Have I Mentioned That All-Century Election?) Robinson
2. Barry (See Ya in Cooperstown) Larkin
3. Ken (Every Day Is Father's Day) Griffey Sr.

RED SOX
OVERRATED
1. Carl (Thank Heaven for Fenway) Yastrzemski
2. George (Not So Booming) Scott
3. Jim Lonborg—it was all downhill (literally) after he hit that ski slope

UNDERRATED
1. Babe (You Mean He Could *Hit* Too?) Ruth
2. Dwight Evans—was there a steadier Red Sox outfielder than this guy?
3. Jackie Jensen—nominated by the Great Mr. Gammons himself

ROCKIES
OVERRATED
1. Vinny (Mile High Heaven) Castilla
2. Neifi (They Should Have Kept My *Off*-Base Percentage) Perez
3. Denny Neagle—$51 million, 19 wins

UNDERRATED
1. Steve (Best Pitcher in Rockies History) Reed
2. Todd (Even Great at Sea Level) Helton
3. Armando Reynoso—less bothered by Coors than any Rockies hurler ever

ROYALS
OVERRATED
1. "Bye-Bye" (If Only My Career Had Been As Great As My Nickname) Balboni
2. Clint (I Didn't *Ask* to Be on That Cover) Hurdle
3. Bo (Life Is a Highlight Reel) Jackson

UNDERRATED
1. Hal (More Than Brett's Trusty Assistant) McRae
2. Dan (Not Just Another Quipster) Quisenberry
3. Jeff (Did They Win *Any* Games I Didn't Save?) Montgomery

TIGERS
OVERRATED
1. George (Home Runs Are Overrated) Kell
2. Denny (Life *Didn't* Begin at 30) McLain
3. Jose (Lima Time Wasn't Win Time) Lima

UNDERRATED
1. Hank Greenberg—the greatest ninth-ballot Hall of Famer who ever lived
2. Lou (How'd I Get Bumped Off That Hall Ballot?) Whitaker
3. Alan (At Least I'm Still *on* That Hall Ballot) Trammell

TWINS
OVERRATED
1. Cristian (Still Looking for My 200th Walk) Guzman
2. Dan Gladden—grit was great; 100 runs would have been better
3. Gary (Lowest OPS in the 300-Homer Club) Gaetti

UNDERRATED

1. Bert Blyleven—3,701 strikeouts, 10 fruitless Hall of Fame ballots
2. Tony (Where Were Those Knee Surgeons When I Needed Them) Oliva
3. Joe (The Mariano of the Midwest) Nathan

WHITE SOX
OVERRATED

1. Luis (Should Have Read *Moneyball*) Aparicio
2. Ray (At Least I Didn't Throw the World Series) Schalk
3. Bobby (One-Hit Wonder) Thigpen

UNDERRATED

1. Hoyt (Possibly the Best Reliever Ever) Wilhelm
2. Minnie (Man of 1,000 Comebacks) Minoso
3. Mark Buehrle—the most top-secret ace in baseball

YANKEES
OVERRATED

1. Phil (Holy Cow, We Still Love Him) Rizzuto
2. Dave Winfield—not Mr. May, but not Reggie, either
3. Don (How Do You Live Up to Perfection?) Larsen

UNDERRATED

1. Goose (Eight Hall of Fame Elections, Still No Plaque) Gossage
2. Yogi (An Even Better Ballplayer Than Humorist) Berra
3. Paul O'Neill—heart of the dynasty